Yugoslavia and the Nonaligned World

YUGOSLAVIA
AND THE
NONALIGNED WORLD

By

Alvin Z. Rubinstein

PRINCETON, NEW JERSEY
PRINCETON UNIVERSITY PRESS
1970

219175

To our friends in Yugoslavia
in gratitude for the warmth
with which they opened their hearts and country
and in the hope that they may prevail
in their search for a more just society

Contents

CONTENTS

Preface

ON JUNE 28, 1948, Yugoslavia was expelled from the then monolithic Communist camp. Not since the signing of the Nazi-Soviet Pact had a decision of Stalin's so startled the Western world; in time its consequences were to be more momentous.

Josip Broz Tito was the most militant and pro-Soviet Communist ruler in Eastern Europe. But having come to power without Soviet assistance, he refused to accept the role of a satrap in his own country. Frictions between the Yugoslav Communists and Moscow had developed during the war when Stalin insisted unrealistically that the Yugoslav Communists form a common front with incompatible and bitterly hostile political groups, when he belittled the military performance of the Partisans, and when he showed himself prepared to join with Great Britain in dividing Yugoslavia into Soviet and British spheres of influence. After the war resentment deepened over Moscow's high-handed, crude dealings with Yugoslavia: Soviet spies tried to infiltrate the Central Committee of the Yugoslav Communist Party; slander and blackmail were used to compromise Yugoslav Communists who would not place Soviet interests above those of their own country; Moscow pressed for the establishment of joint-stock companies and preferential trade treaties designed to exploit Yugoslavia economically. Stalin also mistrusted Tito's efforts to promote integration in the Balkans. But above all, there was Tito's refusal to turn Yugoslavia into a Soviet satellite.

Expulsion from the Soviet bloc forced Yugoslavia to look for security in new relationships with non-Communist countries. During the initial years of excommunication from the Cominform, the years of maximum military threat, it was to the West that Belgrade turned; however, by the early 1950's, the danger from the East had receded, and Belgrade looked to the Third World for congenial friends to whom it could relate politically and economically, for influence and a new role in world affairs, and for support against future threats to its existence and stability.

This study focuses on the origins and development of Yugoslavia's foreign policy toward the nonaligned world. A story of many dimensions, it examines the determinants which shaped Belgrade's turn to the new nations of Asia and Africa and its role in pioneering nonalignment; it discusses the policies of Yugoslav leaders, their aspirations and tribulations in the quest for security, influence, and a voice in the revamping of international relationships; it traces Tito's relations with Nasser, and the many ways in which Yugoslavia has established close ties to the nonaligned nations and acquired as a consequence a position of prominence in the nonaligned world; it explores Belgrade's role in the Moscow-Peking rift as manifested in the Third World; and finally, it evaluates the Yugoslav impact on nonalignment and nonalignment's changing role in the international relations of the postwar era.

A Communist country, Yugoslavia is a leader among the nonaligned—the only European country so accepted. A stalwart of the Soviet Union until excommunication from the Cominform in 1948, it has since been more often than not anathema to the oligarchs of Byzantine communism. As Yugoslav leaders charted a nonaligned course, their outlook and attitudes underwent dramatic changes in response to nonideological determinants; and in the process Yugoslav ideology adapted, and with it the perceptions and values of the generation that made the revolution. The metamorphosis was at once a precondition for influence-building among the developing nations and a tangible bar to renewed membership in the Soviet bloc. Forced to go its own way, Yugoslavia staked out a role in international relations that has kept it in the forefront of major developments in the United Nations and nonalignment during the past two decades. Its experience illustrates the potentialities, as well as the limits, of small nation activism in world politics.

The research for this study entailed an exhaustive examination of Yugoslav writings on nonalignment and international relations, and the Yugoslav record in the United Nations. Beyond that, an extensive program of personal interviewing was carried out in order to obtain—from such an intractable subject as the foreign policy of a Communist country—insights into changing perceptions, determinants, and priorities, insights that could not be gained through a rigid *a priori* research design.

Four categories of officials were interviewed. The first included more than sixty Yugoslavs, most of whom were the Party or government officials who had been directly involved in the formulation and implementation of Yugoslav policy toward the Third World at some time during the 1948-1968 period. These interviews were on an average one hour long; they were conducted mainly in Yugoslavia during the course of two visits, one from October 1965 through May 1966 and another in March 1968. The second group was composed of diplomats from more than a dozen non-aligned countries which have been the targets of Yugoslav courtship. Thus, in Belgrade I discussed nonalignment and Yugoslavia's role in it with officials at various Asian and African embassies; in Cairo, in June 1966, I spoke with Egyptian officials about Yugoslav-U.A.R. relations; in Geneva, New York, and Washington I interviewed Afro-Asian diplomats. Third, civil servants of international organizations in New York, Geneva, and Vienna provided information on Yugoslav policy and interaction with non-aligned countries. Finally, I have benefited from the evaluations of the Western diplomats who have had extended contact with Yugoslavs or with the countries most courted by them.

Out of this composite data bank of written and oral resources, I have attempted to elucidate the aims, the achievements, the disappointments, and the dilemmas of the Yugoslav leadership wending its way from the wings of Stalin's empire to a respected position on the international stage.

It is with gratitude that I acknowledge my debt to the in-

xiii

dividuals and institutions in various countries who made possible the research for this study. I benefited greatly from the willingness of Yugoslav officials to share with me information and insights not generally available in the public record. Resident diplomats in Belgrade and officials—national and international—in Cairo, Geneva, New York, and Washington contributed valuable perspectives on Yugoslav policy; they helped educate an educator to the complexity and elusiveness of international politics and to the need for attention to the ideas, ideals, and hidden trends which move man and history. I would like to express my appreciation to Mr. Leo Mates, Director of the Institute for International Politics and Economy, and his staff for their hospitality during an eight-month stay; to the John Simon Guggenheim Memorial Foundation for making possible an uninterrupted year of research in Europe; and to the American Philosophical Society for providing a grant for an additional period of interviewing in Yugoslavia.

I have benefited from the critical and helpful suggestions of a number of friends and specialists: Mr. Anton Bebler of the Institute of International Politics and Economy (Belgrade) ; Dr. John C. Campbell of the Council on Foreign Relations; Professor George Ginsburgs of the New School for Social Research; Professor William E. Griffith of M.I.T.; Mr. Mahmoud El-Okdah of the Arab States Delegations Office in New York; Dr. Amos Perlmutter of the Center for International Studies, Harvard University; Dr. Dimitrije Pindić and Dr. Obrad Račić of the Institute of International Politics and Economy; and Professor Oles Smolansky of Lehigh University. The editors of *Orbis*, the quarterly published by the Foreign Policy Research Institute of the University of Pennsylvania, kindly granted me permission to use my article that had appeared in their journal. Working with the staff of Princeton University Press has been a pleasure: Mrs. Carol Orr skillfully edited the manuscript; and William J. McClung, the Social Science Editor, was helpful throughout. Mrs. Nancy McCloskey typed the manuscript at different stages of completion. Finally, I express my deepest affection and sense of good fortune to my wife, Frankie Ruda Rubinstein, for her constant encouragement and vital spirit.

Alvin Z. Rubinstein

Philadelphia
June 9, 1969

Yugoslavia and the Nonaligned World

CHAPTER I

The Uncertain Years, 1948-1952

THE EXCOMMUNICATION of Yugoslavia from the Soviet world on June 28, 1948, compelled Yugoslav leaders to forge new policies which in time would rest on new assumptions and new alignments. It exposed the rupture that had barely been forestalled in the interval since Kardelj's abortive effort four months earlier to convince Stalin of Tito's fealty and wholehearted acceptance of Soviet leadership of the socialist camp. But Tito's unwillingness to relinquish control of the country and the Yugoslav Communist Party to the Soviet leadership infuriated Stalin and moved him to escalate the dispute. The Cominform statement excommunicating Yugoslavia declared:

. . . by their anti-Party and anti-Soviet views, incompatible with Marxism-Leninism, by their whole attitude . . . the leaders of the Communist Party of Yugoslavia have placed themselves in opposition to the Communist Parties affiliated to the Information Bureau [Cominform], have taken the path of seceding from the united socialist front against imperialism, have taken the path of betraying the cause of international solidarity of the working people, and have taken up a position of nationalism. . . . The information Bureau considers that, in view of all this, the Central Committee of the Communist Party of Yugoslavia has placed itself and the Yugoslav Party outside the family of fraternal Communist Parties, outside the Communist front and consequently outside the ranks of the Information Bureau.[1]

Stalin expected one of two things: Tito's abject surrender or his deposal by the Muscovite faction in the Yugoslav Party. His condemnation aimed at isolating the Yugoslav

[1] Royal Institute of International Affairs, *The Soviet-Yugoslav Dispute: Text of the Published Correspondence* (London, 1948), pp. 68-69.

Communist Party leadership from the Yugoslav people, and the Titoists from the Muscovites.

Clearly not willing to make any concessions to Moscow, the Central Committee of the Communist Party of Yugoslavia (CPY) responded forcefully on the following day, asserting that the criticism levelled against it by the Cominform was "inaccurate and unfounded" and that "the greatest historical injustice" was being perpetrated against the Yugoslav Communist Party. Stubbornly disclaiming any responsibility for the traumatic turn of events, the Yugoslav leadership contended "that it bears no responsibility for all these phenomena as it did not provoke them by any act of its own."[2] This was quickly followed by an editorial in *Borba*, the official organ of the Communist Party of Yugoslavia, demanding to know in what way the Yugoslav comrades had not supported Soviet policy or had jeopardized the solidarity of the socialist camp.[3]

After these two immediate unrepentant responses to the Cominform's denunciation, Yugoslav statements and editorials assumed a subdued, respectful tone during most of the next six months. Thus, on July 5 *Borba* stated that "to consider the possibility of constructing socialism in one country without the cooperation of the USSR and the other democratic countries—is as absurd as to believe that other friendly socialist states can, alone, remain socialist states in an imperialist world":

> It is understood that if Yugoslavia would rely on the imperialists for "defense" of its independence from the USSR, that would be anti-Soviet. It would also be anti-Soviet if the Yugoslavs would, as a bribe, act on the idea or behave in practice as if the USSR and the imperialist states were the same. That would lead directly to imperialism.[4]

On July 20, *Borba* declared:

> Our country, like the other countries of the Peoples' De-

2 *Ibid.*, p. 79.   3 *Borba*, July 1, 1948, p. 1.
4 *Borba*, July 5, 1948, p. 1.

4

mocracies, can exist and develop only by building social-ism according to the principles which Marx, Engels, Lenin, and Stalin set forth, by remaining in fraternal union with the USSR and the other Peoples' Democ-racies, and by developing further that union.[5]

On July 22, 1948, at the Fifth Congress of the Communist Party of Yugoslavia, Tito affirmed Yugoslavia's complete accordance with the foreign policy of the Soviet Union "be-cause that policy corresponded and corresponds to the in-terests of our country and the interests of peace." He noted that after the liberation of the country, the first meas-ures taken by the Yugoslav leaders were "to associate Yugo-slavia as closely as possible economically, politically, and culturally with the Soviet Union and the Peoples' Democracies":

> The creation of pacts of friendship and mutual assistance, all-around cooperation, the drawing up of economic and other contracts were all done at our own initiative, with-out anyone driving us to it. We considered it to be pre-cisely the most correct way toward the peaceful develop-ment of our country, toward the consolidation and pres-ervation of peace in the world, and toward the strengthening of democracies in other lands—such as Poland, Czechoslovakia, Bulgaria, Hungary, and Romania. . . .

> We have remained to this very day faithful to all our obligations toward the Peoples' Democracies. On the other hand, we have emphasized the need for cooperation with other countries as well because we consider it to be one of the contributions to the consolidation of peace in the world, because we considered it to be useful for Yugo-slavia which suffered so terribly in the great war for lib-eration. But this [attitude] has never gone beyond the limits of a strict adherence to our principles of loyalty to Marxism and loyalty to our friends—the USSR and

[5] *Borba*, July 20, 1948, p. 2.

the countries of the Peoples' Democracies. In this connection I must emphasize that we, that is Yugoslavia, have been most fiercely scored and attacked by the entire international reaction. . . .[6]

As if to underscore Yugoslavia's loyalty and pro-Soviet orientation, Tito concluded his speech with a ringing "Long Live Stalin!"

For more than three months after expulsion from the Cominform, Yugoslav leaders—with the exception of the two initial responses noted previously—repeatedly acknowledged the leading position of the Soviet Union in the socialist camp and reiterated their loyalty to Stalin, the Soviet Union, and Marxism. At the Danube Conference in Belgrade in August they supported the Soviet Union in its plan to eliminate Western influence from the lower Danube by restricting the membership of the reconstituted Danubian Commission to riparian states. Above all, they curbed their pens, avoiding any criticism of the Soviet Union.

Leadership Strains

The abrupt halt to the initial spirited rejections of Cominform charges and the assumption of a conciliatory tone during the ensuing months require explanation. The restraint of public statements and commentaries mirrored the deepening dilemmas and turmoil of Party leaders, who began to ponder the isolation they now found themselves in. The restraint may also have reflected an insecurity among the leaders of the Central Committee, some of whom were experiencing second thoughts. The Yugoslavs, alarmed at being set adrift in a hostile capitalist sea, were reappraising the consequences of obstinacy. They were also weighing alternatives, not in terms of their ability to survive apart from the socialist camp—an alternative that apparently was not consciously or seriously considered by the Yugoslav leadership until late 1948 or early 1949—but in terms of

[6] *Borba*, July 22, 1948, p. 4.

6

the areas in which they could make concessions to the Soviet Union without surrendering their independent existence. Reconciliation with the Cominform was regarded as a distinct possibility by segments of the leadership in the months immediately after June 28. The leadership's uncertainty was heightened by their fear of the internal consequences of the split with the Soviet Union. They had no sure feeling of the popular mood in those anxious days. The discrepancy was vast between the harshness of Stalin's demands and aims—which the leaders had come grudgingly to comprehend—and the enormous enthusiasm for Stalin and the Soviet Union in the country and Party at large, particularly in Serbia, Montenegro, and Macedonia. It was not at all clear whether the Party itself would hold together, for the threat from the East was not readily understandable to the man in the street. Two important Party officials, Andrija Hebrang and Sreten Žujović, had been removed from power on the eve of the split, but the loyalty of the Party to Tito had still to be proved.

At the third session of the U.N. General Assembly in September 1948 the Yugoslav delegation fully supported and unstintingly praised the Soviet Union. *Borba* echoed *Pravda:*

> the democratic camp led by the Soviet Union will oppose all attempts to convert the U.N. into a tool of U.S. aggressive imperialist policy, struggling consistently for the principles of international cooperation and decision-making by consent which alone can secure true peace and thwart the attempts of warmongers to provoke new bloodletting.[7]

The Yugoslav delegation adhered to the Soviet position, whether on the admission of new members, the control of atomic energy and general disarmament, or the Greek, Korean, and Indonesian questions; and on all key issues and votes its public stand was one with the Soviet Union. Yugoslav delegates harshly criticized Western policies. In their

[7] *Borba,* September 22, 1948, p. 1.

comments on developments in Indonesia, India, and Burma they spoke the language of the Cominform and diligently toed the mark on the Zhdanov line (the two-camp thesis formally enunciated in September 1947 at the founding of the Cominform), postulating the bipolarity of the international environment. Nehru, for example, was termed a "hypocrite" whose arbitrariness was "a transparent device behind which lie concealed the interests of Indian reactionaryism, British colonialists, and foreign companies."[8]

Stalin was lauded as the great leader of the socialist camp. On the occasion of his 69th birthday Tito sent a warm congratulatory telegram, *Borba* featured a full page story and photograph, and a member of the Central Committee said at a meeting of the Society for Cultural Cooperation Between Yugoslavia and the USSR:

> There are no kinds of difficulties, no matter which side they come from, that cannot be set aside from the road to the building of socialism and the struggle against imperialism, and on that road we must always keep before our eyes the enormous experience of the USSR which is elaborated in the works of Stalin.
>
> Long live the leader of progressive mankind, Joseph Vissarionovich Stalin.[9]

However, before 1948 drew to a close, expressions of defiance also appeared in the Yugoslav press. One editorial astringently dismissed the allegations emanating from the Cominform that Yugoslavia had become part of the imperialist camp:

> It is not the Central Committee of the Communist Party of Yugoslavia which isolates Yugoslavia from the democratic countries, but the leadership of these countries, making use of the incorrect excuse that the Central Committee of the CPY will not acknowledge errors, which is isolating Yugoslavia.[10]

8 *Borba*, November 2, 1948, p. 3.
9 *Borba*, December 21, 1948, p. 3.
10 *Borba*, October 3, 1948, p. 2. Later in the month Milovan Djilas wrote in a pamphlet denying Cominform accusations that, though no

The Turn from Moscow

Late in December Tito made his first public criticism of the Cominform's economic hostility. He told the National Assembly that Yugoslavia would prefer to have the help of the Peoples' Democracies in modernizing and industrializing, but made it clear that "if our allies from the Peoples' Democracies will not help us in that, then it is understood we must sell our raw materials elsewhere, even if that would be to the capitalist countries, so that we can buy various types of machinery which are needed for the mechanization of our industry."[11] He defended trade with capitalist countries as in no way signifying the surrender of sovereignty or the improper granting of political concessions, and observed that the very countries which accused Yugoslavia of such actions themselves traded with the West. Further, in an allusion to the United States' return of impounded Yugoslav gold after outstanding claims had been settled, he noted that the East European countries, too, had reached agreements with the West on financial questions. Tito's speech left no doubt of the Yugoslav leadership's continued determination not to be cowed by the Cominform and, perhaps more important as a reflection of inner-Party thinking, of their dawning realization that limited coexistence with the West was a viable alternative which would not jeopardize their domestic system.

In a speech a few days later, Edvard Kardelj, who had replaced Stanoje Simić (a holdover from the pre-1945 regime) as Minister of Foreign Affairs shortly after the Cominform crisis erupted, elaborated on a theme that was to become of increasing importance for the Yugoslavs: the need to strengthen the United Nations. Acknowledging the shortcomings of the U.N., he emphasized that it could nonetheless contribute enormously to the maintenance of peace:

---

one denied the authority of the Central Committee of the Soviet Communist Party, this authority should not be used to prevent the truth from being known. See *O neistinitim i nepravednim optužbama protiv KPJ* (Belgrade, 1948).

[11] *Borba*, December 28, 1948, p. 1.

. . . in spite of its great weaknesses, this organization is nevertheless useful and can serve as a serious obstacle to those who are prepared for their own selfish aims to push mankind toward the catastrophe of a new world war.[12]

His concluding remarks dealt with the nature of future relations between socialist countries and the methods that would be necessary to create the unity of socialism. Outlining what was at a later date to be known as the "many roads to socialism" doctrine, Kardelj set forth the theoretical justification for each socialist country deciding for itself the best way to achieve socialism:

We are entering an epoch when the building of socialism is no longer a matter only for one country, but when socialism encompasses new countries, new peoples, numerous new millions of working masses, who have been brought up in different conditions, with different levels of economic development, on various levels of general culture and with different mentalities.[13]

The argument that the principles of Marxism-Leninism could be realized only through concrete experience which reflected the historical uniqueness and complexity of each adherent to socialism was instrumental in the mid-1950's in attracting the new nations of Africa and Asia to the Yugoslav views on and model of socialism. Kardelj implicitly rejected the heretofore unquestioned Stalinist tenet that the Soviet experience in building socialism was prerequisite for all members of the socialist camp. "Only ruthless dogmatists," he boldly stated, "can think that this process can go in one way, according to one design and without difficulty." If Yugoslav insistence on governing its own country free from Soviet interference was politically antithetical to Stalin's chauvinist mentality, then obviously Kardelj's assertion that *each* country should be permitted to find its own road to socialism, though guided by the theoretical experience of the Soviet Union, was considered heresy. The

[12] *Borba*, December 30, 1948, p. 1.   [13] *Ibid.*, p. 3.

point of no return had been reached, though several more months were to pass before Yugoslav leaders fully accepted the finality of the new relationship.

During the first half of 1949 the Cominform's verbal assaults against Tito intensified, with the ironic effect of making him more and more a symbol of Yugoslav patriotism, a defender of national independence, even in the eyes of those not well-disposed toward the Communist Party; they also alienated growing numbers of the Party rank-and-file and, in the words of one American writer, helped Tito "to dislodge pro-Soviet sympathies in all but the most stubborn of Party affiliates."[14] Thus, Stalin's crude campaign of psychopolitical overkill backfired: instead of precipitating a Party coup against the "Tito clique," it consolidated Party and popular support behind Tito and his lieutenants.

In the U.N. Yugoslav delegates continued to support Soviet positions, but this seeming unity of outlook was increasingly belied by the spirited response of the Yugoslav domestic press to Cominform charges. While Soviet condemnations of NATO and eulogies to the Red Army were duly published, and while the Yugoslav Government purported to find "astonishing" the fact that it was neither informed in advance of nor invited to participate in the founding conference of the Council for Mutual Economic Aid (CMEA)[15] (Moscow's gesture at establishing an equivalent of the Marshall Plan for Eastern Europe), Yugoslav commentators defended themselves forcefully against Cominform allegations that they were betraying socialism.

Following the Soviet lead, Yugoslav officials deplored the establishment of the NATO Pact, terming it a "serious threat to peace and international cooperation" and, more specifically, "a plan for the forcible establishment of Anglo-American world domination."[16] Further, they criticized reactionary Western propaganda for spreading "the word that Soviet troops are concentrating around Yugoslavia and

[14] Charles P. McVicker, *Titoism: Pattern for International Communism* (New York: St. Martin's Press, 1957), p. 20.
[15] *Borba*, February 2, 1949, p. 1.   [16] *Borba*, April 3, 1949, p. 6.

that the USSR is preparing an attack on Yugoslavia."[17] But though they publicly stated that such allegations were started by the West to divert world attention from its own aggressive ambitions, privately Yugoslav leaders were not quite sure. They had reports of troop movements but were uncertain what conclusions to draw from them. Tito was still not willing to accept the West's view of Stalin; moreover, even if he had been, he was not then prepared to accuse the Soviet Union of warlike behavior, to give Stalin any pretext for using these troops against Yugoslavia. By mid-1949 the entire general line of Yugoslav foreign policy was in flux, and with it ingrained ideological and emotional links and assumptions, and the dreams of men who had come to political prominence revering Stalin and Soviet socialism.

That Tito would not, however, pay just any price for a reconciliation with the Soviet Union was clear from the growing frequency with which Yugoslav officials emphasized, concomitant with their equilibrating criticisms of the West, that Yugoslav foreign policy was based on the principle of the sovereign equality of socialist states, which implied equality in economic relations as well. In a word, Yugoslavia was not willing to accept the status of a compliant satellite, exploited by Moscow for the exclusive benefit of the Soviet state. At the Third Congress of the National Front of Yugoslavia on April 9, 1949, Tito demonstrated consummate diplomatic skill. Dismissing the political attacks against Yugoslavia, he stated "that if our 'critics' [in the Cominform] or international reaction [the Western powers] are waiting for us to lose courage under the impact of all these lies and slanders, and take indiscreet steps that would be contrary to our revolutionary beliefs, to our principles, then they will be bitterly disappointed."[18] On the one hand, he flailed "the reactionary elements in the capitalist countries" who thought that Yugoslavia would

[17] *Borba*, March 30, 1949, p. 1.
[18] *Borba*, April 10, 1949, p. 4.

join the West in combination against the Soviet Union, because of the hostile attitude of the Eastern countries. On the other hand, he told the "critics" and all who did not wish Yugoslavia well that they would wait in vain for its moral or physical collapse. Rejecting political or military alignment with the West in order to avoid open provocation of the Soviet Union, he tried to convince Moscow of his determination to resist Cominform pressures while he simultaneously offered expressions of political loyalty and ideological kinship—mollifications for a possible reconciliation. He was not yet ready to embark Yugoslavia on a foreign policy course independent of the Soviet Union.

It is not possible to pinpoint the moment when the top Yugoslav leadership realized the finality of the rift with Stalin, perhaps because among themselves they came to perceive the irrevocability of their involuntary isolation from the socialist camp at different times during the year after June 28, 1948. A number of Yugoslav officials who in the 1948-1949 period were important in the Party, close to Tito, and primarily concerned with foreign affairs, when asked in retrospect of the time that each personally had seen the futility of trying to heal the rift, gave differing dates and events. But all agreed that by the summer of 1949 it was evident to everyone. A noted American writer of Yugoslav descent, Louis Adamić, was in Yugoslavia in 1949 from mid-January to late August and met often and informally with all the key Communist leaders, including Tito, Kardelj, Djilas, Ranković, and Pijade. He wrote: "I sensed every once in a while that vestiges of the old hope-against-hope sentiment [for a reconciliation with Stalin] clung on. In Tito and Kardelj they lasted until the end of June [1949]."[19]

If June was indeed the month of no return, then the catalyst that angered and shocked the Yugoslavs as nothing had since the June 1948 rupture was the Soviet decision to drop its support of Yugoslav claims to the Carinthian area

---

[19] Louis Adamić, *The Eagle and the Roots* (New York: Doubleday and Company, 1952), p. 260; see also pp. 254-255.

of Austria. When Andrei Vyshinsky, the Soviet Foreign Minister, announced at the Paris meeting of the Council of Foreign Ministers (the United States, Great Britain, France, and the Soviet Union) that the USSR no longer would uphold the Yugoslav position, Belgrade immediately protested the refusal of the Foreign Ministers to hear the Yugoslav case, but to no avail. The last lingering illusions about Stalin's intentions dispelled, the Yugoslav leaders began now systematically and unequivocally to counter Soviet charges and Cominform hostility, though still wary of provoking a Soviet military response.

During the summer, as relations with the Soviet Union worsened, Yugoslavia adopted a conciliatory position toward Greece and sealed the border, thus depriving the Greek Communist rebels of sanctuary in Macedonia. (That the Yugoslavs had previously assisted the Greek Communists in the Civil War seems indisputable, though the degree of assistance is a matter of controversy.) Relations with the Greek Government slowly improved.

Beyond all this loomed the broader question: whither Yugoslav foreign policy in a bipolar world? In a speech to the Politburo of the Central Committee, Moshe Pijade, the Party's leading theoretician, derided the Cominform for thinking that two months after the Resolution of June 28, 1948, Yugoslavia would lose its independence and become a colony of the "imperialists." He noted that, on the contrary, resistance to Cominform pressure had ensured national independence and made certain that Yugoslavia would not "become a colony or someone's province": "On the theoretical side, that prophecy is in general not intelligent, and historically it is unjustifiable." Continuing in a vein that was in a few years to find formal expression in a new conception—nonalignment, he asserted that "there is no justification at all for the view that small nations must jump into the mouth of this or that shark. If that were a social law, there would not today be any small states."[20]

[20] *Borba*, July 9, 1949, p. 2.

Yugoslav "Discovery" of the United Nations

Because of mounting incidents and troop movements along its borders with the Soviet satellites, by late summer of 1949 the Yugoslav Government had become so thoroughly concerned over its security and survival that it decided to place the causes of the Yugoslav-Soviet rift before the United Nations and make explicit the fundamentally political character of what had hitherto been viewed in the West as largely an ideological split. A hint of Yugoslavia's intention to air its complaints against the Soviet bloc came on September 22. During discussion of the proposed agenda, and specifically of the item dealing with "Observance in Bulgaria, Hungary, and Romania of Human Rights and Fundamental Freedoms," the Yugoslav delegate abstained, saying for the first time that "some of the countries in question had violated their obligations towards Yugoslavia under existing peace treaties and had also violated several other agreements with Yugoslavia."[21]

On September 26 Edvard Kardelj, the Yugoslav Minister of Foreign Affairs, sharply reversed his uncritical support of the Soviet Union of the previous year and opened with a blistering attack on Soviet interference in Yugoslav affairs. This was the first time the dispute with the Soviet Union had been raised in the United Nations. No longer, he asserted, could the dispute be cloaked in make-believe:

> In order to establish a hegemony over Yugoslavia, every form of pressure, backed by a campaign of lies and slander unparalleled in history, had been brought to bear on it. Organized economic pressure had all but brought about a complete economic blockade of Yugoslavia by Eastern European countries. An attempt was being made to terrorize people with weak nerves by means of notes which were of inordinate length and which were not in accordance with diplomatic practice. That was accompanied by countless frontier incidents and by troop movements amounting to military demonstrations.[22]

[21] U.N., General Assembly, *Official Records*, Fourth Session, p. 19.
[22] *Ibid.*, p. 68.

15

Kardelj challenged the Soviet Government to put into practice the principle of the equality of rights between states, which it consistently championed, and he called upon the small nations, not just the Great Powers, to participate actively in efforts to preserve peace.

His speech marked the shift to a new policy. Heretofore, Yugoslavia's mooring had been the Soviet Union. Now that the line was cut, it was clear that Yugoslavia would have to seek another mooring point. The severing process, which had started in March 1948 with the first Cominform representation to Yugoslavia, and continued with the Cominform resolution of June, had not cut all Yugoslav ties to the USSR; some legal and diplomatic threads still linked the two. By the fall of 1949 the process was completed.

Kardelj's speech also indicated a turning point in the attitude of Yugoslav leaders toward their own people. For the first time the Soviet Union itself was identified as a threat to Yugoslavia and accused of trying to subvert the Tito regime. By September 1949 the Yugoslav leadership apparently felt that their people had caught up with the new international conditions in which the country found itself, that the emotional ties and political loyalty to the Soviet Union, which were particularly strong in the traditionally pro-Russian sections of the country, were no longer a cause for concern. Tito had used the year wisely. He had understood the need to minimize dissidence in the country and isolate pro-Soviet agents; he had given Party and military cadres, many of whom had been reared on loyalty and devotion to the Soviet Union and Stalin, time to absorb the shock, to become accustomed to its implications, and to reformulate their views. A period of reeducation and reindoctrination had been necessary; hence the obeisance paid to Stalin in the early period after the Cominform resolution. According to one Yugoslav Party official, "This public obeisance contrasted with the internal image held by the leadership and with the realistic evaluation that they had of the situation and of the impossibility of returning to the former relationship. But a time lag had

16

to be endured during which the lower echelon cadres had to be brought up to date." By September 1949 Tito felt confident that the general population would support him against the Soviet Union and the socialist camp. The Party leadership had survived the trauma of isolation and ideological rejection and had forged a sense of national unity.

Two days after Kardelj's speech, the Soviet Government cancelled the Soviet-Yugoslav Treaty of Friendship and Mutual Assistance and Postwar Cooperation, which had been signed on April 11, 1945 in Moscow. The kingpin of the Yugoslav security system was gone. In search of a diplomatic alternative, Yugoslav leaders turned to the United Nations. As if to underscore Yugoslavia's determination to present its case and seek support in the U.N., Marshal Tito told a group of six hundred Army officers at the conclusion of military maneuvers:

> They [Soviet leaders] hoped that we would slink into a bench in the United Nations and be silent, while they, undisturbed, would strike us there, lash us and slap us. And why should we be silent? (*We will not, we will not!*) We spoke not because of the Western reactionaries, because they are not better, but only because it was right. We are obliged to say that they [the Western reactionaries] only talk, but the others [the Soviet leaders] work against us. (*Acclamation and applause.*) We have the right to defend our country and not permit our people to be isolated, for then it would be even harder on them. And we will not permit it. (*Prolonged acclamation.*) We will speak out in the future in all international meetings and forums. If the Soviet Union will at times be right, we will be with them. If they will not be right and their statements will be false, we will say so, and not otherwise. (*Unanimous powerful ovation.*) [23]

On October 5, 1949, the Yugoslav delegation in the U.N. offered a proposal, the "Declaration of Rights and Duties of States," which was intended to ensure national security

[23] *Borba*, October 4, 1949, p. 1.

through elaboration and codification of the principles of the U.N. Charter; in particular, the sovereign equality of states, the right to self-determination, and the guarantee of the security of each state were to be converted into formal conventions having a binding character under international law. Though the Sixth Committee (Legal Committee) of the General Assembly had discussed this general subject since the Panamanian delegate had raised it in 1946, the Yugoslavs invested the issue with urgency. The Yugoslav spokesman, the distinguished jurist Milan Bartoš, acknowledged that the Charter laid down the principles which should govern relations between states and that no one openly denied them, but he said that actual conditions showed deeds fell far short of words;[24] the behavior of certain powerful states diverged markedly from the basic principles of the U.N. While under no illusions that the adoption of a Declaration on Rights and Duties of States would eliminate the use of pressure in relations among nations or would oblige any government which refused to do so to refrain from interfering in the internal affairs of other states, Bartoš insisted, nevertheless, that "the existence of such a Declaration would, however, make it more difficult for possible aggressors to justify their aggression before their own peoples by hypocritical propaganda, and would enable public opinion to assess correctly the actions of aggressor governments."[25]

The political motivation of the Yugoslavs was clear: fearing attack by the Soviet Union, they hoped to gain widespread support through the United Nations for their position in the dispute and thereby to deter the Soviet Union. Any additional margin of security, however tenuous, was desperately welcome. Henceforth, the United Nations became perceptibly important to Yugoslav foreign policy.

The irony of the Yugoslav position was not lost on the

[24] U.N., General Assembly, Sixth Committee, *Official Records*, Fourth Session, p. 191.

[25] *Ibid*. See also Vladimir Popović, "The Equality of Rights of Peoples and the Struggle for Peace," *Komunist*, Vol. IV (March-May, 1950), pp. 108-123.

Greek delegate, who noted that the Declaration was only the result of the present Yugoslav difficulty with the USSR and not the expression of profound legal conviction. The Yugoslav Government, he observed, had not abided by the key provisions of its Declaration during the 1947-1948 period when it had materially abetted the rebels in the Greek Civil War. The British representative expressed his sympathy with the motives which prompted the Yugoslav proposal, but regretted that the principles set forth therein had not been applied to the situation in the Balkans, and deplored the attempt to graft onto the corpus of international law proposals which had an immediate and specifically political relevance. Though the Yugoslav draft proposal was not adopted, it did strengthen the Yugoslav case against the Soviet Union. More significant for long-term Yugoslav policy in international organizations, the proposal marked the beginning of a persistent Yugoslav effort to gain universal acceptance of political principles and policies which it espoused, e.g., the codification of the principles of peaceful coexistence. One factor which has militated against Western acceptance of these proposals in the U.N. has been the convenient exclusions and interpretations. Thus, the injunction against interference in the internal affairs of another country becomes subordinated to the right of self-determination when the Third World sees the issue as one of anti-colonialism which is always construed as anti-Western.

One consequence of the Yugoslav-Soviet rupture was seen in the filling of a non-permanent seat in the U.N. Security Council. As a candidate, Yugoslavia fervently sought election to buttress its diplomatic position vis-à-vis the Soviet Union. It needed the support of the Western powers but felt uncertain of their reliability. Reports in The *New York Times* of a Soviet willingness to settle the Greek problem with the Western states in return for their support of the Soviet candidate received prominent attention in the Yugoslav press, reflecting the leadership's anxiety.

Andrei Vyshinsky, the Soviet Foreign Minister and head

of the delegation to the General Assembly, bitterly argued that the Yugoslav candidacy did not accord with Article 23 of the Charter, which holds that due regard should be given to the principle of "equitable geographical distribution" in the election of nonpermanent members of the Security Council. Evidently he no longer considered Yugoslavia part of Eastern Europe. He assailed the contravening of the tacit gentleman's agreement, which had been applied during the previous elections of 1946, 1947, and 1948, to the effect that candidates for the rotating vacancies be nominated by states belonging to the geographical areas concerned. On October 19 Mr. Acheson of the U.S. delegation rejected the Soviet contention, adding: "Yugoslavia is East European; it is Slav; it is Communist. The only thing it lacks is domination by the Kremlin, which is not referred to in the U.N. Charter or any other agreement as a condition for membership of the Security Council." In search of votes, the Soviet delegation tried various blinds including, in the wooing of the Argentinian delegation, a description of the Argentinian dictator Juan Peron as a great democrat.[26] However, these efforts failed; and unmoved by Vyshinsky's insistence "that gentlemen should honour a gentleman's agreement,"[27] the General Assembly, on October 20, 1949, elected Yugoslavia on the second ballot, along with Ecuador and India, to a two-year term. *Borba* regarded the development as a major deterrent to Soviet aggressive designs: observing that "the problem of peace, of the free development of each state, is not so much a matter of the difference in social structure between states, as in the suppression of hegemonistic tendencies within the social structure," it said the election showed the Soviet Union that the international community would resist attempts to impose Soviet hegemony.[28] Yugoslavia's election to the Security Council was providential because it was during this period of 1950-1951, in which Yugoslavia came into

[26] *Borba*, October 18, 1949, p. 1.
[27] U.N., General Assembly, *Official Records*, Fourth Session, p. 103.
[28] *Borba*, October 24, 1949, p. 1.

intimate and prolonged contact with the newly independent nations of Asia and Africa, that the seeds of nonalignment germinated.

Policy Options: 1949

On December 28, 1949, Edvard Kardelj addressed the Eighth Session of the National Assembly on the foreign policy of Yugoslavia. Disclaiming any intention of entering into "secret agreements" or "gentlemen's agreements," he said Yugoslavia's policy was open and clear: Yugoslavia "does not belong to any military blocs nor will it be a participant in any kind of aggressive planning against any country."[29] Kardelj desired to persuade the Soviet Union that Yugoslavia was not contemplating membership in NATO, and also to disabuse those in the West who believed that this course of action was now logical and the only one open to Yugoslavia. Above all, Kardelj's words were intended for the Kremlin.

According to a Yugoslav official who was then privy to the thinking of the inner circles of the foreign policy decision-makers, "Yugoslavia was well aware during the period of greatest immediate danger between 1948 and 1951 of the danger that the Soviet Union might misinterpret the position of Yugoslavia and overreact to anything that Yugoslavia might do or say. The government therefore was very careful not to take actions which might occasion a precipitous Soviet response. Since there was a strongly felt need for Yugoslavia not to be misunderstood by the Soviet Union, one essential characteristic of the Yugoslav leadership at this time was a heightened sensitivity to Soviet perceptions of, and probable responses to, Yugoslav policies and statements. During this crucial period, Yugoslavia was not able, nor indeed did it seek, to maintain a position equidistant between the Soviet Union and the Western Powers; very often, it would support the Soviet position in the United Nations, a type of overcompensation, if you will, that was deemed vital at the time."

[29] *Borba*, December 28, 1949, p. 2.

A high-ranking Croatian Communist Party leader said that Soviet officials considered Yugoslavia's accession to NATO inevitable. In this one perceives the influence of the Zhdanov two-camp thesis. Periodically, there were Western pressures on Yugoslavia to align itself formally against the Soviet bloc. However, Yugoslav officials invariably compliment the United States Government for its awareness of the nuances and dilemmas of the Yugoslav situation and for never having pressed the point. The assignment in December 1949 of George V. Allen as U.S. Ambassador in Belgrade proved felicitous. Though lacking background on Soviet and East European affairs or on communism in general, Allen worked smoothly with Yugoslav officials to make U.S. aid possible. An intimate of President Truman's, he ensured the Yugoslavs of a sympathetic listening in Washington and effectively espoused the case for economic and military assistance to Yugoslavia among Congressional leaders at a time when differentiation between Communist regimes was not generally accepted.

The Kardelj-Vyshinsky confrontation at the 1949 session of the General Assembly dispelled whatever illusions may have remained in the upper and middle echelons of the Yugoslav leadership about the possibility of an understanding with Stalin. The untenability of the choice between a return to the Cominform fold and accession to NATO was made clear in a major article which appeared shortly after Kardelj's speech.[30] Written under the pseudonym A. B., it was recognized as the work of Aleš Bebler, the Deputy Minister for Foreign Affairs, and as such, a reflection of official thinking at the highest levels. In the article, Bebler attributed the threatening rise in international tension and the danger of a new world war to the global rivalry of the Soviet Union and the United States and to their policy of interference in the internal affairs of other countries. He declared "an illusion" the Soviet contention that agreement among the Great Powers would end international

[30] A. B., "The Struggle for Peace—One Yugoslav View," *Trideset Dana*, Vol. VIII, No. 48 (January, 1950), pp. 1-6.

tension and the danger of war. He observed that their war-time cooperation had collapsed once the Axis Powers were defeated because of the frictions that arose over the division of spheres of influence which the Allies drew up among themselves. Noting that the division of spoils encompassed not only enemy territories, but allied and sovereign ones as well, Bebler argued that "harmony based on the assignment of spheres of influence was an edifice built on sand, indeed, even on quicksand." As long as the small nations refuse to consent to be only the objects of Great Power policy, struggle, instability, and war are inevitable. Any policy of interference, whether by the Soviet Union or the West, enhances the danger of war. From this concept stemmed the condemnation of blocs and the untoward pressures that flowed from their influence in international relations. According to Bebler, the solution lay in the application of the principles of the U.N. Charter, especially the equality of large and small nations and recognition of the right of all nations to self-determination.

There was as yet no thought of acting in concert with other small nations to realize these principles and no attention to the potentials of diplomacy outside the purview of Great Power rivalries. In Belgrade, contingency planning dominated the 1949-1951 period; there was no time or thought consciously given to long-term policy prospects. Yet, the aversion to membership in military blocs was taking hold as a cardinal principle of Yugoslav foreign policy.

A return to the Cominform was impossible, for it would have entailed surrender to Stalin, the deposal of Tito, and satellitization of Yugoslavia. The possibility of an out-and-out military alliance with the West was unacceptable for a number of reasons: it might have precipitated a crisis within the Yugoslav Communist Party and provoked the latently pro-Moscow faction to open revolt; it would have weakened Tito's position in the Party and in the country at large by seeming to substantiate Moscow's charges that he had betrayed socialism and become the lackey of the capitalists; it was too traumatic an alternative to contemplate ideologically for leaders who were, after all, long-time Comintern Communists, reared to overthrow, not embrace, capitalism; and perhaps most important, Yugoslav leaders believed such a move would be interpreted in Moscow as the beginning of a military countermove by the West against the still insecure Soviet position in Eastern Europe, and would have surely resulted in a Soviet armed intervention against Yugoslavia. During an election speech in early 1950, Tito went out of his way to allay Soviet fears on this point: "We declare, and we have been so declaring since we broke with the Cominform, that we have no intention of joining any other camp. We are not in any camp, nor are we in any bloc. . . ."[31] In a more general vein, he emphasized Yugoslavia's opposition to spheres of influence and its belief that all disputes should be resolved in the United Nations. Under no illusions that the two blocs would suddenly disintegrate, the Yugoslavs groped for a way of gradually transcending the bipolar, ideologically motivated constellations controlled by the Great Powers, and of creating an instrumentality for giving the small nations a voice in their destinies. In retrospect, one can detect in this line of thinking the embryonic policy of nonalignment.

Early Interactions with Developing Countries

The first impressions that Yugoslav officials formed of national-liberation developments in Asia were conditioned by their novitiate relationship to the Soviet Union. Having had no pre-1945 experience with Asian communists or socialists, the Yugoslavs viewed them in the light of their knowledge of the European counterparts. Contacts in the early postwar years were sporadic and meager. Yugoslav officials met Asian communists and socialists through Communist Front and Communist Party organizations in Western Europe and youth groups such as the National Youth Organization of Yugoslavia. For example, Burmese delegates to the British Empire Communist Conference held in

[31] "Tito's Speech at Titovo Užice," *Medjunarodni Problemi*, Vol. II, No. 1 (March, 1950), p. 14.

London in February 1947 returned home via Yugoslavia, where they were apparently impressed by the mobilization of young people for public works projects.[32] In July 1947, when cooperation still existed between the Burmese White Flag Communist Party and the dominant socialist AFPFL Party, the Yugoslavs played host to U Kyaw Nyein, the leader of the Burmese Socialist Party and then Minister of the Interim Government for Home and Judicial Affairs. That he knew about and sought to incorporate aspects of Yugoslavia's socialist system is evident from his statement that Burma's Draft Constitution, which had been drawn up by the AFPFL and was under consideration by a special committee of the Constituent Assembly, "embodied certain important features of the Yugoslav Constitution, particularly those clauses relating to minorities."[33] Burmese jurists were also attracted to the economic provisions of the 1946 Yugoslav Constitution. Ironically, the Burmese Communists took exception to using the Yugoslav Constitution as a model because it granted compensation for expropriated property, a point they argued with Yugoslav Communists at the Calcutta Conference in February 1948. Their preference for the Soviet Constitution was overridden by socialist Prime Minister Nu, who justified the inclusion of this principle in the Burmese Constitution by citing the example set by Yugoslavia, "a leading Communist country."

Prior to the Cominform crisis, a few Yugoslavs met with Burmese leftists in India in early 1947 as part of a Youth Delegation from the World Federation of Democratic Youth, a Communist Front organization, and in February 1948 at the Calcutta Conference of Asian Communists. After June 1948 the Burmese Communists lost interest in the Yugoslavs, who, on their part, became preoccupied with their relations with the Soviet Union and even more iso-

[32] I am indebted to Mrs. Anne (Rauch) Mochizuki for the insights into Burmese contacts with Yugoslavia during the 1945-1948 period.

[33] "U Kyaw Nyein at Yugoslav Capital," *The Burman*, July 17, 1947. Quoted in "Yugoslav Relations with Burma and Their Impact on Burmese Domestic Politics," an unpublished paper by Anne Rauch, p. 6.

lated from the complexities of South Asian internal developments. The Burmese socialists, however, retained a continuing interest in Yugoslav socialism, particularly in the system of Workers' Councils adopted in 1951 and in decentralization. Prior to 1954-1955, Burmese interest in and knowledge of Yugoslavia far exceeded that of the Yugoslavs concerning Burma.

In the two years after excommunication from the Cominform, Yugoslav perceptions of developments in Southern Asia betrayed their Soviet antecedents. The fighting in Kashmir between Pakistan and India and "the invasion" of Indian troops into the Princely State of Hyderabad were seen as examples of "imperialist efforts" to retain a foothold on the Indian subcontinent.[34] In consonance with Soviet views, the Yugoslavs maintained that the Western colonial powers were fomenting "religious and chauvinist conflicts," using the local bourgeoisie to convert India into a base for aggression. Nehru was viewed as a handmaiden of the Indian reactionaries and British colonialists. Throughout 1949, and probably as late as the Korean War period, Yugoslavia considered the Indian Government subservient to British and American interests,[35] a view which did not preclude it from negotiating its first trade agreement with India on December 29, 1948. In evaluating the uprising in Burma, the Yugoslavs mirrored the Cominform thesis, sided with the rebels, and criticized the U Nu regime for suppressing the Communist Party—"the real leader of the revolutionary movement."[36] Similarly, when the uprising of the Indonesian Communist Party (PKI) broke out in Madiun in September 1948, the Yugoslav press quickly expressed its sympathy for the rebels and hinted at a sellout to the Dutch by the incumbent government: "the Sukarno and Hatta regime has sold the republic to the Dutch and converted it into a Fascist state."[37] By early 1949, the press lamented the fall of Indonesia into the hands of the bourgeoisie, com-

[34] *Borba*, November 2, 1948, p. 3.
[35] *Borba*, April 4, 1949, p. 3.   [36] *Borba*, October 31, 1948, p. 5.
[37] *Borba*, September 22, 1948, p. 3; *Borba*, October 3, 1948, p. 7.

prising "feudal aristocrats, old bureaucrats who had served the former Japanese and Dutch regimes, and even Fascist elements [Sukarno] from the Japanese occupation period";[38] and in an obloquy only once removed from standard Cominform diatribes of the period, it deprecated the Indonesian leaders for sharing the same outlook "as a Nehru, an Ali Jinnah, a Pibul Songgram, a Syngman Rhee, and other narrow-minded bourgeoisie of the East." Though castigating the Hatta-Sukarno regime for "carrying out the dictates of American imperialism" and maintaining that the national-liberation struggle could be successful only if led by the Communist Party, the Yugoslav delegation in the United Nations, following the policy of the Soviet Union, voted to support the Indonesian republic against the Netherlands.[39] The stance in the U.N. bore little relevance to the domestic appraisal of the situation in the newly independent colonial countries. Yugoslav writings both on Western policy and on developments in the underdeveloped areas mirrored the assumptions and outlook of the Soviet Union and the Leninist theory of imperialism.[40] Only as a consequence of intimate and extended contact with delegates from these new nations and the needs of its own national policy did Yugoslav perceptions and policies change, departing from the Soviet view of the Third World and anticipating by several years the post-Stalinist modification of doctrine and outlook.

The Impact of the Korean War

The outbreak of the Korean War on June 25, 1950, heightened Yugoslavia's sense of insecurity and expectation of a Soviet attack. As a member of the Security Council, Yugoslavia was drawn into the vortex of deliberations aimed at ending hostilities, a process which expedited the shed-

---

38 *Borba*, March 26, 1949, p. 4.

39 *Borba*, May 14, 1949, p. 3.

40 "Crisis of the Colonial System," *Medjunarodni Problemi*, Vol. II, No. 2-3 (1950), pp. 46-91. This article was apparently a collective effort of the group on colonial affairs of the newly established, quasi-official Institute of International Politics and Economy in Belgrade.

ding of its ideological armoring against international realities and alerted it to the unexplored possibilities of
systematic collaboration with other small nations. Con-
comitantly, on a bilateral basis, Yugoslavia edged toward
closer military cooperation with, and dependence on, the
Western nations, since the fighting in the Far East seemed
linked to the intensification of provocations along its borders with Hungary, Romania, and Bulgaria. Thus, during
1950-1952 Yugoslavia began receiving military as well as
economic assistance from the United States and, even more
important, it felt assured of generous American support in
the event of a Soviet attack.

1. *The Yugoslav Position*

Yugoslavia supported the majority position in the Security Council and the initial moves which were taken to
repel the North Korean invasion. However, it resisted, as
dangerous and self-defeating, the prevailing American attitude of pressing for punishment of the aggressor and, when
the prospect seemed within grasp after the Inchon landing
in September, of crossing the 38th parallel and reunifying
all of Korea by force.

Uneasiness at the limited range of policy options, the
consequence of military and ideological bipolarization, was
expressed by Edvard Kardelj at the Fifth Session of the General Assembly in September, 1950. He described the aggressive policy of the Soviet Union and other East European
governments with regard to Yugoslavia as one of the principal causes for world tension, but made the United States,
too, culpable for seeking to exploit the Korean war to
mount a crusade against communism. Kardelj argued for
separation of general ideological antipathies from concrete
military threats. "Peace," he said, "cannot be preserved by
means of a crusade against socialism or against the strivings
of peoples towards freedom and independence. On the contrary, peace can be preserved only by combatting domination and aggression wherever they appear, regardless of the
chief political and ideological slogan behind which they

conceal themselves."[41] Anticipating themes which were to become the mark of nonalignment, he called for cooperation among nations with different social and political structures, opposition to Great Power hegemony, and an independent and enlarged role for the small nations. Implicit in his rejection of permanent commitment to either bloc and his insistence upon the equality of small and large states are the conceptual underpinnings of nonalignment:

> The peoples of Yugoslavia cannot accept the assumption that mankind must today choose between the domination of one great power or another. We consider that there is another path, the difficult but necessary path of democratic struggle for a world of free and equal nations, for democratic relations among nations, against foreign interference in the domestic affairs of the people and for the all around peaceful cooperation of nations on a basis of equality. . . . [42]

2. *Anxiety Over Soviet Intentions*

Anxiety over Soviet intentions prompted Kardelj to propose a draft resolution on the Duties of States in the Event of the Outbreak of Hostilities. Adopted by the General Assembly on November 17, 1950,[43] it aimed at forestalling a Soviet armed intervention against Yugoslavia under the guise of self-defense. It obligated any state engaged in military operations against another state to declare publicly within twenty-four hours its readiness to halt hostilities and withdraw its armed forces from foreign territory, provided the opposing side made a similar declaration. A state failing to act in accordance with this procedure would be adjudged the aggressor and would incur the responsibility for breaking the peace. The Yugoslav delegation also supported the Uniting for Peace Resolution, adopted in October 1950, since it invested the General Assembly with authority to act in situations where the Security Council was stymied be-

[41] U.N., General Assembly, *Official Records*, Fifth Session, p. 72.
[42] *Ibid.*, p. 69.   [43] General Assembly Resolution 378 (v).

cause of a veto by one of the permanent members. However, Yugoslavia strongly opposed carrying the war across the 38th parallel:

> The aim of the Security Council's action had been to prevent the alteration by force of a given situation, and not to use armed force to change the de facto situation existing at the beginning of hostilities, which would establish a precedent to justify any intervention in a country's internal affairs.[44]

Its expectation that the attempt to unify Korea by military means would complicate the task of easing international tension proved warranted.

The following year Yugoslavia brought a formal complaint against the hostile activities of the USSR and the Peoples' Democracies before the General Assembly. Having exhausted all normal diplomatic channels for eliminating the threat of Soviet attack, and having published a "White Book" cataloguing Cominform provocations along the Yugoslav border, Yugoslavia justified this extreme step as essential because of "the systematic organization of frontier incidents, the concentration of troops, the economic blockade, the creating of a special diversionary network within Yugoslavia, the call to subversion and acts of terrorism."[45] On November 26 and 27, 1951, Milovan Djilas, the delegate in the *Ad Hoc* Political Committee of the General Assembly, set forth the basis of the Yugoslav case against the Soviet bloc. The perceived gravity of the situation coupled with firm assurances of Western support in the event of attack impelled the Yugoslav leadership to bring maximum diplomatic and psychological pressure to bear on the Soviet Government and to abandon its previous relative forebearance. Soviet rejoinders concentrated on trying to raise doubts abroad about the socialist character of the Yugoslav regime and on labelling it a renegade regime. On

[44] U.N., General Assembly, Political and Security Committee, *Official Records*, Fifth Session, p. 39.
[45] U.N., General Assembly, *Official Records*, Sixth Session, p. 95.

December 14, 1951, the General Assembly took cognizance of the Yugoslav complaint and passed a resolution directed at the Soviet bloc countries which called on them to conduct their relations with other states in accordance with the provision of the Charter; to follow the usual laws and practices of diplomacy; and to solve all border difficulties through a mixed border commission or some other peaceful means.

Although aggressive provocations persisted until after Stalin's death, the imminence of an intervention receded in 1952. Yugoslav officials cited the overwhelmingly favorable vote of the General Assembly on the Yugoslav complaint as crucial in deterring aggression by signifying to the Soviet Union the readiness of the international community to take appropriate action to safeguard Yugoslavia as it had done in Korea.[46] What they left unsaid, and what was no doubt a restraining consideration in Moscow, was the growing U.S. commitment to Yugoslavia.

Outside of the U.N., the Korean War had two short-term effects on Yugoslav foreign policy: first, it led the Yugoslavs reluctantly to explore a closer military relationship with their pro-Western neighbors. Negotiations initiated by Yugoslavia with Greece and Turkey led to the signing of a Treaty of Friendship and Cooperation—a step toward entente which, it may be noted, called only for consultation—in Ankara on February 28, 1953. (A formal military alliance—the Balkan Pact—was signed at Bled on August 9, 1954.) Second, the Yugoslavs redoubled their efforts to settle fractious border disputes with Italy and Austria. In their growing dependence on American economic and military assistance and their eagerness to improve relations with non-Cominform neighbors, they made concessions on the Trieste and Carinthian issues which ended these troublesome frontier disputes and ushered in a period of generally excellent relations with Italy and Austria. The Trieste problem, in particular, was a major stumbling block. An

[46] M. I., "The Significance of the Yugoslav Complaint in the U.N. Against the Soviet Bloc," *Medjunarodni Problemi*, Vol. IV, No. 1 (January-February, 1952), pp. 5-6.

American Ambassador who had served in the Balkans during this period observed that "basically the West was unfair to Yugoslavia in not giving an inch because of the internal politics and situation in Italy. But the Yugoslavs settled anyway on the West's terms." By late 1953 Yugoslav political horizons beyond the Balkans loomed increasingly important in official thinking.

3. Changed Perceptions of Newly Independent Colonial Countries

In his speech before the Yugoslav National Assembly on December 29, 1950, Foreign Minister Kardelj presented a detailed explanation of Yugoslavia's support for the U.N.'s policy of thwarting "the adventurist policy of the North Korean Government," but of voting against its interventionist actions in pressing beyond the 38th parallel. Kardelj also used the opportunity to offer some general views on Yugoslavia's foreign policy. Specifically, his speech is noteworthy because the principles enunciated therein correspond so closely with the platform on active peaceful coexistence which emerged in 1955. He reaffirmed the government's opposition to all forms of Great Power interference in the internal affairs of other states, to aggression and the agents of aggression, and to attempts to transform national-liberation, progressive movements into instruments of this or that Great Power; and he called for a strengthening of the United Nations, the development of peaceful economic, political, and cultural relations among nations on the basis of equality, and renewed efforts to promote agreements among the Great Powers, "but on the basis of respect for the U.N. Charter and the right of each nation to self-government and independence in its internal and foreign policy."[47] Kardelj also gave greater emphasis to the principles of providing "international economic assistance to underdeveloped countries" and supporting "national-liberation, democratic, and progressive movements in all countries"

[47] Edvard Kardelj, "The New Yugoslavia in the Contemporary World," *Komunist*, Vol. v, No. 1 (January, 1951), p. 17.

than he had several months earlier in his speeches in the United Nations. Apparently, by late 1950 Yugoslav perceptions of the politically independent character of such newly independent countries as India, Egypt, Burma, and Ceylon began to undergo important changes which were to reshape Yugoslav foreign policy in the decades ahead.

More than any single event, the Korean war wrought a major change in Yugoslav views of the newly independent nations. Hitherto accepted assumptions came under searching review. Thus, the belief that economic dependence meant political subservience was contravened by the independent positions which nations such as India, Burma, and Egypt adopted toward the Korean war, despite their continued close and dependent economic links to the former metropole. Prior to June 1950 the belief was widespread among Yugoslav officials that India, though nominally independent, was part of the West. But India's position on Korea made it evident that India was in fact an independent country. Yugoslavia came to appreciate the independent stand of these new nations, not only on this issue, but on disarmament and colonial questions, on the seating of Communist China, and on the urgency of promoting the economic development of the less-developed countries.

The Yugoslav reaction to Soviet pressure did not automatically usher in an era of new perceptions and policies. Of crucial importance were the physical contacts and interaction with other countries also in quest of an independent position outside the two blocs. Thus, the basis for Yugoslavia's future friendly relations with India and Egypt were laid while all were members of the Security Council in 1950-1951. The consultations among the chief delegates—Aleš Bebler of Yugoslavia, Sir Benegal Rau of India, and Mahmoud Fawzi of Egypt—started on the Korean question and were carried forward to other issues of mutual interest. The three tended to vote or abstain together on most questions pertaining to the Korean war. This collaboration was continued and expanded even after they were no longer members of the Security Council.

In late March 1951 Sir Benegal Rau told Dr. Aleš Bebler that Prime Minister Nehru, speaking in the Indian Parliament, had called for an unaligned policy.[48] Josip Djerdja, assigned to New Delhi in February 1950 as Yugoslavia's first Ambassador to India and accredited as Ambassador to Burma when diplomatic relations were established in February 1951, informed Belgrade of the similarity of sentiments, aspirations, and outlooks that he found in Nehru, U Nu, and the Indonesian officials with whom he came into contact in New Delhi. In 1951 the Yugoslavs organized a conference in Zagreb of representatives of various movements and groups from Europe and Asia to discuss the idea of coexistence and, specifically, ways of ending the Korean war. Though unproductive, it demonstrated to the Yugoslavs the deep-rooted interest in all areas of the world in a policy not tied to either of the Great Power blocs. In October 1951 Dr. Joža Vilfan, another important Yugoslav official whose involvement in foreign policy has continued to the present, headed the first goodwill mission to Ethiopia and was treated cordially. Soon afterwards, the Minister of Industry and the Chief of the General Staff visited Ethiopia, initiating close relations in several areas. The visit of Emperor Haile Selassie to Yugoslavia in July 1954, the first by an African leader, was an outgrowth of the ties developed and expanded as a result of the Vilfan mission. Each of these events had a similar effect: the communication to decisionmakers in Belgrade of the existence in Asia and Africa

[48] During the course of a discussion of foreign policy, Prime Minister Nehru deplored the prevalence of the view that India had to be aligned in the Cold War. In words that foreshadowed the spirit of Bandung and nonalignment, he expressed disquiet at attempts to pressure every country to take sides with one bloc or the other: "I am not concerned for a moment with the policies of this group or that. But my simple policy—and it is not a negative policy, it is not a passive policy—is that first of all, as far as possible, [of] doing our utmost for the avoidance of world war, or any war; secondly, of judging issues on the merits and acting accordingly."

He argued against alignment of any kind on the ground that it would result in India's following policies which were not formulated with India's needs or views in mind. Lok Sabha, *Parliamentary Debates* (March 28, 1951), pp. 5289-5290.

of leaders who were all trying to find a way of survival for their independent nations and who shared a sense of the fragility of their countries' newly won independence.

Within the U.N. the interest in economic development reinforced the beginnings of regular consultations among the unaligned nations. In 1947, UNRRA was disbanded and Yugoslavia cast about for alternative sources of assistance within an acceptable multilateral framework. Unlike Poland and Czechoslovakia, it did not even conceive of exploring the possibilities of the Marshall proposals of June 1947. For Yugoslav leaders the prospect of accepting aid from the United States implied inevitable control by U.S. capital. In the General Assembly Committee for Economic and Financial Questions, Yugoslav delegates responded favorably to the proposals of Dr. Hernan Santa Cruz of Chile and Dr. V.K.R.V. Rao of India, in particular, for a system of international financing. Though concerned with its own immediate needs, Yugoslavia participated in the early discussions which proceeded from the first within a broad framework and were in 1951 to give birth to the SUNFED proposal. The combination of active cooperation in trying to arrange for a truce for the Korean war and extensive discussions about common economic needs contributed to the development in the unaligned countries of an awareness of themselves as independent and not unimportant actors on the international stage.

Yugoslav writings on the situation in Asia gradually became less doctrinaire. As early as September 1950 an important Yugoslav journal acknowledged that though India and Burma were still dependent economically on the Western imperialist powers, they had nonetheless refused to become members of either bloc and were searching for an independent path in world affairs.[49] By 1952 articles appeared in *Borba* which departed drastically from Soviet interpretations of developments in Southern Asia. One piece deserves

[49] "The Significance Underlying the Rise of New States in South and Southeast Asia," *Review of International Affairs*, Vol. 1 (September 27, 1950), p. 13.

mention because it was written under a pseudonym by Josip Djerdja, then recently returned from his tour as Ambassador in India, and is an example of the economic evaluation on which nonalignment was to be based. Approaching the economic situation in South Asia on a realistic basis, Djerdja stressed the quest of these countries for independence from former metropoles; the usefulness for them of a mixed economy which, though socialistic in aspiration, retained many capitalistic elements; the socialistic outlook that had nothing to do with Soviet socialism or Soviet influence, which was virtually non-existent; and the possibility of cooperation between Yugoslavia and these countries.[50]

The End of the Cominform Threat: Observations

By late 1952 the Yugoslavs no longer feared a Soviet attack. Western aid under the Tripartite Agreement of 1951 was arriving in generous amounts; the Korean war was not the opening gambit of a new Soviet expansionist drive, as many had believed in 1950; the military provocations of the Soviet satellites tapered off, though the economic blockade and hostile propaganda continued; the United Nations had proved a valuable instrument for enhancing Yugoslav security, and the overwhelming majority of nations there had supported Yugoslavia against Soviet pressures; and the virtual isolation and friendlessness of 1948 were relics that had been replaced by friendly relations with most of the non-Communist nations of the world, and especially with the leading new nations of Asia and Africa.

In retrospect, Yugoslavia's expulsion from the Soviet bloc may be seen as the crucial turning point in its postwar evolution. Its suddenness and harshness compelled the Yugoslavs, who were probably the most orthodox and zealous Communists in Eastern Europe, to shed illusions that if acted on would have meant greater backwardness and a role on the periphery of the Soviet empire, entailing decades

[50] Djordje Jerković (pseudonym for Josip Djerdja), "On Certain Problems of Contemporary Developments in Asia," *Borba*, May 18, 1952, p. 3.

of political subservience. Necessity led Yugoslav leaders to reevaluate underlying doctrinal and political assumptions hitherto not questioned. The consequences of the distorted Stalinist image of the world were understood and acted upon. Reevaluation bred revisionism. A process started which shaped a new outlook characterized by a greater realism in international affairs, and a disposition to depart from the canons of the Soviet developmental model and to experiment with new forms of economic, social, and political institutions in the construction of a socialist society.

By being set adrift on the international scene, Yugoslav leaders discovered the importance of the United Nations for a small nation. They became acquainted with the U.N. as a forum for arousing "international public opinion," that chimerical but occasionally useful device for inducing a measure of additional constraint in ambitious nations. Through General Assembly resolutions, expanded concepts of international law, and sympathetic voting majorities, the Yugoslavs helped to pioneer small nations' use of the United Nations as a restraint upon the actions of the Great Powers.

The United Nations became the Yugoslav bridge to the Third World. Contacts and collaboration with the new nations convinced the Yugoslavs that, contrary to Soviet views, many of the new nations were not controlled by the former Western colonial powers and that they, too, shared a desire for national independence, self-determination, and equality. The interaction with the other unaligned nations opened new vistas for Yugoslavia. Threatened from the East and uncomfortable with the West, Yugoslavia sought an association that was ideologically congenial and politically feasible. The Korean war brought out the communality of views among the unaligned nations on the major issues of war, peace, and survival in a bipolar international environment; and discussions in the U.N. made evident the paramountcy of economic development for these nations. This growing consciousness of common political, security, and economic interests intensified communication among them. What was needed was a broad unifying conception.

In a more immediate vein, the Cominform crisis intensified Yugoslavia's efforts to seek a reconciliation with its pro-Western neighbors—Greece, Italy, and Austria. After the war the Communist Party of Yugoslavia[51] had made territorial claims against these countries which, had they persisted, would have poisoned relations for decades. In the interest of security Yugoslavia made compromises that favored its pro-Western neighbors. These peaceful settlements of border disputes, motivated by national necessity, were later made a virtue and a cardinal principle of peaceful coexistence, the ideological essence of nonalignment.

New trends and ideas that emerge fortuitously are not immediately recognized by decisionmakers as the basis for new policies. No special decision concerning closer links with the unaligned nations had apparently been made in Belgrade by late 1952, but a Yugoslav who had been Ambassador in one of the leading countries of Western Europe said that he had by then received instructions to strengthen contacts with nations having similar outlooks, i.e., with India, Burma, the Arab states, Indonesia, and Ethiopia. There was as yet no grand design, no formal policy of organizing with the unaligned, no concentration on the Third World. Yugoslav attention was still centered in Europe, but it began to look beyond the Cold War to developments and possibilities in Asia and Africa.

[51] In line with the trend toward liberalizing the Party and promoting economic decentralization and self-management, the leadership renamed the Party at the Sixth Congress in November 1952. After that time, the Communist Party of Yugoslavia was known as the League of Yugoslav Communists (LYC). This is the name which will be used in subsequent chapters. The change in name signified the retrenchment of direct Party control over economic, government, and social life, and the determination to focus primarily on political and ideological matters.

CHAPTER II

Between Unalignment and Nonalignment

THROUGHOUT 1953 and half of 1954, the central preoccupation of Yugoslav leaders was with those issues which impinged directly on national security. Foremost among these were the Trieste question and the unfriendly relations with Italy, both of which were exacerbated by the bitterness between Belgrade and the Vatican over Cardinal Stepinac, the Croatian Catholic religious leader incarcerated for wartime collaboration with the Nazis and the Ustashi, the Croatian Fascist group; the negotiation and implementation of the Balkan Pact with Greece and Turkey; and, notwithstanding the death of Stalin on March 5, 1953, the continued sense of threat from the Soviet Union and the Cominform countries. Indeed, as late as April 1954, Aleš Bebler, the Undersecretary for Foreign Affairs, was quoted in a Yugoslav journal as maintaining that "it should still be persistently and unequivocally pointed out that the USSR and its foreign policy still constitute the main obstacle on the road to a lasting and solid peace."

Yet, on ancillary levels, Yugoslav interaction with Asian, African, and Latin American countries intensified. Yugoslav political leaders, military and economic missions, trade unionists and artists visited and hosted their counterparts from India and Burma, Ethiopia and Egypt. Cooperation increased in international organizations. Slowly, inexorably, the horizons of upper and middle echelon officials in the Party and government widened beyond the confines of the Balkans, a prelude to the ambitious internationalism of Tito. The purposes underlying this as yet unorchestrated activity were threefold: to reinforce Yugoslav efforts to end its position of relative diplomatic isolation by seeking a political and security community with which it could ideologically identify and associate; to link Yugoslavia to the "progressive" forces in the world; and to develop the markets Yugoslav enterprises thought they saw in the new nations of Asia and Africa.

39

The Asian Socialist Conference

At the first Asian Socialist Conference, held in Rangoon in January 1953, the Yugoslavs made a notable entrance onto the stage of Asian socialism. Seeing that "the central question of foreign policy discussion would be the creation of a third bloc in Asia,"[1] they worked hard to be invited, as did the Israelis, and were the only Europeans to be so honored;[2] both sought to end their diplomatic isolation and cultivate among the Asian socialists support in the U.N. and partnership in trade; both sent high-ranking delegations in accordance with the importance that they attributed to the opportunity.

If the conference entailed recognition by the Asian socialists of the differences both between Yugoslav and Soviet communism and between Yugoslav and West European socialism,[3] conversely, for the Yugoslavs it constituted a stepping stone to cooperation with the socialist, rather than the Communist, parties of Asia and an awareness of the deep-rooted desire in Asia for a third bloc, independent "both from capitalism and from Cominformism." In the interval between the organizing sessions in Rangoon in March 1952 and the convening of the conference itself, Yugoslav officials in the region succeeded in communicating to their superiors in Belgrade a sense of the complexity and intense nationalism underlying Asian political currents, and the need to interpret socialism in a manner that often bore little relationship to the Marxist-Leninist antecedents on which the Yugoslav revolutionaries had been reared. Milovan Djilas and Aleš Bebler, the main Yugoslav delegates, stressed three themes deriving from the Yugoslav experience: the possibility of a small nation's preserving its in-

[1] P., "The Rangoon Conference of Socialist Parties of Asia," *Trideset Dana*, Vol. XIII, No. 84 (December 1952), p. 1095.

[2] Clement Attlee, the former British Prime Minister who was instrumental in giving Burma its independence, attended as an honored guest, but there was no official delegation invited from the British Labor Party.

[3] "Pending the Socialist Conference in Rangoon," *Review of International Affairs*, Vol. IV, No. 1 (January 1, 1953), p. 5.

dependence in a world dominated by the hostility of the two Great Powers; the differences between Yugoslav and Soviet socialism, with particular attention to the hegemonistic intrigues and anti-democratic bureaucratism of the Soviet Union; and the role of Workers' Councils and self-management in promoting democracy and socialism.[4] Their purpose was to link Yugoslav developments and aspirations with those of Asian socialists, and not to advance a Yugoslav model of development for Asia.

Shortly after the Conference ended, a Yugoslav editorial observed that the standpoint of the Asian socialists on colonial issues revealed "the existence of great revolutionary possibilities within these parties." It also noted that their principal weaknesses—the absence of a well-prepared program and of fully developed guiding concepts—were being overcome, and suggested that the League of Yugoslav Communists could serve as the link between Asian socialists and their European colleagues, whom they still viewed with reserve and some justifiable suspicion.[5] Two months later Vladimir Dedijer wrote a follow-up article that was important for three reasons. First, having recently completed an authorized biography of Tito, Dedijer presumably expressed views accurately reflecting those of the Yugoslav leader. Dedijer said "there are favorable conditions for promoting contacts between Yugoslavia and the progressive workers' movements in Asia and Africa, particularly as regards the development of socialism in underdeveloped countries."[6] He associated Yugoslavia's economic underdevelopment, history of exploitation by one big power or another, and struggle for national independence with those of the Asian countries. Second, Dedijer deftly substituted the Socialist Alliance for the League of Yugoslav Communists as

[4] Asian Socialist Conference, *Daily News Bulletin*, January 11 and 15, 1953.

[5] "A Good Beginning in Rangoon," *Review of International Affairs*, Vol. IV, No. 3 (February 1, 1953), p. 6.

[6] Vladimir Dedijer, "A Yugoslav View on the Problem of Collaboration in the International Workers' Movement," *Review of International Affairs*, Vol. IV, No. 10 (May 16, 1953), p. 7.

the principal vehicle for establishing contact with workers' parties and other progressive forces working toward socialism in developing countries. The Socialist Alliance encompassed all types of economic, social, and cultural institutions and was the mass front organization which the Yugoslav Communist leadership used to generate and maintain enthusiasm. Shrewdly perceiving that in dealing with non-Communist socialist parties contacts would be easier to establish if ideological and political controversy were minimized, Dedijer's commentary signified the expansion of the Socialist Alliance's role abroad. The term "Socialist" clearly had a favorable connotation abroad which "Communist" did not have, regardless of the vintage. He noted that the Socialist Alliance would, for example, be better equipped to improve relations with the ruling Congress Party in India.[7] Finally, Dedijer cautioned his more zealous comrades against indulging Yugoslav chauvinism in dealings with Asian and African countries: it would not do to have Yugoslavs brag that their country was "the cradle of socialism" or that they were the only ones who had discovered "the touchstone for socialist wisdom."[8]

Yugoslavia participated actively in the work of the Asian Socialist International during the 1953-1956 period. Key officials attended the meetings of the Permanent Bureau (Secretariat), Anti-Colonial Bureau, and the one on Planning; and Yugoslavs contributed frequently to *Socialist Asia*, the journal published by the International. However, after the second Asian Socialist Conference, held in Bombay in November 1956, the Yugoslavs lost interest, in part because the Conference declined to take a strong stand against the aggression of France, Great Britain, and Israel against Egypt. Also, they had by then established firm ties with the leading Afro-Asian countries, and, as one of the leaders of the emerging third bloc, were directing their energies toward the main arena of world politics and the formalization of nonalignment.

[7] *Ibid.*, p. 8.   [8] *Ibid.*

Links to Afro-Asia

1. Ethiopia

Ethiopia was the first African country with which Yugoslavia established close relations. Initial contacts between Yugoslav and Ethiopian officials were made at the Paris Peace Conference in 1947. Both countries shared the common experience of having been victims of Italian aggression and had a stake in the question of reparations. Their consultations in Paris continued in the United Nations, where Yugoslavia supported Ethiopia's claim to Eritrea, and Ethiopia reciprocated on the Trieste issue. In October 1951, a goodwill mission headed by Dr. Jože Vilfan, then Undersecretary for Foreign Affairs, was sent to Ethiopia and Egypt to explore possibilities for extending diplomatic and economic ties and to bring back first-hand impressions of these countries. Regular diplomatic relations were established with Ethiopia in March 1952, and a Yugoslav Legation was opened in Addis Ababa in October; the Ethiopian Legation in Belgrade was opened in May 1954. The following year both governments agreed to upgrade their missions to the Embassy level.

According to one of the members of the Vilfan mission, their most interesting discovery was the varied presence of Western technicians and assistance: a Swedish mission trained the Air Force; a Belgian mission developed the police force; and an American mission assisted in economic development. He said, "This type of diversified Western aid was the first lesson for Yugoslavia in what the West was doing in an African country in the field of technical assistance." Responding to the cordial reception offered them, the Yugoslavs sent a number of government Ministers to promote trade and economic cooperation. The first such agreement between the two countries was signed in Belgrade in August 1953 during the visit of an Ethiopian delegation. In February 1954 General Peko Dapčević, the Chief of Staff, visited Ethiopia as a special emissary from President Tito and extended an invitation to Emperor Haile Selassie to visit Yugoslavia.

The visit in July 1954—the first by an African leader to Yugoslavia—marked the beginning of Tito's active courtship of the most prominent leaders of the unaligned new nations of Africa and Asia; the previous month he had received the invitation he coveted to visit India in December. No longer anxious over his security in the Balkans, and sensing the enormous political potential of the new nations for playing an active and influential role in international affairs, Tito set out on his personal investigation of the possibilities. Haile Selassie's visit had been a great success, and Tito returned it in December 1955. As a result of the visits, economic relations were expanded, several mixed Ethiopian-Yugoslav enterprises were established, and Yugoslav technicians were sent to Ethiopia—the beginnings of Belgrade's economic activities and technical assistance program in Africa.

During the 1954-1961 period, President Tito and Emperor Haile Selassie met six times and frequently exchanged personal views during the Middle East crises of 1956 and 1958 and the Congo crisis of 1960-1961. Commenting on the state of relations between the two countries, a ranking member of the Ethiopian Embassy in Belgrade later stated: "People are always asking me how can an Emperor and a Communist get along well. The answer is simple: they feel a sense of respect and mutual regard; both fought against Italy, against a Fascist invader; both triumphed against adversity; both have sought to modernize their country; both are of the same age; and both have achieved eminence in the world and share many views on important matters." This evaluation is accurate, but incomplete. The friendly relations between Yugoslavia and Ethiopia from 1954 to 1961 can more properly be described as merely cordial after the Belgrade Conference of 1961. This subtle shift has occurred because the Yugoslavs have paid greater attention since then to the "progressives" and radicals of the nonaligned world. As nonalignment assumed a markedly leftist swing during the 1961-1966 period, Belgrade accommodated itself accordingly. To Tito's brew of pragmatism were added the

44

hops of ideological radicalism. The Yugoslavs felt a need to dissociate themselves somewhat from the "conservative forces" in Africa; the Ethiopians, for their part, became more African-oriented and less ambitious for an international role in Asia and Latin America.

2. *Burma*

After 1952 Yugoslavia's fragmentary contacts with Burma assumed a coherent, cordial pattern. Out of Yugoslavia's search for friends and Burma's need for military assistance to combat rebel tribes and the incursion of remnants of Chiang Kai-shek's defeated army into northern Burma, and out of a shared affinity for socialism, close relations developed which lasted until U Nu's final deposal in March 1962. (U Nu led his country from its independence in 1948 until September 1958. Deposed by General Ne Win, who established a military dictatorship for eighteen months, U Nu returned as Prime Minister in April 1960, remaining until Ne Win's second coup two years later.) Unable to obtain from the British or Americans the necessary military equipment to cope with its military-security problems, in part because of the priorities of the Korean War, Burma looked to unaligned and ideologically sympathetic Yugoslavia, Israel, and India. A high-ranking Burmese mission, led by Cabinet Minister Kyaw Nyein and Brigadier Kyaw Zaw, spent a month in Yugoslavia, at which time the invitation for Yugoslavia to attend the Asian Socialist Conference was also arranged. The Yugoslav military mission sent in December 1952 concluded the arrangements for the mortars and mountain artillery the Burmese desired (at about the same time, the Israelis agreed to sell them rebuilt British Spitfires). Thus, at this critical period, the Yugoslavs and Israelis provided armaments vital for Burma's political existence. The Yugoslav military instructors greatly impressed the Burmese: selfless and hard-working, they made no demands for special housing or comforts, living simply and giving fully of their time and expertise.

Yugoslav military assistance and support in the U.N. for

Burma's complaint in March 1953 against aggression by Nationalist China enhanced Belgrade's prestige in Rangoon. Important Burmese officials, impressed by Yugoslavia's socialist program, entertained the desire "to transform Burma into the Yugoslavia of Asia."[9] An eminent British specialist on Burma was led to observe in 1960:

> Certainly the two countries have many affinities: both have federal constitutions and include within their boundaries diverse races and religions, both are situated precariously on the very edge of the Communist world empire, both are endeavoring to take revolutionary strides from a medieval, agricultural society towards a modern, industrialized order; and both are committed wholeheartedly to a policy of neutralism which they hope to galvanize into something dynamic, a positive force among nations.[10]

Burma's regard for Yugoslavia resulted in an invitation to attend the Asian Socialist Conference. Participation enabled the Yugoslavs to establish firm contacts with Asian socialist parties. The decisions and resolutions passed by the conference mirrored the domestic and foreign policy outlook of the Burmese leadership and seemed to the Yugoslavs remarkably consonant with their own. In particular, Burma's espousal of a "Third Force" which would avoid all forms of commitment to either bloc, its rejection of "all military or military-related pacts, e.g., SEATO," and its commitment to the U.N. "as an instrument of peace in the political and socio-economic realms,"[11] led the Yugoslavs, in 1953, to view Burma as the most progressive country in Southeast Asia. This interest heightened as a consequence of Tito's visit in January 1955.

[9] Hugh Tinker, *The Union of Burma: A Study of the First Years of Independence* (London and New York: Oxford University Press, 1961. 3rd Edition) , p. 362.

[10] *Ibid.*

[11] Frank N. Trager, "Burma's Foreign Policy, 1948-56: Neutralism, Third Force, and Rice," *Journal of Asian Studies*, Vol. XVI, No. 1 (November, 1956) , p. 97.

3. *India*

Friendship with India matured slowly, notwithstanding the close relationship developed by Dr. Aleš Bebler and Sir Benegal Rau during their tenure in the Security Council in 1950-1951, and the concurrent attention of their delegations to the prospects for economic development. This friendship was far more important to Belgrade than to New Delhi. Reflecting the disparity, the Yugoslav Embassy in New Delhi was opened on April, 20, 1950, whereas the Indian Government did not accredit a permanent Ambassador to Yugoslavia until October 1954. A Yugoslav goodwill mission, headed by Rodoljub Čolaković, then a member of the Federal Executive Council, visited India from December 14, 1952 to January 12, 1953, and was apparently well-received. At a banquet in honor of the delegation, an Indian Minister graciously attributed to the visit special significance for India "because it is the first [high-level goodwill] mission of a European country which has been sent to our country since independence."[12] Despite reservations about certain aspects of India's internal and foreign policy, the Yugoslav leadership lauded India's refusal to join any military blocs or anti-Communist movements and "its active role in the struggle for peace and in the struggle to realize full equality among nations of different races, ideologies, and continents."[13]

The assignment of Dr. Jože Vilfan as Ambassador to India in the 1952-1953 period was a felicitous one. An astute, empathetic, and humane person, Dr. Vilfan quickly earned the respect of the Indians. During his first summer in New Delhi, when air-conditioning was not yet standard Embassy equipment, he encountered the oppressiveness of the Indian plain. Most of the foreign missions left New Delhi for the highlands to escape the hot season, as had been the custom during the British period. Detecting an underlying unhappiness among the hypersensitive Indians, to whom such be-

[12] "Spoljna Politika," *Yugoslovenski Pregled* (1958), p. 31.
[13] "India's Day of Independence," *Review of International Affairs*, Vol. IV, No. 3 (February 1, 1953), p. 4.

havior smacked of the colonial tradition, Vilfan and his wife remained in New Delhi. The incident itself was of minor importance, but it helped to distinguish Vilfan in Indian eyes. It was also symptomatic of Yugoslav sensitivity to the fragile egos of the new nations and to the small matters that often condition the outlook on the substantive issues of international affairs—a sensitivity that has generally characterized Yugoslav diplomacy.

During his service in India, Vilfan worked closely with the Indians in helping to arrange the truce in Korea. He became friendly with Dr. Sarvepalli Radhakrishnan, then Vice-President of India, and was instrumental in obtaining an invitation for him to visit Yugoslavia in July 1953 to meet Tito, who expressed his interest in seeing India and in exchanging views with Nehru personally. In late June 1954 Madame Vijaya Lakshmi Pandit, Nehru's sister and then President of the General Assembly, visited Yugoslavia. As Secretary to the President, Vilfan arranged for her to meet with Tito; and at that meeting an invitation was extended to Tito to visit India in December. Thus, the initiative for the first summit meeting between these two leaders came from President Tito.

On October 25, 1954, on the eve of his departure for India and Burma, President Tito delivered a lengthy address to the Federal Assembly on the solution of the vexatious Trieste question, the normalization of relations with the Soviet Union and Eastern Europe, and the negotiation of the Balkan Pact. Toward the end of the speech, he alluded to his forthcoming visit to Southern Asia, emphasizing the considerations which motivated him in this new undertaking: the past cooperation with these countries and their past understanding of Yugoslavia's plight and unique political situation; the similarity of views on various world problems; the common heritage of struggle against foreign rule and the shared concern for internal development and modernization; and the common interest in peaceful cooperation based on "the principles of respect for independence, nonaggression, and equality," especially in the U.N. Besides these understandable political reasons, it is important to take into account the personality of Tito, about which more will be said in a future section.

The Genesis of Yugoslav Credibility in the Third World

When the policies of two nations coincide, it is difficult to ascertain whether their motives also coincide. In the early sessions of the United Nations, before the Cominform break, both Yugoslavia and the Soviet Union opposed colonialism and supported independence for Afro-Asian countries, though for different reasons. But it took more than excommunication from the Cominform for other nations to differentiate between Yugoslavia and the Soviet Union.

During the 1950-1954 period, the Yugoslavs participated actively in the work of the Trusteeship Council, making constructive proposals and establishing sound ties with the new nations; they were in the forefront of efforts to promote economic assistance to the underdeveloped countries within the framework of the U.N., and helped shape the 1951 SUNFED proposal; and during the Korean War they cooperated with the unaligned countries to end hostilities. Despite this commendable record of constructive behavior in the U.N. and despite the realization by the new nations of the genuineness of the clash between Belgrade and Moscow, it took time for Yugoslavia to gain widespread acceptance among the unaligned countries as an independent, socialist, and *responsible* nation.

Ironically, Yugoslavia's principal difficulty was not in demonstrating its friendship for the new nations, but in convincing them that it was neither being too anti-Soviet nor trying deliberately to intensify the Cold War, which these nations sought to abate, and that its complaints against the Soviet Union were justifiable, based on reality and not on ideological chauvinism. One longtime Yugoslav correspondent at the United Nations, commenting on his country's decision in 1951 to bring the issue of Soviet pressure to

49

the attention of the U.N., said that the Indian delegation had thought Yugoslavia was behaving like an *enfant terrible*, making the East-West rapprochement that India was seeking to effect even more difficult. Krishna Menon, the Indian delegate, did not understand the Yugoslav position in 1951; he considered Yugoslavia's formal complaint unnecessarily provocative. He was quite unfamiliar with the specifics of Yugoslavia's border disputes and, moreover, was perhaps piqued by this added complication to his self-assumed role of mediator between the Soviet Union and the United States. At the same time, while intensifying his pressure against Yugoslavia, Stalin shrewdly dropped hints of interest in a lessening of tension with the West, thus making it even more difficult for the Yugoslavs to justify their decision to bring the complaint before the U.N. The problem for Yugoslavia was to convince India and the other unaligned nations that it was not a provocateur; certainly no one believed it a pawn of Moscow.

In 1951-1952 the detachment of the unaligned states from a situation that the Yugoslavs perceived as precarious, and their occasionally placatory gestures toward the Soviet Union provoked Yugoslavia into criticisms that seem, in the light of Yugoslav policy since 1955, curiously unreal. The Asian-Arab countries' support of Czechoslovakia rather than Yugoslavia for the seat on the Economic and Social Council in November 1952 impelled Belgrade (which was wary of unduly affronting these nations even in the days before nonalignment became the cornerstone of Yugoslav foreign policy) in a rare outburst of anger to condemn their "unprincipled dalliance with the Soviet Union, the expression of readiness to grant unnecessary concessions to the Soviet bloc. . . ."[14] Acknowledging the undeniable historical importance of the emergence of Africa and Asia, Belgrade nonetheless took them to task for their short-sightedness in not appreciating the indivisibility of nationalist

[14] "Activities of the Asian Arab Bloc in the UN," *Review of International Affairs*, Vol. IV, No. 22 (November 16, 1952), p. 8.

aspirations in all parts of the world and the interdependence of all struggles for freedom from Great Power
domination.

Important though the U.N. was in facilitating Yugoslavia's interaction with the new nations, the manifestations
of friendship on the bilateral level—over and above the
usual round of economic treaties and exchange of missions
—were more crucial to the germination of the relationship.
The clandestine shipments of arms to Burma and Egypt
in the 1952-1954 period, and subsequently to Algeria, facilitated the intimate exchange of views and reshaping of
the attitudes on international affairs; they also helped dispel lingering reservations stemming from different ideological orientations, especially in the case of Egypt.

The Yugoslav and Egyptian delegations in the Security
Council conferred frequently and agreed on many issues;
however, in matters of policy, they could not press beyond
the point of confluence of their two countries, and the
Egypt of King Farouk, heavily dependent on the West and
under the shadow of British military power in the Suez
Canal area, exercised only limited independence in foreign
affairs. In November 1951 the Vilfan goodwill mission, returning from Ethiopia, spent a few fruitless days in Cairo.
The Yugoslav Legation had few contacts with the Farouk
regime, and these were curt and unpleasant, in part because of the fractious activities of a political émigré group of
former Ustashi and Chetnik personnel bitterly hostile to
the Tito Government. Also, as a Communist country Yugoslavia found itself under suspicion by Egyptian officials,
who generally viewed communism and the Cold War
through British eyes.

The overthrow of Farouk in July 1952 by a group of
Army officers angered by the military defeats in Palestine
in 1948-1949 and by the corruption and ineptness of the political leaders was evaluated by Yugoslav officials in Cairo
as a genuine expression of Egyptian nationalism and not,
as assumed by most foreign diplomats, as a conservative mil-

itary clique supplanting an equally conservative but hope-
lessly venal political one.[15] Unsigned articles appeared in
Yugoslav journals—most likely the observations of Yugoslav officials and journalists in Cairo—calling attention to
episodic domestic developments which, they speculated,
might presage a major internal political transformation.
One article noted, before Western commentators did, that
General Naguib, the head of the military junta, was under
pressure from some in his immediate circle to adopt a more
radical line toward Great Britain.[16] Yugoslav analysts saw
Naguib's military dictatorship as one that nonetheless
aimed at becoming a parliamentary democracy. They
called Belgrade's attention to Naguib's unsuccessful search
for arms in Western Europe in the spring of 1953 and to the
strong likelihood of his turning to the Soviet bloc.[17] In
August 1953 the first Egyptian military mission visited Yugoslavia, touring Army units and factories. The ground was
prepared for the sale of small arms to Egypt. Notwithstanding British and American pressure, Belgrade went through
with the sale, significantly enhancing its standing in Cairo,
as much for the political courage as for the arms.[18] Through
its willingness to provide arms to Burma, Egypt, and the Algerian FLN at a time when no major power would, and its
readiness to incur Western displeasure at possible political
and economic disadvantage to itself, Yugoslavia took giant

[15] Considerable credit for alerting Belgrade to the importance of
post-1952 developments must go to the Yugoslav Ambassadors: Jože
Brilej (1952-February 1953) and Marko Nikezić (March 1953-May
1956) ; and to Zdravko Pečar, the chief Yugoslav correspondent in Egypt
between 1952 and 1957. Each has distinguished himself in the past
decade: Brilej served as Ambassador to the United Kingdom and in
other posts in the Ministry of Foreign Affairs; Nikezić served as Foreign
Minister (1965-1968) ; and Pečar emerged as a leading specialist on
Egypt and North Africa, particularly on Algerian affairs, and was appointed Ambassador to Mali in 1967.

[16] "On the Eve of Internal Changes in the Near East Countries,"
Review of International Affairs, Vol. IV, No. 2 (January 16, 1953) , p. 4.

[17] "Looking for New Paths," *Review of International Affairs*, Vol. IV,
No. 11 (June 1, 1953) , p. 23.

[18] For a detailed treatment of this phase of Yugoslav-Egyptian relations see Chapter VII.

steps toward establishing its credibility among these new nations at the time of their greatest uncertainty and sense of political weakness.

Tito in South Asia

In a message to the Yugoslav people on the eve of his departure for India and Burma aboard the yacht "Galeb," President Tito explained that such trips greatly benefited the country, by enabling leaders abroad to gain a greater understanding of Yugoslavia's internal development and outlook on international issues. Hitherto, his visits had been to countries directly involved in the strengthening of Yugoslavia's national security: Great Britain, Greece, Turkey. For the first time Tito moved out of Europe. The seeds of Tito's internationalism, implicit in his outlook and ambitions, were now sown in areas where the yields would soon far exceed his boldest expectations. That Tito placed great hopes upon this venture is evident:

> I wish to emphasize that I consider this visit of ours to be of special significance precisely because it is taking us to those far-away countries which in their internal efforts and development bear a great resemblance to our country and whose stand on international problems and the consolidation of peace is similar to ours; to countries with whom we can cooperate to the great advantage not only of ourselves and themselves, but [to the advantage] of that which today represents the most important quest of people in the world: the consolidation of peace and international cooperation, that is, a peaceable active coexistence between states and nations with differing systems which we regard as the sole road for avoiding new wars and destruction of mankind.[19]

1. *India*

Tito visited India from December 16, 1954 to January 3, 1955, and again from January 20 to 25 on his return from

[19] *Tito Speaks in India and Burma* (New Delhi: Ananda Press, published by Yugoslav Embassy, 1955) , pp. 5-6.

Burma. His most important speech was delivered to the members of the Indian Parliament on December 21, 1954. Setting the pattern for Tito's style during the years leading up to the Belgrade Conference of September 1961, it introduced into the pronouncements of the unaligned nations an activist ingredient hitherto absent. After sketching Yugoslavia's postwar domestic development, calling attention in particular to the "democratic and socialist" character of its one-Party system, he discussed the evolution of Yugoslav relations with the Western and Soviet blocs, and the limitations of looking to either bloc in the present era of spheres of influence, inequality between nations, Great Power interventions, and colonialism. He argued that the gravest peril to world peace inhered in the formation of blocs along military and ideological lines and stated that only "in the coexistence of nations and States with differing systems" could catastrophe be averted:

> What I have in mind is not a sort of passive coexistence, but an active cooperation and a peaceful and agreed settlement of different problems, as well as the removal of all elements liable to impede a broad cooperation between States, large and small.[20]

As if to illustrate the "practical possibility" of coexistence, Tito linked the normalization of relations between Yugoslavia and the Soviet Union to the sweeping changes in outlook of the post-Stalinist Soviet leaders. At one and the same time he disarmed his critics and reassured the Indians of his continued commitment to a policy of nonalignment:

> The initiative in this respect came from the Soviet Union, and was followed by a statement on the part of the present Soviet leaders to the effect that Yugoslavia had been wrongly treated and condemned in 1948. Such statements, as well as others which will one day become known to the world, have assisted towards our accepting to establish normal relations, all the more so as it was in keep-

[20] *Ibid.*, pp. 30-31.

ing with our wish to cooperate with all countries desirous, on their part, to do so and respectful of the principle of equality.[21]

Finally, he derided as erroneous the supposition that the purpose of his visit to India and Burma was "to set up a third bloc." Yugoslavia did wish "to increase the number of States and of nations who place the safeguarding of peace above all else and who struggle for relations based on equality, for peaceful cooperation among nations and for an active coexistence of States with different social systems," but he insisted this did not imply the creation of a third bloc.

The following day, Tito and Nehru issued a joint communiqué setting forth their areas of accord. First, they proclaimed adherence to a policy of nonalignment. They reiterated, as each had on numerous occasions, that nonalignment was not synonymous with "neutrality" or "neutralism," with the passivity and fatalism implicit therein, but rather was "an active, positive and constructive policy seeking to lead to a collective peace on which alone collective security can really rest." Henceforth, the term "nonalignment" came into vogue, subsuming under it both noninvolvement in any of the Great Power blocs and the desire for an independent policy in foreign affairs.

Second, they enunciated the principles that were to guide the relations of their two countries: respect for each other's sovereignty, independence, and integrity; nonaggression; equality between nations; noninterference in the domestic affairs of each other's and of other countries; and the promotion of peaceful coexistence. These principles had first been set forth in the preamble to the Sino-Indian agreement on Tibet, signed on April 29, 1954, in Peking, and reaffirmed at the meeting between Nehru and Chou En-lai in New Delhi two months later. Nehru hoped the application of these principles "not only between various countries but also in international relations generally" would con-

[21] *Ibid.*, p. 32.

stitute a basis for a stable peace. The Yugoslavs considered "peaceful coexistence" the umbrella, the *geist*, the goal encompassing all the other principles enunciated in the *Panch Shila* (The Five Principles of Coexistence). Tito's assent to the *Panch Shila* was a compromise, a subtle acknowledgment of the preeminence of Nehru. Tito went along because Nehru, in addition to being the senior statesman of the Asian world, was a world-renowned figure and provided Yugoslavia with a solid link to the emerging Afro-Asian group. Nehru, on the other hand, regarded "peaceful coexistence" as a cumbersome and imprecise formulation. However, at the end of the communique mention was made of "the necessity of peaceful coexistence not merely as an alternative, but as an imperative"—a concession which apparently satisfied Tito. But in the emergence by 1961 of "peaceful and active coexistence" rather than *Panch Shila* as the doctrinal formulation of nonalignment, one may discern Yugoslav tenacity and political persuasiveness. Indeed, by 1961 Tito overshadowed Nehru as the driving force behind nonalignment, and more than any other individual personified the quest of the new nations for influence in world councils.

Third, they repudiated the "erroneous conception which has become prevalent in some quarters" of the creation by the nonaligned countries of a "third bloc." They declared, "This is a contradiction in terms because such a bloc would involve them in the very system of alignments which they regard as undesirable."[22] Ironically, their disavowal of any intention to establish a third bloc was interpreted by the Western countries and by the Soviet Union as signifying the exact opposite. The protagonists of the Cold War were discomforted by the convening of the Bandung Conference, the propensity toward group voting in the U.N., and the growing frequency of Nonaligned Summits; despite their power, they shared an uneasiness about the efforts of the nonaligned nations to forge a collective position to maximize their influence in diplomatic bargainings with the

[22] *Ibid.*, p. 39.

Western and Soviet blocs. The Great Powers did not see that the cast of nonalignment was still plastic, differing in important details from the familiar die of blocs in an era of Cold War, e.g., that the contacts among the nonaligned had an *ad hoc* character; that no permanent Secretariat nor organizational machinery existed; that no rules for ordering priorities or positions had been reached; that no financial agreements had been discussed.

Tito and Nehru met four times in the course of the visit; three of their talks were completely private, with only Krishna Menon and Jože Vilfan present. From all reports the talks were candid and comprehensive. Though the outlooks of the two leaders differed in important respects, there existed a common basis for cooperation. For Tito, the visit came at a propitious moment. Several months earlier, Nehru had been persuaded by the Indonesian Prime Minister, Ali Sastroamidjojo, of the importance of convening an Asian-African Conference. Disturbed by Dulles' introduction of Cold War alignments into Asia through the Manila Pact, which established SEATO in September 1954, and by the danger of war stemming from the isolation and ambitions of Communist China, Nehru was receptive to Tito's suggestions for broadening the activities of nonalignment. Tito's formulation for nonalignment proved more viable and valuable than the all-encompassing racial-political format of the architects of Bandung. It was some time before this became clear to Nehru, U Nu, Nasser, and Sukarno. In the meantime Tito took the initiative, demonstrating the efficacy of personal contacts and summitry for the leaders of the nonaligned as a new factor in international relations, thus laying the groundwork for the activist phase of nonalignment. In so doing, he gained ready acceptance for Yugoslavia as a founding member of the nonaligned group.

2. *Burma*

During his visit to Burma, January 6-17, 1955, Tito was given a welcome unequalled by that of any other foreign

dignitary. One newapaper compared Tito to the revolutionary leader of Burmese independence, Aung San:

> Marshal Tito has often been referred to as the Aung San
> of Yugoslavia, and in turn *Bogyoke* [Aung San] has been
> called the Tito of Burma.[23]

His fame as a wartime hero and as the David who con-
founded the Soviet Goliath, coupled with the interest of
Burmese leaders in Yugoslav socialism, assured an enthusiastic press:

> The decentralization of control in industry and the crea-
> tion of workers and producers councils are ideals which
> welfare-minded Burmese leaders have been striving to
> achieve here in Burma.[24]

In addition, Yugoslav military assistance, which had enabled the Burmese army to cope with the Nationalist
Chinese troops in the mountain areas of northern Burma,
reinforced the attachment to Tito.

In his speech at Rangoon University on January 16, 1955,
Tito specifically included references to the common revolutionary heritage and quest for security and independence
of the two countries. Sensitive to Burma's precarious position, to its anxiety over the ambitions of powerful neighbors, to its internal divisions and low level of economic
development, he expounded more forcefully than in India
the underlying philosophical and theoretical propositions
of his thinking. Tito called attention to the vast changes
that had been wrought by decolonization and the attendant
problems of creating in these new nations political systems
that were genuinely independent, stable, and economically
self-sustaining. Criticizing those who would cast the political systems of these nations in familiar or "classical"
molds, he said that each nation should adopt forms and institutions of development suitable to its own specific conditions, that there are many roads to democracy and socialism. The emergence of the new nations strengthened the

[23] Tinker, *op.cit.*, p. 362.
[24] *New Times of Burma*, January 6, 1955, p. 4.

forces for peace in the world because they, more than others, knew how essential peace was to overcome economic backwardness. Accordingly, they were admirably suited for a more active role in international relations: "In general, the role of these countries in international life helps to smooth away antagonisms and serves as a useful counterbalance to the extremes of one or the other side."[25] The new nations, in concert, could help democratize international relations by championing each nation's right to self-determination, equality, and freedom from interference in its domestic affairs, and by advancing the economic development and integration of all nations. Only through the implementation of the principle of peaceful coexistence could these objectives be realized.

On his departure Tito made Burma a gift of military material to equip a brigade. One Burmese official described this as a gesture to induce Burma to establish a "Tito Brigade" and purchase more arms from Yugoslavia. As it turned out, most of the uniforms and equipment for the brigade were not suitable for Burmese conditions, or else were considered inferior to the material then being supplied in adequate quantities by Great Britain. The gift was accepted politely, but stored and never used. In keeping with U Nu's concept of independence and his penchant for reciprocity, a "gift" of rice was given the Yugoslavs for the value of the military equipment (during the Khrushchev-Bulganin visit in December 1955, Soviet "gifts" of a technological institute and hospital were also matched with a comparable "gift" of rice). However, Yugoslavia did provide some much coveted arms for mountain fighting. Moreover, the firm *Yugoimport* has maintained a representative in Burma and become a regular supplier of small arms as the Yugoslav arms industry has grown.

Yugoslavia was interested in expanding economic ties for several reasons, including the belief of many Yugoslav enterprises that they could find a ready market for their goods in Burma. During U Nu's visit to Belgrade in June 1955 trade and technical cooperation agreements were

25 *Tito Speaks, op.cit.*, p. 96.

negotiated. Trade levels did jump, but the absolute amounts involved were never significant for either country, nor did they have any noticeable long-range impact on Burmese politics. Traditionally, Burma, as a colony, had dealt primarily with Great Britain, and was well acquainted with the quality and practices of British firms. By contrast, the Yugoslavs were not good businessmen, seldom delivering goods on time; and the quality of their products left much to be desired. Also, with the settlement of claims against Japan, Burma used the reparations to expand trade with that country.

Relations between Yugoslavia and Burma were especially cordial until March 1962, when U Nu was removed from power for the second and final time. This deprived Tito of a close and convinced proponent of active nonalignment and presaged Burma's retreat, under General Ne Win, into a stringent isolation. In a sense, the deposal of U Nu represented the beginning of the end of the era of the charismatic nationalist leaders who, by dint of personality and diplomatic adroitness, imbued nonalignment with an aura that mesmerized the international community in the decade after 1954 and helped make it an important factor in world politics of the period.

3. *Impact*

Of Tito's many visits to African, Asian, and Latin American countries in the years since 1954, none matched the drama and impact or had the significance for Yugoslav foreign policy of this first one to India and Burma, which included his meeting with Nasser in the Suez Canal in February 1955. First, Tito established a pattern for personal consultations with the leaders of the nonaligned countries. He had been known to Nehru, U Nu, and Nasser as a revolutionary and Communist who had maintained his independence in the face of severe Soviet pressure. However, as a result of the personal meetings, he impressed them with his ideas and sincerity, as well as with his human qualities, and established a relationship which expedited his entree into the leading circles of Asian and African nationalism. Association with these men was a crucial factor in Tito's metamorphosis from revolutionary to statesman in the eyes of the world.

Second, through these personal relationships and the force of his own personality, Tito influenced the outlook of Afro-Asian leaders toward coexistence.[26] Tito's call for cooperation among the countries outside the orbit of Cold War blocs and his assertion of the inseparableness of peace, economic development, and international stability fell on receptive ears, coming as it did on the eve of the Bandung Conference. While these were not new ideas, Tito gave them an urgency and a substantiality that were instrumental in the crystallization of nonalignment as a functioning entity in international politics.

Third, Tito's visit presaged the emergence of Yugoslavia as an intimate of the unaligned Afro-Asian nations and as an influence in international affairs, transcending the confines of Europe. Undeterred by limited power resources, Yugoslav foreign policy assumed global pretensions, hitherto the preserve of Great Powers.

Fourth, Tito's trip came at a moment when the orientation of Yugoslav foreign policy was at a crossroads: Stalin was dead and relations with the Soviet bloc were in the process of normalization; relations with the Western countries were excellent; and decisions were pending in the Party on the extent to which decentralization and liberalization should be expanded and accelerated. In the search for security and an opportunity to play a prominent role in world affairs, Tito perceived in nonalignment the "constituency" he lacked in Europe, and the unifying policy internally that was not afforded by the other options available to him. Politics, personality, and promise interacted to make 1955 a critical year of choice for Yugoslav decision-makers.

[26] Vojan Rus, "The Peoples of Asia and Africa as Exponents of Coexistence," *Medjunarodni Problemi*, Vol. VIII, No. 1 (1956), p. 14.

The Bandung Illusion

The Bandung Conference of twenty-nine Asian and African countries, held in Indonesia in April 1955, is generally acclaimed a success. In the words of one Western scholar, the five sponsoring powers (Burma, Ceylon, India, Indonesia, and Pakistan) believed they had succeeded in achieving their primary purposes: to create an environment which "would serve as a moral restraint against possible Chinese tendencies of aggression"; to decrease the likelihood of war between China and the United States; and, by regaining "their personality and international dignity," to assert the determination of Asia and Africa "to share more fully with the West in decisions affecting the interests of their countries."[27] Agreement was reached on a number of broad issues: anti-colonialism; universality of membership in the United Nations; condemnation of apartheid in South Africa; and disarmament and the prohibition of nuclear testing. The Conference also contributed to Afro-Asia's awareness of itself as a factor in world affairs and served notice on Washington and Moscow of the emergence of a new force that they would have to reckon with.

These accomplishments, however, were more apparent than real. The Conference lacked machinery for implementing its resolutions. Moreover, it was composed of disparate political elements which foreclosed cooperation: frictions between the unaligned, nonbloc majority (among which India, Burma, Indonesia, and Cambodia were most prominent) and the bloc-affiliated minority (in particular, Pakistan, Turkey, and Iran) were papered over only with difficulty. A platform of priorities could not be implemented as long as important segments of the drafters pursued antithetical policies. The Cold War could not be exorcised from planning considerations for the future by well-intentioned speeches; peaceful coexistence among the

[27] George M. Kahin, *The Asian-African Conference* (Ithaca, New York: Cornell University Press, 1956), pp. 36-38.

conglomerate of committed and uncommitted countries was possible in principle, but effective political and diplomatic action was not. As realization of this truth filtered through the platitudes about Asian and African unity, a major re-casting of the group seemed essential. Nonalignment, which was not mentioned in the final communiqué, alone held out the promise of maximum political cohesiveness within a broadly based but internally congruent constellation. Thus, Bandung may be considered to have been a necessary stage in the evolution of nonalignment. By its ineptness it demonstrated the impotence of an Asian-African constellation encompassing all political outlooks, and inadvertently led the unaligned members to reassessments which coincided greatly with the views expressed so forcefully by Tito during his talks with Nehru, U Nu, and Nasser. The fleeting utility of Bandung may be seen in the insurmountable difficulties the original sponsoring nations have had in convening a second Conference of Bandung powers, in accordance with the recommendation of the April 24, 1955 communique. Ten years later, a second "Bandung" was scheduled for Algiers, but the deposal of the host, Ben Bella, in mid-June, resulted in its cancellation. Meanwhile, the nonaligned Afro-Asian nations (a grouping which included Yugoslavia) held two mass conferences—at Belgrade in 1961 and Cairo in 1964—in addition to several summits and bilateral meetings among the most prominent figures of nonalignment. The congeries of Afro-Asian states occasionally function as a bloc in the U.N., but it is the nonaligned segment which more frequently holds together on most issues.

Yugoslavia, though not invited to Bandung because it did not qualify as an Afro-Asian country, was a major beneficiary of the Conference's inability to establish a workable basis for cooperation. It perceived the frustration of the politically uncommitted majority at being stymied by the Afro-Asian "client-countries" of the West. Out of its own bitter experience with blocs and consequent desire to remain uncommitted to East or West as a matter of national necessity, Yugoslavia detected the underlying communality of interest between itself and these unaligned nations—an interest in maintaining their independent positions on a plane of equality with all nations, in asserting themselves in international relations in a constructive and influential manner, and in participating actively in the decisions that affected their future. More than any other country, Yugoslavia helped to make of Bandung a prologue to political action rather than a footnote to futility.

The Resolution of a Dilemma

On the eve of his departure for India, Tito cautioned Moscow against expecting Yugoslavia to improve its relations with the Soviet Union and the East European countries to the detriment of ties to the Western countries, especially where economic agreements were concerned:

> We cannot now retract all we have said and done so far. . . . We have numerous trade and other agreements with them, we have been granted many credits and have a number of other obligations towards them which we have not yet even begun to fulfill; we still receive aid from some Western countries, like the United States, Great Britain, France, for instance, and so far these countries have not shown themselves to be our enemies; they have proved to be friends in need. We therefore consider them as such and have no reason to sever, nor the slightest intention of severing, our relations with them.[28]

On his return Tito stated in a speech in Zagreb that the country's future lay with the uncommitted countries, Yugoslavia's "true allies and . . . greatest friends,"[29] a commendation far beyond any made in the past.

On May 14, 1955, the Yugoslav Government announced

[28] *Review of International Affairs*, Vol. v, No. 112 (December 1, 1954), p. 3.
[29] Geoffrey Barraclough and Rachel F. Wall, *Survey of International Affairs, 1955-1956* (London: Oxford University Press, issued under the auspices of the Royal Institute of International Affairs, 1960), p. 55.

that a meeting "at the highest level" would soon be held in Belgrade between Soviet and Yugoslav leaders. Convened at Moscow's initiative, it was the dramatic culmination of the normalization of relations that had been proceeding for almost a year and a complete vindication of Belgrade's policy. Tito reaffirmed Yugoslavia's intention to maintain the close ties which had been cultivated with the West since 1948, but praised the constructive acts of Soviet diplomacy: in addition to the rapprochement with Yugoslavia, Moscow prepared to sign the Peace Treaty with Austria and withdraw its military bases from Finland, tabled a comprehensive disarmament proposal, and agreed to meet with the Western Powers in a Summit Meeting in Geneva in July. With a portentous revamping of Soviet foreign policy evidently underway, the Yugoslav leaders were confronted with a situation that taxed their skill to the utmost: as relations with the Soviet bloc improved, eventually leading to the reestablishment of Party-to-Party relations in June 1956, some segments of the Yugoslav Communist Party pressed for a restoration of intimate ties to the socialist camp; others argued for a pro-West European orientation; still others, probably a minority at the time, pressed for active association with the unaligned countries of Asia and Africa. Tito himself purported to see Yugoslavia functioning as "the bridge between East and West," implying alignment with the Third World.[30] But the allure of collaboration with the Soviet Union on a presumed basis of equality, with Yugoslavia linking the socialist camp to the unaligned world, forestalled a clearcut decision. As an old Communist, Tito had a strong desire to be able to operate within the international Communist movement (especially within Eastern Europe, in particular against such enemies of his as Rakoši) and thereby to increase Yugoslav influence. By the time the Moscow Conference of eighty-one Communist Parties met in November 1957, however, the Yugoslavs

[30] *Borba*, August 3, 1955. Quoted in Fred Warner Neal and George W. Hoffman, *Yugoslavia and the New Communism* (New York: Twentieth Century Fund, 1962), p. 428.

realized that the Soviet leadership was not willing to deal with the Yugoslav Communist Party on a basis of equality, that it was not ready for the partnership and ideological flexibility which Yugoslavia regarded as essential for any genuine "commonwealth" of Communist nations. In the summer of 1955, however, the dilemmas were real and the options tantalizingly attractive.

What all Yugoslav leaders could agree on after the normalization of relations with the Soviet Union in May 1955 was that the Balkan Pact of August 1954, which had superseded the Treaty of Friendship and Cooperation, signed a week before Stalin's death, was an anachronism. In June 1953 Tito had termed the Treaty "a necessary measure" that "represents a powerful bulwark of peace," and had given assurances that Yugoslavia would remain a loyal member and not weaken it. But by March 1955 Yugoslavia preferred to shelve any efforts to infuse life into the Balkan Pact, in part because of the rising difficulties between Greece and Turkey over Cyprus, but primarily because Yugoslavia's situation had completely altered: its border disputes had been amicably resolved; the nonaligned countries had become more important in Yugoslav thinking; and, most relevant, the Soviet Union was no longer regarded as hostile or threatening. The military alliance fell into a state of desuetude. Increasingly, it became an embarrassment rather than a guarantee. To date, despite its opposition to military groupings, Yugoslavia has not formally abrogated the alliance, which remains in effect, at least juridically speaking, until 1974. The Soviet invasion of Czechoslovakia in August 1968 and Moscow's subsequent threatening attitude toward Yugoslavia have raised new interest in Belgrade in the Western commitment inherent in the Balkan Pact.

During the 1955-1957 period, some Yugoslav officials toyed with the possibility of a return to the socialist camp; their inherent emotional attachment to the Soviet Union and to the internationalism implicit in Marxist-Leninist ideals predisposed them to view the changes in Soviet outlook and policy over-optimistically. Soviet endorsement of the principle of noninterference in the internal affairs of other countries, open admission of past injustices to Yugoslavia, and readiness to extend generous long-term loans on favorable terms led them to interpret the relaxation in Eastern Europe, the constructive Soviet diplomatic overtures aimed at a *détente* with the West, and the normalization of relations with Yugoslavia as portents of irreversible liberalization. Khrushchev's destalinization speech at the Twentieth Congress of the C.P.S.U. in February 1956 accelerated the de-satellitization of Eastern Europe. It also persuaded Tito to reestablish formal Party-to-Party relations in June 1956, at the time of his visit to Moscow and the seeming acceptance by Soviet leaders of the principle of "many roads to socialism." With the reconciliation, the pro-Moscow segments of the Yugoslav leadership, and Tito himself, envisaged a grand coalition of the socialist countries and the "progressive" nonaligned nations of Afro-Asia, with Yugoslavia the bridge between the two groupings.

But Tito underestimated Khrushchev's obstinacy, as Khrushchev did his. Both had signed the agreements in 1955-1956 for tactical reasons. Tito was prepared to support Soviet policy toward the West "and to use Yugoslavia's growing influence in the Third World to promote the long-term interests of communism as he saw them"; and Khrushchev fully expected Yugoslavia to adhere to the Soviet line, taking it for granted "that the power of the lesser parties should be narrowly circumscribed, and that once unity had been restored, Yugoslavia would revert to its proper status as a junior member of the team."[31]

Destalinization was an untidy process. The Poznan riots at the end of June 1956 brought in their wake Soviet attempts to arrest the slackening of Party controls in Eastern Europe. To the disquiet of the Yugoslavs, Moscow circulated a secret memorandum on September 3 to all East European Communist Parties warning them of the Titoist

[31] John L. H. Keep, "Belgrade and Moscow: A Calculating Courtship," *Orbis*, Vol. x, No. 3 (Fall 1966), p. 757.

virus of "many roads to socialism" and reaffirming the ideological correctness of the Soviet model. Tito and Khrushchev hastily exchanged meetings in Brioni and the Crimea to iron out ideological differences. They failed, and the sudden disintegrative developments in Poland and Hungary —in particular the Soviet repression in Hungary—wiped away the facade of unity. Notwithstanding his desire to help Khrushchev fend off the attacks of opponents in the Kremlin who opposed the rapprochement with Yugoslavia, Tito, in his speech at Pula on November 11, 1956, strongly criticized the Soviet intervention in Hungary; in the United Nations, Yugoslav diplomats deplored the Soviet action and the incarceration of Imre Nagy, the Hungarian Prime Minister who had left his asylum in the Yugoslav Embassy in Budapest, presumably on receiving a guarantee of safe conduct, only to be abducted and executed by Soviet authorities. Unhappy over Tito's criticisms and preoccupied with the need to restore bloc unity, Khrushchev was in no mood to cater to the Yugoslavs. For his part, Tito (and presumably the majority of the pro-Soviet segments of the League of Yugoslav Communists) drew appropriate conclusions about the limits of Yugoslavia's ability to influence the Soviet leadership and about the mercurial nature of Soviet permissiveness.

In a concession to Khrushchev, Tito agreed to attend the conference of Communist Parties in Moscow in November 1957. At the last minute, however, he had second thoughts and instead sent Kardelj and Ranković. They had considerable leeway to act and decided on the spot not to subscribe to the Declaration adopted there. Not only were the Yugoslavs uneasy because it condemned "revisionism" (i.e., Titoism), but they were disturbed by the insistence of the Chinese that all the participants acknowledge the "leading role" of the Soviet Union—a proposition contravening Yugoslavia's espousal of equality of all Communist Parties and one the Chinese may well have deliberately proposed to isolate the Yugoslavs, whose views were anathema in Peking.

Like a mirage, the glimmering vision of unity in 1955 had on closer inspection vanished. The euphoria over "liberalization" and "destalinization" in the Soviet Union and Eastern Europe had stimulated illusions in Yugoslav leadership circles that Moscow would drastically alter its internal policies and its attitude toward Yugoslavia. But Soviet leaders were not prepared to accord the Yugoslavs a position of equality in the formulation of bloc affairs; they were not willing (or able) to accept Yugoslavia in the camp on Yugoslav terms. Moscow waited for Belgrade to close ranks in the interests of maintaining the cohesiveness of the Communist bloc, but the demands were too great: Yugoslav society had moved too far from the Soviet model to be reversed without force, which was unthinkable given the high premium the regime had conceded to popular support, stability, and self-management.

Yugoslavia drifted into nonalignment because each of the other two alternatives was unacceptable to influential segments of the Party and because all elements of the Party could accept it as a substitute for a compromise policy. Nonalignment did not enjoy the widespread and enthusiastic support of the broad spectrum of the Yugoslav leadership during the 1954-1957 period that it subsequently did; nor had it yet crystallized as a viable alternative, nor were its potentialities for enhancing Yugoslavia's domestic, as well as international, position yet fully understood.

At the beginning when Tito was evolving the policy of nonalignment he was proceeding on the assumption of continued hostility from the Soviet camp, notwithstanding the death of Stalin in 1953. During the 1953-1954 period Tito had taken important steps toward alignment with the unaligned. The ambivalence of 1955-1956 coexisted with the courtship of the prominent figures of the nonaligned world: Tito sandwiched in Khrushchev's May 1955 visit between hosting U Nu and Nehru; in December, Tito made an official state visit to Egypt and Ethiopia. As a result of Moscow's apology for 1948, Tito's prestige among the Afro-Asian nations soared, giving substance to his contention that nonalignment could play a positive role in reconciling the two blocs and lessening international tension. His prestige also enhanced the appeal that nonalignment began to generate among the new nations and the attention it began to receive in the major capitals of the world. At this moment when Tito's policy of nonalignment with either bloc was crowned with stunning success, he was intrigued by the prospect of using it to amplify his voice in the Soviet camp and to link the socialist camp with the progressive forces in the Third World. In Moscow, Belgrade cited its respected position among the new nations as evidence of the correctness of its approach and argued that the more the Soviet Union promoted reconciliation with Yugoslavia, the more Moscow would dispel lingering suspicions of its intentions among the Afro-Asian nations it was starting to court. Speaking on the occasion of U.N. Day, on October 24, 1955, Kardelj stated "there can be no doubt" that Moscow's making amends to Yugoslavia "has freed many peoples of fears for their independence, and enabled the alleviation of bloc antagonisms, while increasing prospects for international cooperation and the creation of the necessary conditions for active coexistence of peoples with different social systems. . . ."[32] There is reason to believe that until Khrushchev and Bulganin's momentous first visit to South Asia in December 1955 and, indeed, for a few years thereafter, the Soviet leadership was basically unable to comprehend the links that bound Tito to Nehru, U Nu, and Nasser. Soviet perceptions were limited by their "Soviet-ness." In the capitals of the nonaligned countries, Belgrade sought to interpret the meaning of the developments in the Soviet bloc and to give reassurance about Moscow's purposes. One influential Yugoslav official succinctly described the unlimited potential that circumstance had placed in Belgrade's reach:

As [a] European and an independent socialist country, Yugoslavia is in a position to interpret for Europe the

[32] *Review of International Affairs*, Vol. VI, No. 134 (November 1, 1955), p. 1.

strivings of the Afro-Asian world, as well as to represent in that region the just and correct interests of the European peoples . . . [as President Tito did during his] historic visits to India and Burma, and now [December 1955-January 1956] to Egypt and Ethiopia, the basic aim of which is: cooperation and progress of all in creative coexistence.[33]

Though pleased by the results of his meetings with Nehru, U Nu, Nasser, and Haile Selassie and the promise for the future which they opened, and though guardedly optimistic regarding the "objective" character of Moscow's amiability, Tito was particularly impressed by the acceptability of non-alignment to all elements of the League of Yugoslav Communists.

Domestic considerations, too, shaped Tito's decision to opt for nonalignment. It became an attractive policy alternative at the time that the assumptions concerning the Soviet threat, which had prompted the search for friends in the Third World in the first place, were themselves undergoing serious revision. The winds of change and moderation from Moscow in 1954 and 1955 had sent quivers of anticipation through the sizeable pro-Russian wing of the Yugoslav Communist Party. Pressures for a restoration of collaboration with the socialist camp emanated from two sources: those with strong pro-Russian proclivities, heady with optimism over the 1955 rapprochement; and the conservative factions disquieted over the trend toward further internal liberalization. Generally, though not always, these two groups were composed of the same individuals. However, the pressures dropped abruptly as Moscow put the brake on destalinization, suppressed the revolution in Hungary, denounced Yugoslavia for revisionism, and aligned itself with the Chinese against the "Titoists" in an effort to restore monolithism to international communism. With the pro-Russian wing temporarily stymied

[33] Djordje Jerković, "India in The Contemporary World," *Review of International Affairs*, Vol. VI, No. 140 (February 1, 1956) , p. 4.

in its efforts to edge Yugoslavia closer to the socialist camp, with Western military support no longer as essential because of Belgrade's belief that post-Stalinist Soviet leaders would not resort to force against Yugoslavia, and with political strains among the republic Party leaderships intensifying over the issues of decentralization and liberalization, nonalignment offered a way of removing foreign policy from the realm of Party disagreements and possible disruptive rivalry. In addition, the difficulties experienced by neighboring non-Slavic Hungary and Romania weakened the case of the pro-Russian wing for closer ties to the socialist camp: opposition came from the pro-West European wing and the Hungarian and Albanian nationality groups. By appearing capable of reconciling the pressures from the entrenched and contentious Party bureaucracies, especially those in the pro-Russian eastern part of the country with those in the more West European oriented western part, nonalignment promised agreement on foreign policy in a period of accelerating domestic change, and thereby provided important assurance of domestic stability.

By orienting Yugoslav foreign policy increasingly toward the Third World, Tito inadvertently happened upon a formula and policy which admirably suited the peculiar domestic conditions and needs of Yugoslavia at that time. His free hand in foreign policy was due as much to the wide support which nonalignment enjoyed among all wings of the Party as to his unchallenged hold over the country. Indeed, in time, Tito's stature on the world scene reinforced his unique status in Yugoslavia itself.

Thus, it must be stressed, nonalignment and the theoretical justification for it evolved gradually, even fortuitously. As the political wings of the Party argued the foreign policy course of Yugoslavia, they found that nonalignment was a viable substitute, appropriate to the satisfaction of internal political requirements, and to the national purpose of ending Yugoslavia's diplomatic isolation and affording it an important international role.

Another factor more difficult to document is the conscious desire of Tito and the Yugoslav Communist oligarchy of his generation and political vintage to play an active and ambitious role in the spread of socialism. This exalted sense of the role Yugoslavia should play in the world derives, in important measure, from the personality of Tito, one of the significant figures of the postwar period. His presence provides the impetus for Yugoslav activism. More than any other option, nonalignment offered Yugoslav leaders the opportunity for influencing international developments, though this fact was not fully realized until the late 1950's.

According to one republican Party official, a member of the Presidium of the LYC, the disappearance of Milovan Djilas from the political scene was, at least in part, a function of his unpalatable prescriptions for Yugoslavia:

> Djilas remained wedded to a pseudo-anti-Stalinistic outlook at a time when it had no future or support in the Party. He held to the formalistic liberal views of the anti-Stalin period, arguing that Yugoslavia should develop into a two-Party system, along the lines of British parliamentary democracy. Had his views on foreign policy been adopted, the result would have been a much closer association with the Western camp, with a dangerous splintering of the Party. It would also have meant that Yugoslavia would not have been able to play a prominent part in international affairs, but would have had to settle for a subordinate position among the small Western nations.

Clearly, Yugoslav leaders were not interested in "splendid isolation," in making their country "the Switzerland of the Balkans." They sought a role for their country transcending the logic of their geographic location, size, and wealth.

Economically, nonalignment coincided with the growing pressures from Yugoslav enterprises for an expansion of trade with the underdeveloped nations. Even before the politically costly gambles of recognizing East Germany and agreeing to attend the Moscow Conference in November 1957 had weakened Yugoslavia's credit in the West, Yugoslav leaders were urged by many of their most important

73

economic enterprises to expand economic relations with the Third World. When Moscow reneged on a 300 million dollar credit for financing Yugoslav industrial growth and foreign trade, Yugoslav traders and economists pressed for expanded ties with the non-Communist world. Moscow's vindictiveness made a deep impression on Yugoslav officials responsible for creating a viable economic system; it reinforced the conviction that Yugoslavia's long-run hope for economic solvency depended on a competitive position in world markets. And the idea that the underdeveloped countries were assuming a growing economic significance because of their "immense resources of material, manpower, and vast strategic possibilities," that as a valuable strategic reserve they were about to attract the intensive attention and ruthless competition of the two blocs, appeared more frequently in serious Yugoslav journals.[34]

Ideologically, nonalignment marked the coming of age of differentiation in the Yugoslav outlook. In 1948 the Yugoslavs had known that differences existed in the socialist camp. In 1949 their fear of the Soviet Union had driven them to the West into an uneasy and dependent association which, paradoxically, helped to liberate them from the sterile schema of Soviet formulations on international relations, and sensitized them to differentiation both in the West and in the Third World. By 1955 they came to perceive that the West, too, was not the monolith they had once supposed and that they could accept assistance from the Western powers without relinquishing sovereignty or political initiative. Yugoslav officials began to see socialism as a "world process," which was taking place simultaneously in the socialist camp, the West, and the Third World.

Politically, nonalignment ushered in a new era in Yugoslavia's foreign relations. Perhaps more important, for the first time Yugoslavia had a *national* foreign policy.

---

[34] Josip Djerdja, "The Underdeveloped Countries in the World of Today," *Medjunarodni Problemi*, Vol. VI, No. 3-4 (June-December, 1954), p. 5. This was the first time this leading journal of international affairs devoted its entire issue to developments in the Third World.

CHAPTER III

In the Vanguard of Nonalignment

THE FIRST "Big Three" summit conference of the nonaligned leaders was held on July 18-19, 1956, on the island of Brioni, off the Croatian coast. For Tito, it was tangible recognition of his growing stature among the nonaligned and emergence as an international figure; for Nehru, a distinguished personality and generally acclaimed the foremost leader in the Third World, the visit fulfilled a diplomatic obligation, but little else; for Nasser, the junior member and least known of the participants, Tito's invitation meant membership in the inner councils of nonalignment and enhanced prestige in the Arab world. The meeting lent a new vigor to the concept of nonalignment—which was Tito's purpose—even though the term itself was not mentioned in the final communique issued on July 19, 1956.

Also on July 19 the United States Government withdrew its offer of assistance to help construct the Aswan Dam, and a week later, on the occasion of the fourth anniversary of the overthrow of Farouk, Nasser nationalized the Suez Canal, precipitating a major crisis in the Middle East. Yugoslavia promptly supported Nasser's decision; but during the next three months it was India that played a prominent part in trying to forestall a war. India's position as a member of the Commonwealth, rather than its role among the nonaligned, made its attitude important in London and its involvement welcomed in Washington. Yugoslavia had a minor role in the supporting cast of nonaligned states; but by the Middle East crisis of 1967 it occupied an important place on the center of the stage—an indication of how far it had come in the intervening period.

In late 1956 a Yugoslav Government report on foreign policy noted the growing role and number of nonaligned Afro-Asian states in international affairs. With Africa south of the Sahara standing on the threshold of nationhood, with the patent inability of the lesser powers to influence events in the Middle East or Eastern Europe, and with estrangement from the Soviet camp once again highlighting Yugoslavia's relative isolation in the world, Yugoslav leaders scrutinized the political and economic dimensions of nonalignment and saw in them the stuff of which influence is made: strategic and diplomatic importance, untapped markets and resources, surplus manpower, and areas whose friendship the Great Powers coveted for psychopolitical reasons related to the East-West struggle. They perceived both the futility of a Nehru acting alone and by implication on behalf of all concerned small nations, and the scarcely veiled arrogance of Great Powers acting heavy-handedly to preserve their security and political interest with scant attention to the views of the small nations whom they sought to manipulate.

At the Seventh Congress of the League of Yugoslav Communists in March 1958, Yugoslavia formally reaffirmed its decision not to rejoin the Soviet camp and took a giant step toward making nonalignment the mainstay of its foreign policy. Criticizing the bureaucratic and statist deformities of Soviet socialism and deploring the dogmatism dominating the outlook of Soviet leaders, the Yugoslav Program rejected the notions that "Communist Parties have a monopoly over every aspect of the movement of society towards socialism, and that socialism can only find its representatives in them and move forward through them." The Program considered these views "theoretically wrong and practically very harmful." It lauded the role being assumed in many Asian, African, and Latin American countries by "nationalist movements with progressive views" and associated Yugoslavia with them. It attacked tendencies toward "ideological monopoly and political hegemony" and championed diversity within the broad framework of parties and movements aspiring to build socialist societies. The Program committed Yugoslavia to the policy of "active coexistence" which "can only be implemented between states and peoples, and not in relations between blocs," and emphasized that "there can be no coexistence between blocs, for that would not be coexistence at all, but merely a temporary 'truce' concealing the danger of new conflicts." In advancing the policy of active coexistence, it held that "a significant role" can be played by the noncommitted countries," which, by virtue of the fact that they are not aligned with any bloc, can contribute a great deal towards the overcoming of the exclusiveness of the blocs." The ideological rationale for Yugoslavia's commitment to nonalignment having been elaborated, there now remained the task of giving a concrete form and sense of direction that had hitherto been absent.

Yugoslav Objectives

Yugoslavia predicated its long-range security on the expectations of bloc erosion and an end to the Cold War between the Soviet Union and the United States, and on the belief that more and more countries would, in their search for genuine independence, adopt a policy of nonalignment, of nonaffiliation with either Great Power constellation in the Cold War. In this sense, the Yugoslavs consider themselves the first "Gaullists": they were the first to advocate the disbandment of military blocs, believing as they do that blocs breed rivalry and proselytizing along ideological lines, and facilitate the insidious extension of Great Power influence and interference under the guise of assistance.

Nonalignment filled various needs. Through it Yugoslavia acquired friends in Asia and Africa who vote with it on issues it deems important, and with whom it has cultivated a relationship of trust that was impossible for other European countries. Yugoslavia has also been able to encourage those who profess a commitment to the socialist path of development, and through its own example has enhanced the case for nonalignment and market socialism. Certainly nonalignment enabled Yugoslavia to end its diplomatic isolation and afforded it an opportunity for national self-assertion and an activist diplomacy that no other policy alternative could have provided. In the words of one official at the Indonesian Embassy in Belgrade, "Yugoslavia does not really belong anywhere: it is neither of Asia nor of Africa, and it is unwilling to align itself too closely in Europe with either camp. It is trying to find roots with some group, while at the same time playing a prominent role in world affairs. Nonalignment has been a godsend to Yugoslavia."

Involvement in Afro-Asian affairs should not obscure the continuing primacy of Yugoslav attention to European developments. An important objective of Yugoslav policy is to increase its bargaining power with the Soviet bloc. The success of the Yugoslavs in enhancing their prestige among developing countries gave them a lever in bargaining with Moscow. There is some evidence, for example, that during his December 1962 visit to Moscow, Tito was able to convince Khrushchev and the Soviet leaders that Yugoslavia's influence in the Third World and policy of active peaceful coexistence could redound to the benefit of the USSR and the cause of international socialism. The Yugoslavs also used their standing among the nonaligned nations as a defense against pressure from the East. The Sino-Soviet rift has brought Moscow closer to the Yugoslav evaluation of trends in the Third World.

Several factors made economic expansion in the Third World attractive to the proponents of nonalignment. Yugoslavia did not want to become too dependent economically on either bloc, especially in view of the moves toward economic integration in both Western and Eastern Europe. The Yugoslavs were also disconcerted to discover that, in addition to the vagaries they encountered in trading with the socialist camp, they had difficulty in competing favorably in world markets, i.e., in hard currency areas. Their infant industries needed dependable markets for their products; hence the domestic pressures to acquire marketing entree into the new African nations. An Ethiopian official said that this explained the alacrity with which the Yugoslavs, at considerable expense, established Legations and

Embassies in all the mini-states of Africa. Comforting themselves with the notion that Western technology was too sophisticated for developing countries and that Yugoslav expertise and level of development would make Yugoslavia especially attractive to the new nations, the Yugoslavs embarked on an extensive, costly economic courtship. The leadership responded to pressures from the export-oriented enterprises partly out of the conviction that closer economic relations would buttress political ties. Thus were the economic aspects of nonalignment interwoven with the political.

A member of the Sudanese Embassy in Belgrade thought the economic motivation behind Yugoslav policy was more important than the ideological, and at least as important as the political. By way of example, he cited the Ben Barka affair (Ben Barka, a Moroccan opposition leader, was murdered in Paris in late 1965 as a result of collusion between French security police and the Moroccan Minister of Interior). Considering Yugoslavia's vehement opposition to the murder, he noted that its press had been quite restrained in discussing the affair, relying heavily upon Reuter's dispatches from Paris. A few days after the story broke, a Moroccan official came from Rabat to visit Tito, no doubt to give the Moroccan Government's version. Shortly thereafter, the Yugoslav press printed several pieces on Yugoslav-Moroccan economic cooperation. The Sudanese official cited similar Yugoslav restraint in responding to the overthrow of Ben Bella and Nkrumah (despite Tito's abortive attempt to organize a quick Nonaligned Summit to condemn "neocolonialist" intrigues against "progressive" forces). He attributed the circumspect Yugoslav reaction in these situations to its desire to protect its economic stake in these countries. After the overthrow of Nkrumah, the Ghanaian military government moved quickly to evict Chinese and Soviet specialists, but no action was taken against Yugoslav technicians. Whatever their long-range political and ideological objectives might be, he said, the Yugoslavs were clearly pragmatists.

Every nation covets prestige. But prestige, like so many components of national power, is elusive, impermanent, and capricious. It has always been important in the calculus of international competition and conflict, yet never more than in the second half of the twentieth century. The nuclear stalemate, the political consequences of the technological revolution in communications and mass media, the prevalence of volatile nationalism in unstable areas, and the coming of age of declamatory diplomacy in international organizations have magnified rather than dwarfed the role of the individual in conflict-resolution and influence-building. A charismatic figure in touch with his times can have an enormous impact upon the international community, which hungers for leadership. As long as Yugoslavia trailed in the wake of the Soviet Union, she was what she appeared to be—small and weak, Balkan and backward: "In international affairs her voice was not heard, nor did anyone value her opinion. She was an instrument of the big power politics. . . ."[1] With his trip to South Asia, Tito moved boldly into a new milieu and found to his surprise that his views commanded attention. Resisting the pull from the East and widening his internationalism beyond the confining Communist third of the world, he made Yugoslavia a nation respected as much for its independence, courage, and determination, as for its ideas and visions of an evolving world community.

Linkages

Yugoslavia is the only European nation embraced by the nonaligned nations of the Third World. The principles underlying its foreign policy are shared by the developing countries: nonmembership in any military or ideological bloc dominated by one of the Great Powers; a commitment to equality in relations between nations, large and small, powerful and weak; the right of every country to self-determination; and avoidance of force as a method of settling international disputes.

[1] "Tito in India," *Review of International Affairs,* Vol. v, No. 113 (December 16, 1954) , p. 1.

1. *Common Aspirations*

The Yugoslavs are acutely aware of the realities differentiating them from the Afro-Asian states with which they cooperate: geographic remoteness, a different political and cultural heritage, a more advanced economic system, and a distinctive political structure. At first glance, these would seem to preclude intimacy. That the Yugoslavs were readily accepted into the inner councils of the nonaligned—indeed, that they have been accorded a position there of leadership—is testament to the persuasiveness of their ideas, the ability of their officials, and the exemplariness of their behavior. The targets of Yugoslav diplomacy in the Third World are at different stages of economic development, all below that achieved by Yugoslavia; they profess nonalignment, but differ, often markedly, in their approaches to international issues; many have regional interests which transcend their attachment to nonalignment, though these are seldom explicitly articulated in a way that would overtly bring the two into conflict.

While alert to the divisive contradictions inherent in nonalignment, Yugoslavia has emphasized the unifying aspects. Foremost among these is the common opposition to the military-ideological blocs headed by the United States and the Soviet Union and to the tendency of the Great Powers to dominate international relations. The nonaligned countries generally accept the Yugoslav view of Soviet-American rivalry as in essence a struggle between two highly developed imperial systems seeking to encompass in their spheres the less developed nations.[2] Criticisms of Western interventionist proclivities find a receptive audience among nations who have obtained the formal attributes of sovereignty but who remain uncomfortably conscious of their continuing dependence economically and militarily upon the former metropoles. Conveniently for Belgrade, suspicion of the West among most of the former colonies overshadows fear of the Soviet Union, thus enabling Yugoslavia to re-

<hr/>

[2] Djordje Jerković, "Conversations Between the 'Big Two' and Prospects for Further Relaxation of Tensions," *Medjunarodni Problemi*, Vol. XI, No. 4 (1959), pp. 8-15.

tain without burden its identity as a Communist country and its special relationship with Moscow in periods when Soviet leaders are not inveighing against "revisionism." However, when Yugoslav-Soviet relations are poor, Belgrade must proceed cautiously among the nonaligned, lest it appear to be trying to embroil them in ideological squabbles which they do not understand and which could only adversely affect their efforts to derive maximum leverage from the Cold War.

In common with the developing countries, Yugoslavia emphasizes the critical importance of economic development. While at home its social scientists prefer to call Yugoslavia a "less sufficiently developed country" to distinguish it from the less advanced developing countries, abroad they drop the distinction and link themselves to the developing countries and their quest for rapid economic development. Yugoslav leaders have been in the forefront of efforts to generate more interest in the helping of the developing countries; both in the United Nations and in the councils of the nonaligned they have advanced constructive and ambitious proposals. They have established themselves as bold and effective advocates of expanded programs and enlightened policies aimed at accelerated national growth.

Far more effectively than the Soviet Union or Communist China, Yugoslavia has sensed the power of the term "socialism" and has strengthened ties to the nonaligned countries through an unquestioned commitment to the promotion of socialism in the world. Ambiguous and subject to innumerable interpretations, socialism is the most potent political word of the twentieth century: its electric quality inheres in the striving for social justice, economic improvement, and political democracy that it connotes to the emergent intelligentsia in the new nations and to the previously mute masses who have suddenly found themselves more intimately involved in the process of change than ever before in history. Notwithstanding the sympathetic responses of many American leaders to the aspirations of the emergent peoples of Africa, Asia, and Latin America, large segments of the American political establishment harbor illusory suspicions and fears of men and movements that postulate socialism as their ultimate goal. A refusal to distinguish between socialism and communism, a presentiment that the former must inexorably lead to the latter to the detriment of American national security, and a discomfort with conceptualization in politics all hamper American efforts to establish firm ties with "progressives" abroad. Freed from the onus of past colonialism and independent of Moscow, the Yugoslavs have made their ardent espousal of and belief in the inevitability of socialism the emotional tie between them and the nonaligned nations.

Another shared aspiration which has acquired almost sinister connotations in the United States because of Communist manipulation is the quest for peace. That the United States has permitted the Communist world to preempt the word "peace" is perhaps more a condemnation of the lack of skill of Western publicists and propagandists than a tribute to the imagination or insight of the Communists. But in the Third World the quest for peace is a platform that all support. The Yugoslavs suffered grievously in World War II and know from their sorrow the irreparable cost of conflict. Their stress on the need for peace is understandable. However, in linking as inseparable the prospects for the development of the poorer nations to the establishment of peace, they have skillfully focused attention on the way in which the Cold War directly affects each underdeveloped country: the more the richer nations spend on armaments, the less there is available to assist the developing countries. Hence, argue the Yugoslavs, the enormity of the responsibility devolving upon the nonaligned in the struggle for peace.

Common aspirations often precede mutual respect. Yugoslavia has succeeded in communicating to the Third World the genuineness and depth of its attachment to the same general goals they all share. On returning from his second major trip to South Asia and Africa in March 1959, at a low point in Yugoslav-Soviet relations when the Soviets had denounced him for having spoken ill of their purposes in nonaligned countries, Tito lashed out at Moscow, insisting that "We have not spoken against anyone" nor sought to sow discord between the United Arab Republic and the Soviet Union. More important, he affirmed the strength of the Yugoslav ties to the nonaligned countries:

> We are bound to them by the same aspirations. Those peoples have deep confidence in Yugoslavia just because in our foreign policy we have consistently defended their interests before the United Nations, against colonial designs, and also because we have assisted them as much as we could in their liberating endeavors. They know that in the future, also, we shall be on their side and without ulterior motives, without any desire to extract some personal benefit in the process. They know that Yugoslavia is not a rich country, they know that she is not rich enough to help them as much as some great powers could but do not want to. They know that we would very gladly assist them also materially, if we could afford it. The moral support given to those peoples by Yugoslavia is far more important to them, and precisely this support has created for us positions which no slander whatever and no intrigues can undermine.[3]

2. *Anti-colonialism*

The outsider who is admitted to the Club or Faith or is "passing" as one of the group feels impelled on every occasion to demonstrate his zeal. Yugoslavia has emphasized its nonaligned credentials by impassioned condemnations of colonialism. In practice it has supported the struggle of any nonaligned Afro-Asian country or group marching under the banner of anti-colonialism. Yugoslavia has concentrated its decolonization efforts within the United Nations, where it has been instrumental in marshalling the nonaligned nations on behalf of the movements aspiring toward independence. But though the United Nations re-

[3] *Review of International Affairs*, Vol. x, No. 215 (March 16, 1959), p. 16.

mains nonalignment's basic instrument for championing anti-colonialism,[4] the Yugoslavs have occasionally acted boldly on a bilateral basis, at the risk of their relations with the Western Powers, and have directly assisted several national-liberation movements—even surreptitiously. The most notable case was that of Algeria.

The Yugoslavs became interested in the National Liberation Front of Algeria (FLN) quite early. They made contact with the Algerian rebels in Cairo in 1953-1954 and soon achieved a position of unusual confidence. Yugoslav interest developed for several reasons: the proximity of Algeria and its strategic location on the Mediterranean littoral; sympathy for the FLN cause; very possibly, the desire of the Yugoslav leaders to assist a revolutionary movement actively, in order to demonstrate their credibility to Egypt, Syria, and incipient African national-liberation movements, many of whom had representatives and organizational fronts based in Cairo. From the start of the FLN uprising on November 1, 1954, Belgrade openly expressed its sympathy for the aims of the Algerian rebels. It championed Algeria's cause before the United Nations, and supplied valuable quantities of small arms through Cairo and coastal gunrunners—the only known instance where Yugoslavia secretly provided military aid to a national-liberation group struggling for independence from a colonial power.

In January 1955 the Yugoslav delegation voted in favor of a Saudi Arabian proposal to bring the Algerian problem before the Security Council. Thereafter, it sought to have the issue discussed by the General Assembly, arguing, together with the Afro-Asian delegations, "that in Algeria it was a question of a national uprising and not the action of a small number of extremists, as officially alleged by France."[5] It deplored the French fixation upon a "military solution" and called for recognition of the legitimate as-

[4] Josip Djerdja, "The Policy of Non-alignment in a Divided World," *Medjunarodni Problemi*, Vol. XIII, No. 3 (1961), pp. 7-12.

[5] "Yugoslavia's Attitude Regarding the Algerian Problem," *Yugoslav Survey*, Vol. II, No. 5 (April-June 1961), p. 739.

pirations of the Algerians and their right to determine their own destiny. However, while applauding the formation of the Provisional Algerian Government in Cairo in September 1958, Belgrade did not extend recognition, for fear of alienating France and because of the differences existing within the Yugoslav hierarchy over the future of the FLN: some members of the Yugoslav Central Committee, impressed with the arguments of the French Socialists, headed by Guy Mollet, thought that it would be better to support reform and autonomy rather than revolution and independence, and were skeptical of the ability of the FLN to defeat the French army; others pressed for unequivocal backing of the FLN, which was compared to the Partisan movement in Yugoslavia in World War II (though this parallel was a forced one, since Yugoslavia fought against an enemy invader and not a colonial power, it had a powerful appeal to Tito, who later tended to see Ahmed Ben Bella as a young Tito-in-the-making). Yugoslavia's reluctance at that time to press a hard line against France on the Algerian question stemmed from its effort to counterbalance tense relations with West Germany with close ties to France. West Germany had broken off diplomatic relations with Yugoslavia in retaliation for the latter's recognition of East Germany on October 15, 1957, and not until January 31, 1968, were formal ties restored. Official Yugoslav policy was also constrained by the moderate stand of Ferhat Abbas, the President of the Provisional Algerian Government, who did not ask for the severance of relations with France, preferring to maintain a policy of firmness with restraint.

In June 1959 Tito met with Ferhat Abbas and expressed his wish that both sides, France and the FLN, effect a peaceful solution of the civil war.[6] He carefully refrained from extending diplomatic recognition out of the belief that De Gaulle, who at that time had returned to power, was genuinely seeking a peaceful solution and restraining precipitate action by the "ultras." A Yugoslav journalist, based in Paris, summed up official Belgrade's view with the observa-

[6] "Spoljna Politika," *Yugoslovenski Pregled* (1960), p. 27.

tion that the Algerian problem had to be solved inside France.[7]

De Gaulle's declaration of September 16, 1959, for the first time expressed France's acceptance of the principle of self-determination as a possible basis for a solution. It temporarily forestalled harsh Yugoslav criticisms, since Belgrade hoped for a settlement before relations with France deteriorated irreparably. But Yugoslavia's condemnation of French brutality in Algeria, its mounting insistence upon a U.N.-supervised referendum, and its grants of assistance to the Algerian rebels intensified French hostility and brought relations between the countries to the point of an open split. On February 2, 1962, the French Government demanded the recall of the Yugoslav Ambassador because Yugoslavia had extended *de jure* recognition to the Provisional Government of Algeria at the time of the Belgrade Conference. By 1964, however, Belgrade repaired its links to Paris, whose essential policies of calculated disruption of NATO and opposition to Cold War blocs now seemed remarkably similar to its own.

Yugoslavia embraced the Algerian war of independence with a fervor it never mustered for any other national-liberation struggle. Through the FLN, the Yugoslav leaders vicariously recaptured their finest hours. An account published in 1959 by a Yugoslav journalist who lived with the FLN and observed its revolution from within helped popularize the struggle.[8] By 1960 the scholarly community began to publish extensively on this issue, but most of the articles were historical accounts of Algeria's past, the rise of the FLN, and the pattern of French economic and political control; few reflected first-hand knowledge of the

[7] Gavro Altman, "Algerian Carrousel," *Review of International Affairs*, Vol. IX, No. 207 (November 16, 1958) , p. 11.

[8] Zdravko Pečar, *Alžir* (Belgrade: Kultura, 1959) , p. 302. In a subsequent study, *Alžir Do Nezavisnosti* (Belgrade: Prosveta, 1967) , a mammoth (923 pages) , definitive chronicle of the FLN struggle, Pečar gives considerable details on the background of the 1954 uprising (pp. 343-352) , the extent and character of Yugoslav military assistance (pp. 857-864) , and the extensive character of Yugoslav nonmilitary assistance, including the training of Algerian doctors and therapists and the caring for the wounded in Yugoslavia itself (pp. 598-600) .

area.[9] Military aid was given generously and contributed to FLN successes. Badly wounded Algerian soldiers were treated in Yugoslav hospitals, and Yugoslav doctors helped train Algerian medics and therapists; clothing and food were contributed for Algerian refugees in Tunisia and Morocco; several hundred scholarships were made available for Algerian students to study in Yugoslavia; Algerian folk and drama groups toured Yugoslavia; and FLN observers were honored guests at the Seventh Congress of the LYC in March 1958 and at subsequent Congresses of the Yugoslav Federation of Trade Unions. These ties forged during Algeria's war of independence were intended to bind the two countries in immutable friendship. Tito sought a relationship of political intimacy with Ben Bella comparable to that which he enjoyed with Nasser. A measure of Tito's success was evident in the remarks Ben Bella made on March 6, 1964, during his visit to Yugoslavia:

> I want to stress that it is not by accident that our first visit to Europe is paid to Yugoslavia. We have come to Yugoslavia because of a great similarity in our struggles. We have come because you have selected the road which we regard as correct—the road to socialism. We have come here because you have taken the kind of road to socialism which we regard as the best of all, since it pays attention to democracy and harmonizes socialism and democracy. We have come to Yugoslavia as a small country which, nevertheless, contributes towards the settlement of world problems, and this is characteristic of great nations. We see a picture of ourselves in you, in your courage. . . .[10]

[9] Three characteristic pieces may be noted: Lazar Zdravković, "The Evolution of the Algerian Question," *Medjunarodni Problemi,* Vol. XII, No. 1 (1960), pp. 113-128; Miljan Komatina, "The Algerian National-Liberation Front," *Socijalizam,* Vol. IV, No. 5-6 (1961), pp. 142-171; Vojislav Arsenijević, "The Struggle for the Independence of Algeria and the Problems of Development in the Future," *Medjunarodni Problemi*, Vol. XIV, No. 4 (1962), pp. 81-100.

[10] Joint Translation Service of the Yugoslav Press, No. 3736 (March 7, 1964), p. 26.

However, the deposal of Ahmed Ben Bella on June 16, 1965, cost Tito a protégé-partner and shattered his dream of a special relationship between Yugoslavia and Algeria.

The Congo crisis, too, absorbed the attention of Yugoslav leaders who sensed that "the struggle for the Congo is the struggle for Africa,"[11] but it evoked little of the popular empathy felt for Algeria. In his speech before the U.N. General Assembly on September 22, 1960, President Tito condemned the Western countries for seeking to perpetuate their economic exploitation of the Congo behind a facade of independence and deplored the ineffectiveness of the United Nations in securing the independence, sovereignty, and territorial integrity of the beleaguered Congo. He corresponded with Nehru, Sukarno, Nkrumah, Nasser, Haile Selassie, and Touré, and tried to fashion a common policy which would eliminate the Belgian presence and the invidious use of mercenaries. On December 7, 1960, the Yugoslav delegate at the United Nations informed Secretary-General Dag Hammarskjöld that because of the impermissible attitude of U.N. forces in not actively supporting the legally-constituted Lumumba Government, Yugoslavia "does not wish in any way to bear or share the responsibility for what is now happening in the Congo. . . ." Accordingly, it is withdrawing its diplomatic mission from Leopoldville and "its pilots and all the other personnel stationed in the Congo at the request of the United Nations." With other leading nonaligned countries, Yugoslavia pressed Hammarskjöld to intercede on behalf of Patrice Lumumba, the former premier deposed by Colonel Mobutu and then murdered by his opponents on February 13, 1961. Three days later, it extended diplomatic recognition to the Gizenga faction in Stanleyville, a gesture which placed Yugoslavia squarely on the side of the militant minority of Afro-Asia.

During his visit to West Africa in the spring of 1961, undertaken to dramatize Yugoslavia's partnership in Africa's quest for independence from colonialism, Tito spoke be-

[11] Aleš Bebler, "Concerning the Congo," *Socijalizam*, Vol. VIII, No. 1 (January 1965), p. 96.

fore the Ghanaian Parliament; he was the first foreign leader to be accorded this honor since Ghana had proclaimed its independence in 1957. Tito asserted that "the colonial problem cannot be dealt with any longer in terms of policies employed at the beginning of the Twentieth Century, or in terms of policies employed during and immediately after the Second World War, nor as a question which occasionally is given a place in solemn declarations of great powers":

> The peoples who have freed themselves from colonialism, or are on the way to acquire freedom, have stepped as an active factor on the scene of modern history. Their destiny can no longer be decided upon without their participation.[12]

After reiterating Yugoslavia's active championing of independence for all colonial peoples, Tito dwelt at length on the situation in the Congo. He denounced the Western powers for trying to maintain their former privileged positions and transform the Congo "into a docile instrument of cold war policy," and he eulogized Patrice Lumumba as a great nationalist leader, condemning his criminal murder by Western-propped usurpers. Tito blamed "some organs and officers of the U.N., particularly the Secretary-General," for their moral responsibility for Lumumba's murder and the success of the Western interventionists. Finally, he called for "active action in the U.N. by the nonaligned countries . . . to prevent this world organization from serving the interests of certain groups of countries and to make it pass urgent decisions which would serve the interests of the Congolese people and of world peace only." In one of his most eloquent appeals for cooperation and cohesiveness among the nonaligned countries in the United Nations, he reminded them that the world organization was their instrument of influence in international affairs:

[12] *Tito: Selected Speeches and Articles, 1941-1961* (Zagreb: Naprijed, 1963) , p. 348.

The U.N. is not an international factor for itself, but an organization where members are various States; it is only an instrument for the realization of mankind's objectives such as the liberation of colonies, the establishment of coexistence, the attainment of an agreement on universal and total disarmament, the granting of economic aid and technical assistance to underdeveloped countries and so on. Whether this instrument will serve these ends or the narrow interests of individual groups of countries, will depend primarily on the members of this world organization and their willingness to settle problems of common interest by agreement. On the joint and consistent efforts of all peace-loving and independent countries towards these objectives depends, to a great extent, whether the weaknesses in the functioning of the U.N. will be overcome and whether the U.N. will be capable of fulfilling its present and future tasks, as was the case, for instance, when aggression against Egypt had been committed, and at some other critical moments.[13]

Anti-colonialism has become the Yugoslav credit card to the Third World. Whether in the case of Algeria or the Congo, Angola or West Irian, Goa or South Arabia, Yugoslavia has sided with the efforts of indigenous peoples to break the shackles of foreign rule and, where the issue of self-determination was clouded by partisan loyalties (for example, the dispute over West Irian), always with the non-Western country against the Western one. When a struggle involved two non-Western nationalist factions, as in Yemen, the Yugoslavs favored the faction supported by a nonaligned country on the ground that it was the more "progressive." Anti-colonialism is the engine that keeps Belgrade on the track with the "progressives" of the nonaligned world whose drive for influence in the world is generally not equal to the rigors of the course.

[13] *Ibid.*, p. 354.

91

3. *Exchanges of Visits*

A firm believer in personal diplomacy, Tito is the most travelled nonaligned leader of his time. Time and again he has carried the message of nonalignment and the need for the nonaligned nations to assume an active role in world affairs to Asia, Africa, and Latin America. His odysseys have become a familiar feature of the post-1954 period. Tito clearly expressed the rationale underlying his trips on the eve of his first visit to West Africa on February 13, 1961:

> Visits and contacts between statesmen are extremely important, especially in the present-day situation, and particularly contacts and mutual visits between the responsible men of the unaligned countries, for in direct personal talks it is possible much more easily and constructively to approach the consideration of various problems and, in accordance with an exchange of views, necessary decisions may be taken concerning further struggle for the preservation of peace in the world and other matters.

Personal diplomacy with other countries involves numerous visits both of heads of state and of lesser officials to and from Yugoslavia. Though the actual political impact of the diplomatic *ronde* is difficult to measure, it undeniably offers Yugoslavia repeated opportunities to manifest its friendship for developing countries and explore avenues of establishing new contacts.

The range of Tito's travels to the Third World is impressive. His trip to India and Burma in December 1954–January 1955 was the first by a non-Asian Head of State to that part of the world; in December 1955 he went to Egypt, the first of many official and unofficial visits that he was to make in succeeding years; in December 1958 he left on a three-month voyage to Indonesia, Burma, India, Ceylon, Ethiopia, the Sudan, the United Arab Republic, and Greece; in the spring of 1961 he made a similar trip to Ghana, Togo, Liberia, Guinea, Mali, Morocco, Tunisia, and the U.A.R.—the first Communist Head of State to go to Africa south of the Sahara; and in September 1963 he was the first to visit in Latin America: Brazil, Bolivia, Chile, and Mexico; since 1964 he has made other trips, including the Middle East and India, though their frequency has diminished as a consequence of the elimination from power of most of the nationalist figures with whom he dealt and the inroads of time on his indefatigable energy and boundless curiosity. During this period all the outstanding figures of the nonaligned world visited Yugoslavia. The most frequent guests were Nasser, Nehru, and Sukarno: between 1955 and 1964, the period within which Yugoslavia played its most important part in the evolution of nonalignment, Nasser came five times—July 1956, July 1958, June 1960, August 1961, and May 1963; Nehru came three times—July 1955, July 1956, and September 1961; and Sukarno visited six times—September 1956, January 1958, April 1960, June 1961, September 1961, and June 1963. In addition, other major figures, such as Emperor Haile Selassie, U Nu, Prince Norodom Sihanouk, Sekou Touré, Kwame Nkrumah, Modibo Keita, Julius Nyerere, and Lopez Mateos, have at various times been Tito's guests. To them, Tito urged the need to strengthen mutual ties and make their voices heard while there is time and before the moment "when it will no longer be possible to control whether or not, and where, the first shot will be fired."

Although the visits between Heads of State attract the greater attention, it is the exchanges of cabinet level officials and goodwill missions which establish the bases for systematic cooperation and consultation in functional areas; they result in the implementation of a line of policy and, indeed, often set the stage for the Heads of State to meet. Such missions are frequent and need not be catalogued. For example, in April 1960, by no means an unusual period, there were three high-ranking governmental missions visiting in different parts of the world: the Foreign Minister, Koča Popović, was travelling in Afghanistan, Pakistan, India, and the U.A.R.; a member of the Federal

Executive Council, Jakov Blažević, attended the celebration marking the formal proclamation of independence of Togoland and discussed prospects for improving relations with officials in Libya; and the President of one of the Chambers of Parliament, Dr. Mladen Iveković, headed a parliamentary delegation to Japan and Cambodia. To illustrate the activity of a goodwill mission, its tangible results, and its long-term influence upon the policy initiatives of the Head of State, the experience of the Yugoslav mission to Latin America in 1959 will be examined. The reasons for focusing on this mission are threefold: first, the author had an opportunity to interview the members of the mission and obtain some insights into the venture which are not available in published form; second, an area of marginal Yugoslav interest, Latin America was the object of an ambitious political exploration by President Tito in September 1963; third, the results of this goodwill mission reveal the limits as well as the specific material returns of personal diplomacy.

Yugoslavia has diplomatic relations with most of the nations of Latin America and is the only Communist country to date with such a record. On the other hand, fewer than half of the Latin American countries have accredited representatives in Belgrade. Trade between Yugoslavia and Latin America has increased gradually, but has never reached the levels hoped for in Belgrade. More than 80 percent of its foreign trade in the area is with Argentina and Brazil, notwithstanding intensive efforts to broaden the base of customers. Official Yugoslav delegations visited Latin America in 1946, 1949, and 1954, the latter two times with political as well as economic aims. In 1958 two delegations were sent: one was in search of trade, the other attended the session of the Interparliamentary Union in Rio de Janeiro and did some political fence-building in Argentina, Chile, and Uruguay as well.

The purposes of the 1959 goodwill mission, which left on June 25 and returned on August 19, were to exchange views on international issues and present Yugoslavia's views

on nonalignment and active peaceful coexistence; to encourage the expansion of trade and to establish closer relations with those countries with which Yugoslavia did not
have permanent missions, i.e., Colombia, Peru, Haiti, and
Honduras; and to establish contacts with socialist parties
in Latin America—an objective which, in general, did not
meet with much success at this time. The initiative for the
mission came from the Federal Executive Council of the Federal Government. Headed by Vladimir Popović, then the
Chairman of the Foreign Affairs Committee of the Federal
Assembly, the mission also included Jože Brilej, an Undersecretary for Foreign Affairs; Borivoje Jelić, a member of
the Planning Council; and Stane Juznić, one of Yugoslavia's eminent specialists on Latin America. The pere-
grinating Yugoslavs started in Mexico and moved, succes-
sively, to Costa Rica, Honduras, Cuba, Haiti, Venezuela,
Colombia, Ecuador, Peru, Bolivia, Argentina, and Brazil.
To the Presidents of Mexico, Venezuela, and Bolivia,
they brought personal letters from Tito, measures of esteem
for socialistically-oriented counterparts.

According to the Yugoslavs, they received cordial recep-
tions in almost every country. In Mexico, President Lopez
Mateos, who was just starting his term in office, expressed
interest in broadening political consultations, not only
in the U.N. but on a bilateral level, and was subsequently
to exchange official visits with Tito. Useful contacts were
established with Mexican businessmen; and commercial relations, which had heretofore been meager, increased somewhat. The mission's purpose in Cuba was to establish diplomatic relations with Castro, who had ousted Batista and
come to power on January 1, 1959. Yugoslavia did have a
formal exchange of credentials with the Batista regime but
no Ambassadors had ever been exchanged. At the time there
were few suggestions of Castro's Communist-orientation, and
one member of the mission later expressed amazement at
the ineptness of American policy toward Cuba in those
days: "Nowhere did I encounter anti-Americanism, though
there was understandable criticism of American policies

and business practices." The Yugoslavs were treated politely but distantly. Their session with Castro was useless because he kept leaving them abruptly, returning, and leaving again, making sustained discussion impossible. At the time, they attributed Castro's coolness to the pressures of managing a new regime. However, in retrospect, they thought a more probable interpretation was that Castro mistrusted Yugoslavia, accepting at face value Moscow's charges of betrayal of socialism and reasoning that it was impossible to receive aid from the United States and not be under the thumb of American imperialism. The Yugoslavs were received by President Urrutia, who was deposed the next day. In Haiti, where François Duvalier was commencing his reign, they were shown around the island and given a cordial reception. Despite the absence of prospects for economic relations, the visit was adjudged useful because it was really the first contact historically between the two countries.

In Venezuela, the Yugoslavs were declared "guests of the government" and given VIP treatment. They met with President Betancourt, and Vladimir Popović addressed the Parliament, where he was attacked by the representatives from the Communist Party and defended by the ruling Acción Democrática. Over the years, Yugoslavia has maintained extraordinarily amiable relations with Venezuela and its socialist-oriented political parties. The reporting of the situation in that country by Yugoslav journalists has been subject to vilification from the Venezuelan Communists, but earned the trust of Betancourt and his successors. Yugoslav friendship for Venezuela has brought Belgrade under fire from China and Cuba. For example, when Yugoslavia proposed that Venezuela be invited to the 1964 Cairo Conference of nonaligned nations, Cuba demurred, bitterly criticizing the Yugoslavs. As a compromise Venezuela was invited as an observer. In Colombia the power of the entrenched and conservative hierarchy of the Roman Catholic Church forestalled the establishment of formal diplomatic ties. But the Yugoslavs did expand trade, taking Colombian coffee in return for machinery. In Ecuador, the only country in which they were not received by the President, who was electioneering in the interior, some business contacts were made. The mission was well received in Peru, where there is a wealthy colony of Yugoslavs with extensive industrial and mining interests; the colony dates from before World War I but still feels very attached to the mother country. In Chile, Bolivia, and Argentina, long-established connections with government leaders and socialist elements assured cordial welcomes. The visit to Uruguay was short and wasted: a general strike paralyzed the country making political and commercial meetings impossible.

In general, the mission was considered a success. It explained Yugoslavia's position on world issues, and found Latin Americans aware of and interested in Yugoslavia and its efforts to build socialism, and highly complimentary to Tito as a statesman; it also returned with a greater appreciation of the diversity and distinctiveness of the area. Some improvement in trade resulted, especially with Brazil, Chile, Colombia, Costa Rica, and Mexico. But, as one member of the mission observed, although Yugoslav enterprises were encouraged to explore trade possibilities, they are hampered by distance, by unfamiliarity with the Latin "style" of business with its inordinate predilection for the "personal touch," by the limited possibilities of Yugoslavia to provide them with products, and by the political and economic circumstances of the countries themselves who place a low priority on expanding contacts with Yugoslavia. A separate Ambassador was accredited to Bolivia, but no more permanent legations were established as a result of the trip. By way of explanation, one Yugoslav noted: "We are a poor country and cannot afford to set up missions all over." In all likelihood, the reasons inhered more in the reluctance of the Latin Americans than in the financial demands upon the Yugoslavs, for expense did not deter them from opening missions, legations, and embassies throughout Africa, where political considerations are apparently controlling. The trip was not the lineal antecedent of Tito's tour in 1963, but it was a step in that direction; it brought back firsthand assurance of a generally congenial environment and thus contributed to the overall assessment which convinced Tito to venture into new terrain once the timing seemed propitious.

The Yugoslavs paid greater attention to Latin America after 1959. With the coming of Castro to power, they sensed the beginning of revolutionary ferment. In 1961, the election in Brazil of Janio Quadros as President appeared to presage a sharp turn to the left in domestic affairs and a further whittling away of *Pax Americana* in the Western hemisphere. (He had visited Yugoslavia shortly before the election and been cordially received.) The largest and most populous nation in Latin America veered toward socialism and nonalignment, or so it seemed: Quadros's decisions to resist U.S. efforts in the Organization of American States (OAS) to quarantine Cuba, to support the admission of Communist China to the United Nations, to establish diplomatic relations with Bulgaria, Hungary, and Romania, to reconsider the resumption of ties with the Soviet Union, to orient Brazilian diplomacy towards Afro-Asia and the nonaligned world, and to invite Tito to visit Brazil in 1961 all signified, in the words of one Yugoslav commentator, "a courageous break with conservative traditions, and . . . a new political concept founded on modern, constructive and democratic ideas."[14] The mystifying resignation of Quadros later in the year was a staggering disappointment.

Cuba's defiance of the United States and growing dependence on the Soviet bloc had reverberations far beyond the Caribbean. The Monroe Doctrine would never again be the same. No longer was Latin America an inviolate American

[14] N. Opačić, "Brazil's New Vistas," *Review of International Affairs*, Vol. XII, No. 263 (March 20, 1961), p. 8. Belgrade viewed the inauguration of Janio Quadros on January 31, 1961 as ushering in "a new phase in Yugoslav-Brazilian relations." "Relations Between Yugoslavia and Brazil (1960-1961)," *Yugoslav Survey*, Vol. II, No. 6 (July-September 1961), p. 894.

preserve, off-limits for the duration of the Cold War. Added to this was a pronounced exacerbation of social unrest, political impatience, and dissatisfaction with pervasive American economic influence and the inadequacy of Kennedy's "Alliance for Progress." Belgrade perceived Latin America to be in the process of emancipating itself from the shadow of American political paternalism and believed the time of rubber-stamp resolutions in the OAS was definitely over.[15]

In May 1962 Koča Popović became the first Yugoslav Foreign Minister to visit Latin America. He went to Brazil, Chile, Bolivia, and Mexico, paving the way for Tito's trip, which, however, was delayed by almost a year. Popović stressed a few themes: their common commitment to the preservation of peace, the quest for independence, and the need for accelerated economic development; and the possibilities open to them to make important contributions in these areas if they acted in concert with other lesser powers. He also extended invitations from President Tito to visit Yugoslavia.

Before Tito embarked on his one-month trip in September 1963, the world had passed through a momentous year. International alignments and attitudes had altered dramatically, irreparably cracking the rigid cast of bloc configurations. The Cuban missile crisis of October 1962, which had brought the United States and the Soviet Union to within an eyelash of catastrophe, shook Tito more than any other single event since the Hungarian revolution. NATO's cohesion was undermined by De Gaulle's implacable opposition to Britain's bid for membership in the Common Market and American leadership of the Western alliance, and by his belief that the Cold War was over. The Sino-Soviet alliance was shattered beyond recognition, and the colossi of communism competed bitterly with one another for leadership in the international Communist move-

[15] Stane Juznić, "New Prospects for the Organization of American States," *Review of International Affairs*, Vol. XIII, No. 284 (February 5, 1962), p. 8.

ment. The Chinese attack against India in late October 1962 had shown the tinsel, transient character of *Panch Shila*. Bandung was dead. In Eastern Europe, Romania intrepidly claimed larger measures of autonomy, careful not to strain the limits of Moscow's permissiveness, and in this it received quiet but reassuring support from Yugoslavia in the form of expanded economic ties, cooperation in harnessing the power of the Danube, and political support. To its chagrin Moscow felt restrained from imposing greater unity on the Warsaw Pact members out of its desire to have their support in the sharpening split with Peking. The blocs were breaking up, and the Cold War no longer seemed as politically frozen as before: the Moscow Treaty, signed in August 1963, raised hopes that the limited nuclear-test ban might break the logjam in the disarmament negotiations; the establishment of a "hot line" between Washington and Moscow, and the U.N. treaty barring the orbiting of nuclear weapons in outer space connoted a growing realism on the part of the Great Powers, which the Yugoslavs found reassuring and promising. This was a time of opportunity for Tito, who gave a new emphasis to nonalignment, hoping to make it more palatable to the Latin American countries. The reaction, however, proved disappointing.

In all five countries (Brazil, Chile, Bolivia, Peru, Mexico) Tito dwelt on the familiar: the necessity for peaceful coexistence between all countries, irrespective of their social systems; the need for general and complete disarmament; the elimination of the remnants of colonialism; the closing of the gap between the developed and the developing countries; and the desire of Yugoslavia to expand economic relations. Tito singled out for special attention the proposal, originating in an exchange of letters between President Goulart of Brazil and President Lopez Mateos of Mexico after the Cuban missile crisis, for the denuclearization of Latin America as a step toward world disarmament.

What was new and startling, however, was Tito's assertion that the general movement for peace, and not the elimination of colonialism as he had proclaimed two years earlier at the Belgrade Conference, transcended all other issues. For the moment, Tito concurred with Nehru and the moderates of nonalignment, rather than Nasser, Sukarno, and Nkrumah, the militants. Not only was the division of the world into Western and Eastern blocs obsolete, but, as he stated again in his speech on October 22, 1963, before the U.N. General Assembly, "in view of the changed international situation, it may be said that the term nonalignment has in a way been superseded by the new and positive evolution of international relations." Beyond nonalignment lay "the polarization of the forces of peace, on the one hand, and of the forces of cold war on the other." Traditional bloc alignments are breaking down and countries are taking their stand more and more in relation to the issue of preserving peace and less and less "according to their formal adherence to one side or the other in the cold war, which is slowly but gradually abating and to which an end should be put as soon as possible." In his first public references to the substance of his discussions with Khrushchev, who had been visiting in Yugoslavia just prior to his departure, Tito told President Goulart that Soviet leaders were ready to settle pending problems by peaceful means, that even the question of Berlin was secondary to the preservation of peace.[16] The great issue of the moment, said Tito, is war and peace, and the countries favoring peaceful coexistence have an active and important role to play in the struggle against the "reactionaries" (those seeking to perpetuate the Cold War) and the "dogmatists" (the Chinese Communists and their apostles in other Communist Parties). The question of the type of social system is secondary to the necessity of all the forces of peace working together.[17] In a sense, Tito called for an international Popular Front linking the Khrushchevite and Titoist Communists, the social democrats, the nonsocialist advocates of nonalign-

[16] *The New York Times*, September 21, 1963.
[17] Bogdan Oreščanin, *Vojni Aspekti Borbe Za Mir Nacionalnu Nezavisnost i Socijalizam* (Zagreb: Naprijed, 1964), pp. 13-16.

ment in the Third World, and all other groups favoring an end to the Cold War.[18]

Tito's trip did not have the significance claimed for it by Yugoslav officials:

> As a meeting of statesmen who approach the crucial problems of the contemporary world in a novel way, who add new dimensions and fresh moral force to the policy of peace and coexistence, this visit is certainly as much a herald of the new era in international trends as it is a confirmation of the theory that political polarization in the world is taking place not only on the basis of the criteria of the cold war, but also on that of the concrete problems and needs which link and unite all the forces of peace and progress, regardless of geography, ideology or system.[19]

Yet the trip was not without effect. Economically, it stimulated a modest expansion of trade, always an important

[18] Dennison I. Rusinow, "Yugoslavia Reaps the Harvest of Coexistence." *American Universities Field Staff Reports Service* (Southeast Europe Series, Vol. XI, No. 1, 1964) , p. 13.

Tito's *chef du cabinet*, Bogdan Crnobrnja, insisted that Yugoslavia did not make any attempt whatsoever "to persuade them to make any kind of formal declaration of nonalignment or neutrality, for that is not essential. What is essential is the substance of the policy they pursue, and its consequences. . . .

"Yugoslavia has stressed again and again that peaceful forces exist everywhere in the world. The goal of the policy of nonalignment has been to avoid destroying links with the peaceful forces wherever they exist, rather than to set about making new ones. This is a more practical proposition now than it was earlier, and it is useful to keep this fact in mind.

"Conditions have undergone an obvious change, so that the policy of nonalignment should be implemented in a different way today. What is involved is not a change that would reduce the significance, role and need for 'nonalignment.' On the contrary, the task in hand now is to strengthen, encourage and assist the peaceful forces under these altered and improved conditions, in order to do away with the cold war as radically and rapidly as possible, and to establish more intensive peaceable and equitable collaboration. This is the framework for the initiation of talks for a new conference of nonaligned countries." "In Support of Peace," *Review of International Affairs*, Vol. XIV, No. 327 (November 20, 1963) , p. 3.

[19] N. Opačić, "A Peace Platform," *Review of International Affairs*, Vol. XIV, No. 325 (October 20, 1963) , p. 2.

dividend for Belgrade. Politically, it demonstrated the willingness of Latin American countries to explore foreign policy initiatives outside the OAS framework; it led a few of them (Argentina, Bolivia, Brazil, Chile, Mexico, Uruguay, and Venezuela) to send observers to the 1964 Cairo Conference of nonalignment, thus evidencing, as one official who had accompanied Tito noted, "an indication of some changing conceptions and interests in these countries." But within a few months, coincidental with Nehru's death in May 1964, Tito restored nonalignment to prominence in his political declarations and, with the toppling of Ben Bella, Sukarno, and Nkrumah, and the escalation of the Vietnam war, moved to reinforce his credentials with the militants of nonalignment through identification of "neocolonialism" and "imperialism" as the threats to world peace.

4. *Summitry and Conference Diplomacy*

More than any of the other major figures of nonalignment, Tito consistently upheld the value of summit meetings. At Brioni in July 1956 he succeeded for the first time in convening a "Little Summit." For the next few years, however, he encountered difficulties in his efforts at summitry, largely because of Nehru's belief that India could act alone as mediator between the Cold War contestants. Thus, in January 1958, when Tito tried to generate support for a "Little Summit" of the uncommitted countries to support Khrushchev's proposal for a conference of the Great Powers, he failed because of Nehru's refusal to participate. In an election speech on March 16, 1958, Tito said that if a conference between the United States and the Soviet Union were held, it should include "countries which do not belong to any military bloc or formation," a theme he reiterated frequently.

During the Lebanese crisis of July 1958 Nehru, not Tito, was involved in the chain of consultations with the Great Powers. But with Africa's advance to nationhood, the appeal of nonalignment spread, and then Tito, not Nehru, struck the responsive chord among these new nations. For his ambitious conception of nonalignment and his demonstration of political adroitness, Tito seemed more in tune with the African nationalist movements. More than Nehru, Tito assiduously courted the uncommitted African nationalist leaders in such organizations as the All African Peoples' Congress and the communist-tinged and manipulated Afro-Asian Peoples' Solidarity Movement. But not until after the U-2 incident and the abortive summit of the Great Powers in Paris in May 1960 was Tito able to coordinate the various segments of the nonaligned world. Citing the ever-present danger of war, he called on the United Nations "to act in some way":

> We who are not participating in these talks [at Paris] must not be merely calm observers. We must oppose the fresh straining of relations, and strive to prevent this from jeopardizing the international situation.

On October 1, 1960, at the session of the General Assembly, India, the U.A.R., Ghana, Indonesia, and Yugoslavia attempted to sponsor a meeting between Premier Khrushchev and President Eisenhower. The leaders of the five nonaligned states requested the United States and the Soviet Union to "renew their contacts, interrupted recently, so that their declared willingness to find solutions of the outstanding problems by negotiation may be progressively implemented." With a self-righteous and callous indifference to the sentiments of the nonaligned which characterized American foreign policy during that period, the United States refused, a blunder compounded by its clumsily contrived attempt to have Australia arrange a meeting of the four big powers (instead of the Big Two), which evoked a rare contumely from Nehru: "I don't want one power, or two powers, or four, or six, to finalize anything for the rest of us. No group of powers, however big, can dispose of the destiny of the world."[20] American influence

[20] G. Barraclough, *Survey of International Affairs* (London: Oxford University Press, 1964) , p. 557.

among the nonaligned nations plummeted to its nadir, for the manner of rejection as well as for the rejection itself. A footnote to this is that President Kennedy and Premier Khrushchev did meet in Vienna in June 1961, but without settling any issues; indeed, far from easing tensions, this summit meeting may have emboldened Khrushchev to undertake adventurist initiatives because of his underestimation of Kennedy.

Tito learned of the Bay of Pigs while in Cairo. He and Nasser promptly condemned as nefarious this attempt to overthrow Castro. On April 22, 1961, they issued a joint communiqué in which they expressed, *inter alia*, their anxiety at the ominous international situation and "called for consultations among uncommitted countries, in order to strengthen world peace, preserve the independence of all nations, and remove the danger of intervention in the internal affairs of other countries." Each for reasons of his own desired a conference of the nonaligned countries: Tito to consolidate Yugoslavia's claim to leadership; Nasser to compensate for frustrations in the Arab world and in his policy toward Africa south of the Sahara. On April 26 they sent a joint letter to the heads of twenty-one nonaligned states setting forth their mutual problems and suggesting that a conference be convened prior to the next session of the General Assembly. On May 4 the decision to hold preparatory talks in June was announced. Tito and Nasser were joined as sponsors by Sukarno, whose long-cherished idea for a second Bandung had not been able to muster sufficient support because his close connections with Communist China only assured obdurate opposition from India, the U.A.R., Yugoslavia, and most of the African countries. Nehru was, it may be noted, not one of the original sponsors. Indeed, he officially and reluctantly accepted the invitation only on August 9, "a mere three weeks before Belgrade, and three and a half months after receiving the invitation."[21]

---

[21] G. H. Jansen *Afro-Asia and Nonalignment* (London: Faber and Faber, 1966), p. 289.

Though unhappy over the way the participants had been selected, he could not refuse:

> For India to be absent from a non-aligned conference convened by its friends Yugoslavia and the United Arab Republic, however badly this had been put together, would have called for a degree of toughness and independence that India's nonalignment policy did not display, then or later.[22]

At a mass meeting on July 4, 1961, commemorating the twentieth anniversary of the Yugoslav uprising at Užice, Tito underscored two of his motivations for arranging the Belgrade Conference: first, to prevent the United Nations from going the way of the League of Nations and becoming the instrument of one or another group of Great Powers; second, since the nonaligned countries, acting individually, cannot accomplish "anything really effective with regard to the improvement of the international climate regardless of how correct and just their attitudes may be," it is essential that "united, resolute action by the greatest possible number of countries that do not belong to either bloc" be taken.[23] In his view the conference was "a logical sequel to the unsuccessful efforts made thus far by the big powers to resolve the most crucial issues . . . by themselves without the participation of the small and non-committed countries and outside of the United Nations." Tito wanted the nonaligned countries to be part of the decision-making process whereby the major issues of international affairs were handled, with Yugoslavia playing an active part.

5. *The Belgrade Conference*

The choice of Belgrade as the site for the conference of twenty-five nonaligned countries was not without design. Cairo, too, coveted the honor. At the preparatory meetings in Cairo and Colombo the Foreign Ministers accepted Belgrade to obviate any embarrassing rivalry between Africa and Asia. Yugoslavia's leading role in urging the nonaligned

22 *Ibid.*   23 *Tito, op. cit.,* pp. 381-382.

nations toward a greater activism and in suggesting the conference helped to make this decision seem the obvious one. Also, since the tripartite meeting of Nehru, Nasser, and Tito in July 1956, Yugoslavia had assumed the character of neutral territory satisfactory to both Asia and Africa. At the 1960 session of the General Assembly, Nehru, Sukarno, Nkrumah, Nasser, Sihanouk, and other nonaligned leaders had met at the headquarters of the Yugoslav Mission, where Tito acted as host. As with the decision to meet at Belgrade, it had been so arranged partly because of Tito's initiative, and partly because it was easier meeting there than on the premises of, let us say, the Indian or Indonesian missions. The technical arrangements for the Belgrade gathering of nonaligned states were handled with distinction by Leo Mates, the Secretary General of the Conference. To preclude possible wrangling over seating and seniority, he gained acceptance for the rules of procedure and precedence used in the United Nations. For the many details associated with so distinguished, prestige-conscious, and unpredictable an assemblage, "improvisation was," in the words of one Yugoslav, "the central organizational concept, since improvisation can never break down."

The international mood at the convening of the Conference on September 1, 1961, was not auspicious. Tensions between East and West had escalated dangerously as a result of the erection of the Berlin wall, the limited American mobilization in mid-August, and the new Soviet pressures that spurred Washington to develop a comprehensive nuclear arsenal. Of immediate consequence for Tito was the decision of the Soviet Union to unilaterally abrogate the informal moratorium that had been respected by the United States, Great Britain, and the USSR since October 1958, and resume testing on August 31, the day before the Conference opened. Belgrade was confronted with a "moment of truth."

In his welcoming address Tito avoided the subject. On September 3, however, he spoke on the substantive issues of international concern: disarmament, Berlin, colonial-

ism, economic development, and coexistence. First flailing
France for not complying with U.N. resolutions on the dis-
continuance of nuclear testing, he then blandly observed
that "matters have now reached a point where the Soviet
Government has published a statement on the resumption
of nuclear weapons tests." No criticism, no indignation, no
rebuke. Far from even attempting a dispassionate assessment of the dangers of French and Soviet testing, Tito denounced the French, but had nothing severe to say about
the Soviets. Indeed, he excused Moscow:

> We are not surprised so much by the communiqué on the
> resumption of atomic and hydrogen weapons tests, be-
> cause we understand the reasons adduced by the Govern-
> ment of the USSR. We are surprised more by the fact that
> this was done on the day of the opening of this Con-
> ference of Peace.[24]

With that all too human capacity of national leaders for
imprudent self-deception, Tito could not face up to the
probability that the timing of the Soviet explosions was deliberate, calculated to demean the Belgrade Conference
and its pretensions to political influence in the world and
to remind it of some glossed over fundamentals of politics.
As it was, the justification and preparations for the Conference were virtually ignored by the Soviet press. Had Soviet
leaders felt any regard for the sensibilities or reactions of
the nonaligned, they could have delayed the resumption of
testing until after the Conference without any jeopardy to
national security. Possibly they felt no need to inconven-
ience themselves, anticipating that no criticism would be
forthcoming, certainly from Tito, with whom Khrushchev
was edging toward a new détente as his relations with
China worsened.

By his equivocation Tito, the father of nonalignment,
dealt his creation, at its moment of maturation, a blow
from which it never recovered. His failure even to express
"disappointment" at the Soviet action squandered his re-

[24] *Tito, ibid.*, p. 392.

serves of goodwill with influential American groups and probably contributed more to the disillusionment of American liberals sympathetic to nonalignment than did any other single act of the 1955-1965 period. In echoing the specious Soviet argument that the moratorium was broken because of France's testing, he allowed himself to be maneuvered into a tendentious position. Not only was France's *force de frappe* technologically and militarily infinitely inferior to the Soviet Union's, but, as we now know, Moscow did not regard it as serious enough to bar agreement on the limited test-ban treaty of August 1963, though France (and Communist China) continue to flaunt the international community on this matter. Lying at the heart of Tito's biased comparison of French and Soviet actions is a crucial question: how does Yugoslavia's being a Communist country contribute to shaping its behavior and foreign policy? Tito interpreted France's behavior in the worst possible light so as to reflect adversely on the West as a whole; whereas, he placed the most favorable interpretation on Soviet actions. It takes little imagination to speculate on what the probable reaction of Tito and the majority at the Conference would have been had the United States broken the moratorium. Largely as a result of his position on this issue, the official U.S. attitude toward Yugoslavia altered visibly, and Tito soon spoke of America's "unjustified attitude" and economic pressure against him.

The Conference militants, e.g., Tito, Nasser, Nkrumah, and Sukarno, identified colonialism as the greatest threat to mankind. Nehru demurred, pleading for perspective. He stressed the transcendent priority of the issue of peace and war: "Everything else, however vital to us—and other things are vital to us—has a secondary place." He tried unsuccessfully to wean the gathering away from its excessive preoccupation with colonialism, noting in an aside that "the era of classic colonialism is gone and is dead"—adding the qualification, "though, of course, it survives and gives a lot of trouble."[25] Nehru called upon the Conference to impress

[25] Peter Lyon, *Neutralism* (Leicester University Press, 1963), p. 188.

the Great Powers with the need to negotiate. But his call was drowned by the shrill cry of men who mistook sound for substance and fury for power.

The Belgrade Conference passed into history in the early hours of September 6, 1961, its transcript a matter of record, its achievements a matter of opinion. Nehru came, spoke, listened, but was clearly not impressed. In his report to the Indian Parliament he said that no "high policy" was formulated, that the "local considerations" of the militant majority had prevailed. An African Foreign Minister whose government did not attend wrote that by its partisan position on most issues the Conference "failed to provide any striking proof of the 'non-alignment' of the participating states, or at least of the majority of them."[26]

Whatever its shortcomings, and despite those who were totally critical, the Conference did have a constructive aspect. Neither the 400-word "Statement on the Danger of War and Appeal for Peace" drafted by Nehru nor the identical letters sent to President Kennedy and Premier Khrushchev urging them to resume negotiations had any noticeable effect; yet the Declaration of Belgrade, even if pretentiously offering recommendations on all global problems and in this respect going far beyond the purview of Bandung, did set in motion developments of continuing importance, thereby fulfilling some Yugoslav expectations. First, the Conference represented a landmark in the evolution of non-alignment as a factor in international relations. As the first mass gathering of nonaligned leaders outside the framework of the United Nations, it established a precedent: the adoption by nonaligned leaders of the traditional diplomatic method of consultation in order to reach a common position on key issues. (It was unfortunate that in treating themes that did not directly affect them the participants indulged in "declamatory diplomacy.") Second, the non-aligned countries succeeded in bringing about an enlargement of the U.N. Disarmament Committee in 1962. The

[26] Doudou Thiam, *The Foreign Policy of African States* (London: Phoenix House, 1965), p. 82.

non-nuclear, nonaligned nations were henceforth part of the protracted process of negotiating the small steps to disarmament. In addition, the General Assembly passed a resolution in late 1965 calling for the convening of a World Disarmament Conference. Third, by their implicit rejection of Khrushchev's "troika" proposal for restructuring the office of the Secretary-General, the nonaligned countries contributed greatly to the solution of the crisis which developed when Dag Hammarskjöld was killed in an airplane tragedy in the Congo a few days after the end of the Conference. Fourth, the Conference served as a socializing medium for many of the leaders from the newest African nations. Diplomacy is, in essence, a process involving personal exchanges. But intimacy can as easily heighten areas of fundamental disagreement as facilitate accord, and the interaction between Asians and Africans was not a happy one: "The Asians found the Africans jejune and over-emotional, and the Africans found the Asians hide-bound and patronizing."[27] Time may bring the two groups closer, or it may accentuate the gulf between them—their political and cultural traditions, and levels of economic development. At least the process of interaction outside of the United Nations gained impetus by this further contact. Fifth, the Belgrade Declaration focused attention on the gravity of the economic problems confronting the developing countries, particularly on the accelerating trends toward integration in Western and Eastern Europe, respectively, and their disequilibrating consequences for the nonaligned nations. It set in motion discussions leading to the Cairo economic conference in 1962 and the first UNCTAD (United Nations Conference on Trade and Development) gathering in 1964, which was the most comprehensive attempt made in the postwar period to arrest the growing gap between the developed countries and the developing countries. After Belgrade, the policy of nonalignment assumed economic as well as political dimensions; it became inextricably linked with the entire complex that inheres in the problem of eco-

[27] Jansen, *op.cit.*, p. 306.

nomic development. According to Leo Mates, a former diplomat and presently the Director of the Institute for International Politics and Economy in Belgrade, one result of the conference was that "the nonaligned countries constituted themselves not only as the core of a single wide front against the cold war and for international cooperation, but also as the political activists for a broadly based movement for the solution of the economic problems of the contemporary world."[28]

That Yugoslavia was host to the first conference of the Heads of State of the nonaligned countries was a stunning diplomatic triumph and in itself justified Tito's penchant for summitry. The conference confirmed Yugoslavia's unquestioned credentials as a charter member of the inner council of the nonaligned and Tito's leading role therein. In the nonaligned countries, the personal visits of President Tito contributed greatly to strengthening Yugoslavia's reputation as an independent socialist country. Many of the new nations, mistrustful of the Great Powers, welcomed Tito's initiatives, seeing that he neither sought to interfere in their internal affairs nor had ambitions to dominate them. Tito had become a world figure and a force behind nonalignment. He sought to give form and life to the expectant, eager political force that was at hand.

The Contributions of Tito

Josip Broz Tito was the chief architect of nonalignment. It is true that even before he arrived on the scene seeking ideologically congenial associates and an end to Yugoslavia's diplomatic isolation, the raw material was already present: the desire of newly independent Asian and Middle Eastern nations to stand apart from alignment in the Cold War and to rule their political systems free from foreign meddling. But Tito gave shape and impetus to nonalignment. Gradually perceiving in nonalignment a felicitous mixture of opportunity and feasibility, he infused it with a dynamism and purposefulness that were lacking in

[28] Leo Mates, *Ekonomski Osnovi Neangažovanosti* (Belgrade: Komunist, 1964), p. 72.

the passivity that he sensed in the formulations of Nehru, the erratic emotionalism of Sukarno, and the inexperience of Nasser. He contributed more than any other individual to the development of the major concepts. One Yugoslav accurately likened his contribution to the evolution of non-alignment to the contribution of yeast to the making of bread: it is the yeast that gives form and quality to bread; it is the yeast that makes the bread palatable and provides the energy for expansion and bursting out.

Tito introduced an activism crucial to the transmutation of an idea into a political force. Where there was passivity he brought forcefulness; where there were restraint and fatalism he brought the positiveness of the revolutionary; where goals were set in regional terms, he recast them into a global mold. His trips and official exchanges explored common grounds for cooperation and were the mortar with which he cemented friendships. His demonstrated success in dealing to advantage with both the West and the East impressed the new nations. Just as his personal qualities had engendered the confidence of the West in his determination to remain independent, so did these same qualities facilitate his contacts with nationalist leaders also. Likewise, the dealings of Yugoslav diplomats with their counterparts in other countries were made easier because the presence of Tito at the head of the Yugoslav State enhanced the confidence of foreign officials in what was being proposed—a factor of some importance for day-to-day diplomacy when one realizes that Yugoslavia has been involved in every initiative undertaken by the nonaligned nations.

Tito holds a dynamic view of nonalignment. In his view, which Yugoslavs say Nehru was not quick to accept, the policy of nonalignment is predicated on the assumption of a changing world in which peace is not a static thing to be bought by freezing the status quo. Inherent in the Yugoslav conception of peace is unceasing *struggle* against the conditions that breed war. "Nonalignment," said a long-time associate of Tito, "is not the soul of his policy: the soul is the active struggle for a new pattern of international relationships."

In emerging from the chrysalis of self-isolating Cominformist Marxist-Leninist orthodoxy, Tito opened the way for the psycho-political transformation of the Yugoslav elite's outlook. Though there was general support in the mid-1950's for Tito's *political* courtship of the nonaligned countries, there were reservations in the Party and enterprises against the *economic* implications internally of his policy of extending credits and expanding trade with Asia and Africa. While wanting the benefits of such economic relationships, certain interest groups were uneasy over the domestic implications of Tito's policy. Yugoslav enterprises were accustomed to a protected milieu and had no experience in a competitive foreign-trade situation. Tito's policy of nonalignment reinforced the bent toward internal economic liberalization, thereby loosening the political and social constraints of the Party over society. Nonalignment inadvertently promoted the liberalization of the Yugoslav society.

Tito also forced a new dimension into Yugoslav political thinking by arguing that the Party could not look at the new countries through the prism of European socialist and Communist experience: that political parties in Asia and Africa differed from those in Europe; that non-Communist Parties, e.g., the Congress Party of India and the Arab Socialist Union in the U.A.R., were more "progressive," and more deeply rooted in the people than were the cloistered local Communist Parties, and hence deserving of support. By his travels and hospitality to visiting Heads of State from non-Communist countries, he helped normalize close cooperation with all types of political systems. The story is told that during one of Emperor Haile Selassie's visits to Yugoslavia the representative of one Workers' Council in Slovenia started his welcoming speech by saying, "Welcome Comrade Czar."

Tito and Nehru: An Evaluation

Two men figured prominently in the entrance of Asia and Africa onto the world stage: Nehru and Tito. Jawaharlal

Nehru was one of the giants of the century. A revered national leader and renowned international statesman, he led his country through its first seventeen years of independence and bequeathed a commitment to democracy, socialism, and humanistic political values. Despite his preoccupation with world affairs he had little to show by way of achievement. He spoke of an unaligned policy for India as early as 1946 but, with the patrician's distaste for proselytizing or popularizing, neglected to consider the needs of his weaker neighbors.

At Bandung, Nehru defended India's policy of nonalignment and spoke eloquently of self-reliance, peace, and security; he condemned blocs, saying it was intolerable for him to think that the countries of Asia and Africa had "come out of bondage into freedom" only to prostrate themselves in the blocs of the Great Powers. But he did not go beyond this point. He spoke as an idealist, not as a political leader; certainly, not as a leader who understood that his universe was basically as threatened and precariously situated as that of the smallest nation, notwithstanding physical discrepancies in size, population, and potential wealth. Nehru spoke principles, not politics; he spoke of policies which seemed to the small nations to leave them to their enemies. Nehru offered neither leadership nor succor to the weak. The Iraqi delegate pinpointed the flaw in Nehru's position:

> Are you ready to bring us together—the weak and small nations—and form another bloc, so that we carry on our work uninterruptedly and also have protection? But by not doing that you leave us alone in small entities, cut to pieces and our existence threatened every moment.[29]

It remained for a European to appraise the mood of the new nations and their need for cooperation, and to provide the impetus for Afro-Asia's political assertiveness on the international scene.

Tito, the Croatian metalworker, accomplished what

[29] Jansen, *op.cit.*, p. 210.

Nehru, the Brahmin aristocrat, thought beyond reach: the vitalization of nonalignment. Tito made nonalignment a serious factor in international politics. The two men differed in outlook, temperament, and aspiration. Whereas Nehru foresaw the rise of Afro-Asian states as a factor in world politics, Tito acted to fashion a segment of them into a potent force; whereas Nehru was a reluctant conference-goer, Tito relished the endless round of political discussions; whereas Nehru was generally opposed to nonaligned summits because of his impatience with protocol and platitudes and the premium placed on consensus and the end-of-conference show of hollow unity, Tito regarded frequent face-to-face meetings as a prerequisite for crystallizing common purposes and reaching accord on a common platform; whereas Nehru was contemplative, skeptical of nonalignment's capacity for sustained, constructive cooperation, Tito was an activist, optimistic over the future of nonalignment and the spread of socialism, and found reassurance in the ability of this heterogeneous, unwieldy group to agree on international issues.

Both Nehru and Tito disclaimed any intention of setting up a "third bloc." Nehru, however, sought for India the *de facto* role of a great power, mediating between East and West, and his coolness toward acting in combination with the nonaligned countries stemmed from this insistent chimera. Only toward the end of his life did he concede the insufficiency of India's power for such a policy. Awakened from the reverie of *Panch Shila* by China's belligerency in 1959 and 1962, and impressed with the urgency of cultivating diplomatic support in the Third World in the face of growing Chinese inroads there, he acceded more readily after October 1962 to proposals for meetings of nonaligned leaders. Tito was not without his own dreams: to serve as the link between the Soviet camp and the nonaligned countries, moderating the views of the former and allaying the suspicions of the latter; and to organize a grand coalition of "socialist" and "progressive" forces. When all is said and done, Nehru proved in practice a consummate conservative defending India's national interests and greatly constrained by the imperatives of domestic politics. Secure in the Balkans, Tito was more genuinely internationalist in what he tried to accomplish, in part because of his Communist background, and in intangible measure because of the personal drives of the man himself.

There is little reason to doubt Tito's crucial role in non-alignment's coming of age. This process was experienced by non-European countries, yet its catalyst was European. That the leader of a small, weak, insufficiently developed country in the Balkans could have an impact far beyond the logic of his power position needs to be mentioned, for whatever importance nonalignment had in the past, holds presently, or aspires to in the future inheres in a central consideration of diplomacy: its human ingredient. This truth has been obscured by the preoccupations of contemporary social scientists whose bent is to depersonalize international politics and reduce the explanation of inter-nation interactions to impersonal levels of knowledge. In diplomacy one is inevitably influenced by the dynamic personality; he who can put forth in cogent and persuasive fashion ideas that seem to accord with the best interests of one's own country will be listened to, regardless of where he comes from or what is the actual strength of his country. Tito's ideas fell on receptive ears; he struck the right note with the right audience at the right moment in time.

Finally, going a step further, why did the Great Powers take the nonaligned countries as seriously as they did during the 1955-1964 period, the heady moment of nonalignment's importance in international relations? Reason alone cannot unravel this riddle. One explanation is that the United States was unsure of itself and of its standing in relation to the Soviet Union. Thinking it had less power than it actually did, it sought reassurance in voting victories in the United Nations and clients who would support American policies in the Cold War. And the Soviet Union was similarly unsure of itself and it, too, looked for new supporters in the beckoning Third World. Another explanation is that both countries sensed the existence of stalemate in Europe, Korea, and Vietnam, and turned increasingly to the Third World to gain a hoped-for strategic advantage and to deny it to the other. But both have come to see that catering to unstable clients is expensive and not very useful politically. An astute French diplomat likened a nation to an individual: "Both are subject to complexes and psychological problems; if you do not give help, you are not liked; if you do give help, you are not liked because it is generally not enough; and if you provide ample help, it creates even more serious problems. A nation, whether rich or poor, wants to be liked." Nonalignment exerted its greatest influence at a time when the Great Powers perceived it as important. After 1964 the leading powers adopted a lower-keyed approach, and this, coupled with major changes which occurred within the nonaligned nations themselves, has had important consequences for nonalignment.

CHAPTER IV

Yugoslav Diplomacy at the United Nations: The Political Dimension

DURING THE heroic period of nonalignment, roughly 1955 to 1964, it was in the United Nations that the new nations came of age. It was there that they aired views, made friends, formed coalitions, and learned consensual politics, U.N.-style. By weight of numbers in the General Assembly, the nonaligned nations dominated U.N. proceedings and pressed for decolonization, disarmament, and development. Yugoslavia unequivocally supported them and helped mobilize their every major initiative during that decade. The list of achievements is impressive: the acceleration of decolonization, the participation of the nonaligned in the disarmament talks in Geneva from 1962 on, the growing attention to economic development, the creating of UNCTAD —all concrete and constructive, all owing their realization in some recognizable measure to the diligence and skill of Yugoslav diplomacy.

The Meaning of 1948

When Stalin expelled Yugoslavia from the Cominform, the United Nations became the main arena for Yugoslav diplomatic initiatives. It has so remained. Yugoslav officials credit the forthright posture of the United Nations in discussing and supporting their 1951 complaint against Soviet-engineered border provocations with helping to frustrate Stalin's designs. They do not discount the importance of the military assistance extended for Cold War reasons by the Western Powers and the overarching security guarantee that this implied, but they add that the extraordinary sympathy manifested for Yugoslavia in the United Nations effectively countered Soviet strategic-political aims, and that even Stalin was impressed by the universal support enjoyed by Yugoslavia.

Generalizing from its own experience—a propensity of individuals and national elites alike—Yugoslavia has championed the view among the nonaligned that only within the framework of the United Nations can the small countries find an effective forum for their legitimate demands; only in the U.N., in conjunction with like-minded members of the international community, can they muster sufficient support and thus acquire the importance that will induce the Great Powers to accord them a voice in the formulating of international decisions. Not only has the U.N., according to one Yugoslav official, "enabled the small emergent and uncommitted countries to establish their equality and to gain increasing influence on a wider plane of international relations," but it has, by its very universalist "democratic framework," contributed in a not unimportant fashion to the shaping of nonalignment.[1]

Yugoslavia demonstrated that a small country need not become a member of an alliance dominated by a Great Power in order to retain its independence. At a time of bipolar bloc configurations it stood aloof from blocs and provided dramatic proof of the utility of the United Nations as a meeting ground where alignments without alliances could be nurtured. The United Nations helped Yugoslavia retain its independence and exercise maximum diplomatic flexibility. For nations emerging from colonial rule, the Yugoslav example was attractive, promising as it did independence and a distinctive international role. A pariah to the East and a maverick to the West, Yugoslavia made a virtue of adversity. To end its isolation, it pioneered nonalignment. The conditions were ripe and the prospective members were increasing, but without Yugoslavia nonalignment would very likely not have taken hold as quickly and firmly as it did. In Tito there coalesced the combination of example, purposefulness, and determination that gave essential form and direction to the new nations. Underlying the Yugoslav approach to nonalignment, both within and

[1] N. Djurić, "The United Nations and the Uncommitted Countries," *Review of International Affairs*, Vol. XII, No. 268 (June 5, 1961), p. 6.

without the United Nations, is the assumption that intelligent, concerted activism by the weak and less-developed nations can influence the policies of the strong and developed nations. Though this cooperation has been difficult to realize with any degree of consistency on all major issues because of conflicting conceptions of national interest and existing rivalries within the nonaligned group, it has been successfully generated on numerous occasions.

Since our purpose here is analysis of Yugoslav interaction with, and impact on, the nonaligned countries within the framework of the United Nations, some of the issues to which the Yugoslav government has accorded protracted and serious attention will be mentioned only briefly because of the low priority that they hold *in practice* for delegations from nonaligned countries. For example, Yugoslavia has closely followed the entire spectrum of disarmament issues from attempts to define the term "aggression," to halting nuclear testing, to prohibiting the orbiting of nuclear weapons in outer space. A firm stand by the nonaligned countries in the General Assembly resulted in six nonaligned nations being added to the expanded U.N. Disarmament Commission in 1962. According to Arthur S. Lall, former Indian delegate to the Eighteen-Nation Disarmament Conference, "the debates on disarmament have ceased to be dialogues between the political West and East and have become world debates in which the two sides have been increasingly under pressure to justify their proposals and attitudes to the third world."[2] Yet, with the exception of Yugoslavia, India, and the U.A.R., none of the nonaligned countries has tried to keep abreast of all the ins-and-outs of the technical problems regarding nuclear weapons and their control, both because of lack of staff and because few of them believe they can affect the outlooks or positions of the Great Powers in that vital area; and even the three leaders of non-alignment may not fully grasp the

[2] Arthur S. Lall, *Negotiating Disarmament: The Eighteen Nation Disarmament Conference: The First Two Years, 1962-1964* (Ithaca, New York: Cornell University, 1964), p. 3.

awesome complexities of all the technical problems under review. At the twentieth session of the General Assembly in 1965, Yugoslavia succeeded in obtaining adoption of a resolution calling for the convening of a world disarmament conference in 1967. The conference has not been convened, in part because it is not a priority issue for small nations, who know the limits of their capabilities and do not wish to assign scarce diplomatic resources to an undertaking that promises little payoff for them. They realize, but prefer not to admit publicly, that disarmament is the subject least susceptible to nonaligned intervention. Of the nonaligned countries only India and the U.A.R. have systematically shown the catholicity of Yugoslavia, and on a host of political, organizational, and economic issues have taken well-defined positions based not only on general political-ideological predilections but on carefully researched and reasoned arguments. Even they have serious doubts about the value of a world disarmament conference without Communist China and without some signs of tangible interest by the United States and the USSR.

Four issues have been selected in this chapter to illustrate the range and impact of Yugoslav activity in the United Nations: decolonization; the codification of the principles of peaceful coexistence; peacekeeping; and organizational matters. Each of these issues shares three characteristics: each has been given a consistently high level of sustained attention by Yugoslavia in particular and by the most active and militant nonaligned countries in general; each is an area in which Yugoslavia has played a leading role, or at least has intimately associated itself with the prime movers behind the issue; and each has been a topic of controversy and importance within the United Nations.

Decolonization

After 1945 national self-determination for colonial areas became a perennial issue at the U.N., as nationalist elites in Asia and Africa agitated there for independence. The leading Western imperial powers—Britain, France, and the

Netherlands—weakened by war and threatened by the spectre of Soviet expansionism, grudgingly acceded to demands for statehood, though not without protracted attempts at delay.

Yugoslavia embraced anti-colonialism very early. A staunch and forthright advocate of independence for all colonial peoples, it persistently supported colonial and former colonial countries against the metropole, often at some cost to its own diplomatic situation. Thus, in the early 1950's it sided with Iraq and Iran in the U.N. in their oil disputes with Great Britain, thereby jeopardizing the continuation of much-needed British support against the Soviet bloc; in the mid-1950's Yugoslavia upheld independence for Algeria, even though at the time it wished also to cultivate France as a friend. (Note: the Soviet Union was also intimately associated with early postwar anti-colonialism, but it failed to reap many benefits until the Khrushchev period because of Stalin's inflexible policy toward national-liberation movements, the insular and secretive demeanor of Soviet diplomats, and the gap between Soviet declarations and deeds.)

The acme of decolonization was the fifteenth session of the General Assembly at which seventeen new nations—sixteen from Africa—were admitted to membership. Speaking on September 22, 1960, Tito welcomed "the powerful upsurge of national liberation movements in Africa and elsewhere" and stated that the emancipation of former colonies was "a historical necessity." He urged encouragement of decolonization and assistance to enable the new states "to emerge as constructive members of, and active factors in, the international community." Though his speech harmonized with the mounting militancy of the assembled delegates, it was the Soviet delegation who captured the imagination of the anti-colonialist forces by proposing on the very next day the addition to the agenda of a "Declaration on the Granting of Independence to Colonial Countries and Peoples." The Assembly subsequently passed a more moderate Afro-Asian version. The Yugoslavs applauded the Declaration on Decolonization, noting that not only did it supersede "the obsolete formulation of Chapter XI of the Charter, which does not stipulate the abolition of colonialism, or the right of colonial peoples to independence," but it shows that certain parts of the Charter can be modified, "through the influence of progressive forces."[3] They noted that the Declaration corrected a deficiency in the U.N. Charter by unequivocally asserting the right of each nation to self-determination. Under General Assembly Resolution 1654 (XVI), the Special Committee on Colonialism was established in 1961,[4] with Yugoslavia as a member. Operating with a solid anti-colonial phalanx, the Committee spearheaded the Afro-Asian drive to abolish colonialism.[5] Yugoslav spokesmen have moved with the nonaligned and Afro-Asian nations to condemn every remnant of colonialism: *inter alia*, they have condemned Portuguese rule in Africa and Southern Rhodesia for denying political democracy to the black African majority, supported an International Convention on the Abolition of all Forms of Racial Discrimination, and even agreed in principle to support the use of force against these recalcitrant regimes—an indication of the extreme to which they are prepared to venture in their perceived need to stay with the militant vanguard and preserve their unique position as the only European country within the nonaligned group.

The willingness to sanction intervention by the U.N. against a colonial power on behalf of a subjugated colonial people led Yugoslavia to tailor its position on noninterference to the political outlook of the Afro-Asian states. The

[3] Leo Mates, "U.N., the Great Powers and the Nonaligned Countries," *Review of International Affairs*, Vol. XIII, No. 284 (February 5, 1962), p. 2.

[4] The official title is the Special Committee on the Situation with Regard to the Implementation of the Declaration on the Granting of Independence to Colonial Countries and Peoples, and it is also referred to as the Special Committee of Twenty-four.

[5] David A. Kay, "The Politics of Decolonization: The New Nations and the United Nations Political Process," *International Organization*, Vol. XXI, No. 4 (Autumn 1967), p. 795.

principle of noninterference in the domestic affairs of another country (Article 2, paragraph 7, of the Charter) was reconciled with the U.N.'s transcendent responsibility for involvement in situations affecting international peace and security, Yugoslavia arguing that, in fulfillment of its responsibility to ensure peace and security, the U.N. could not remain indifferent to injustice. A nation violating the Charter cannot be permitted to find sanction for repression in the Charter. Intervention by the U.N. was permissible, subject to the qualification that it be designed to promote national self-determination of colonial areas. The General Assembly, by adopting the Declaration on Decolonization, had assumed a specific and solemn obligation to advance the independence of dependent territories.[6] Thus intervention by the U.N. in a "just" cause was, by implication, a justifiable course of action.

Yugoslavia's narrow interpretation of Article 2, paragraph 7, had emerged from its early postwar affiliation with the Soviet Union. However, during the period in which it was under pressure from the Soviet bloc, though still upholding the principle that the United Nations should generally refrain from dealing with questions that fell within the domestic jurisdiction of member states, it nonetheless contended that the consistent and flagrant violation of human rights constituted a threat to international security which could not be ignored and which justified discussion and appropriate recommendations by the General Assembly (as in the case of the December 1946 resolution, calling upon members to ostracize Franco Spain). Thus, Yugoslavia had argued as early as November 1947 (before the Soviet-Yugoslav split) in favor of an Indian resolution calling for the protection of the Indian minority in South Africa, rejecting the view that the situation "was purely a domestic matter."[7] On this basis, too, Yugoslavia declared

[6] A. B., "Yugoslavia's Activity in the United Nations Committee on Decolonization," *Yugoslav Survey*, Vol. IV, No. 14 (July-September 1963), p. 2082.

[7] U.N., General Assembly, Political and Security Committee, *Official Records*, Second Session, p. 326.

in October 1950 that it "would not oppose an international investigation into the systematic violations of human rights and fundamental freedoms in Bulgaria, Hungary, and Romania."[8] It took the position that once an internal question acquired an international dimension "it ceased to be a matter within a State's domestic jurisdiction and outside the competence of the United Nations."[9] As it became involved with the unaligned new nations, Yugoslavia insisted that the quest for independence of colonial areas, such as Tunisia, Morocco, and Algeria, was as much within the legitimate purview of the U.N. as racial discrimination in South Africa.

Upon reconciliation with the Soviet Union in 1955, Yugoslavia restricted its agitation for U.N. intervention exclusively to questions involving colonial areas. In most instances its stand was easily taken: support for the dependent area against the Western colonial power. Support for Afro-Asian countries tied in with Yugoslavia's national interest in establishing a firm affiliation with the nonaligned countries.

Where loyalty to a political ally conflicted with commitment to a political principle, the latter, not unexpectedly, was conveniently overlooked. Thus, at no time did Yugoslavia criticize the U.A.R.'s military intervention in the Yemeni civil war during the 1962-1967 period: friendship with Nasser has been a key element in Tito's courtship of the nonaligned countries since 1956. Perhaps an operational definition of "friendship" in relations between nation-states is a readiness to interpret the behavior of one's friend in the best possible light: for the Yugoslavs the struggle in Yemen involved a "progressive" movement—empirically identified as the faction propped up militarily by the United Arab Republic, and a "reactionary" one—defined as the faction relying on pro-Western and feudal Saudi

[8] U.N., General Assembly, *Ad Hoc* Political Committee, *Official Records*, Fifth Session, p. 34.

[9] U.N., General Assembly, Political and Security Committee, *Official Records*, Seventh Session, p. 215.

Arabia. They overlooked the violence that was being done to the principles of noninterference in the domestic affairs of other states and focused instead on the nature of the internal struggle, the characterization of which was depicted in accordance with standard ideological stereotypes. Whatever reservations existed among Yugoslav leaders were kept tightly in rein.

The options became more complex when all the contestants in a given situation were Afro-Asian. For example, the issue of independence for Mauritania placed the Yugoslavs in an awkward position. A sparsely settled land of about one million with rich iron ore reserves, Mauritania was granted independence by France on November 28, 1960, and applied for admission to the United Nations. Morocco advanced historical arguments claiming that Mauritania was in fact an integral part of Moroccan territory. With the exception of Tunisia, the Arab states led by the U.A.R. supported Morocco's claim, despite the conservative character of the Moroccan regime. On the other hand, the black African states (except for Guinea and Ghana), and in particular those of French Africa, supported Mauritania's claim. For Nasser Arab brotherhood superseded African brotherhood. Ethnic and linguistic affinities proved stronger than religious ones. The Yugoslav delegation sided with the Arab states. While upholding the right of Mauritania to self-determination and calling for a peaceful solution to the problem, it voted for the draft resolution favored by the Arab states, which stressed the historic ties of Morocco and Mauritania, and France's tacit recognition in the past of the integral character of the two areas. Though not happy about the need to choose between two African states, Yugoslavia aligned itself with the U.A.R. position—an example of Belgrade's partisan support of Cairo.

On the general issue of anti-colonialism Yugoslavia has maintained a consistently principled position,[10] though at times it has been needlessly doctrinaire and even damaging

[10] Aleksandar Božović, "United Nations and the Decolonization Process," *Medjunarodni Problemi*, Vol. xv, No. 2 (1963), pp. 53-66.

to constructive efforts to deal with colonial problems in the U.N. Moreover, the complex politics of Africa increasingly confront the Yugoslavs with dilemmas of loyalty. However, as long as Tito and Nasser enjoy a special relationship, and as long as Yugoslav leaders regard the United Arab Republic as the most prominent country in Africa, Yugoslavia will look foremost to Cairo. Economically, this could prove shortsighted because the markets of Africa south of the Sahara may offer more possibilities for Yugoslav industries and exports in the decades ahead. However, politically, as long as Yugoslavia aspires to a major role among the nonaligned countries, it may be expected to nurture relations with the United Arab Republic to the occasional detriment of those with the countries of black Africa. With most of the formerly dependent peoples now politically independent, the decolonization drive is running out of steam, though colonialism—or its contemporary variant "neocolonialism"—is too useful a bogy to relegate to mere ceremonial status. Yet to their credit, the Yugoslavs sense that the long-term viability of the nonaligned countries depends on cooperation on positive, future-oriented issues, rather than on a preoccupation with obsolescent issues; and they seek to give leadership in a variety of political and economic areas which they consider important for nonalignment and for their own national aims.

Codifying Constraints on the Great Powers

Since 1949 Yugoslavia has sought to augment the security of small nations and circumscribe the power of strong nations by U.N. resolutions and international conventions. Among the possibilities offered by the U.N. was the prospect of a more effective role for international law. However, the road to two world wars abounded with instances of indifference by the Great Powers toward the legal rights of small nations, and poignant reminders of tattered treaties and unfulfilled obligations were not difficult to find. All the greater, therefore, the impressiveness of the Yugoslav feat in generating interest in recent years in developing international norms of behavior which will be accepted by the powerful as by the less powerful; this interest also inheres in the recognition by the major powers of the mortal hazards of another global war in a nuclear-missile age, and in the new premium they now place on competitive maneuvering and influencebuilding among the smaller nations.

The focus of Yugoslav efforts has been the Sixth (Legal) Committee of the General Assembly and the International Law Commission, a body established by the General Assembly in 1947 and assigned the responsibility for developing and codifying international law. On October 7, 1949, the Yugoslav delegation introduced a draft Declaration on the Basic Rights and Duties of States, which aimed at formulating rules guaranteeing states against aggression by spelling out and systematizing the provisions in the U.N. Charter prohibiting war. Acknowledging that a declaration would not abolish "imperialism or any other kind of expansionism," the Yugoslav delegate maintained that it would alert public opinion to impending preparations for aggression and mark an important step toward the development of international law.[11] The Yugoslav proposal went beyond an earlier Panamanian draft in calling for the right to self-determination for all peoples and the outlawing of wars of aggression, themes calculated to broaden the base of support among the new nations. Its adoption in November 1950[12] served the immediate Yugoslav purpose of mobilizing opinion in the U.N. against the threats from the Soviet bloc. Encouraged by the result, the Yugoslavs pressed

[11] U.N., General Assembly, Sixth Committee, *Official Records*, Fourth Session, p. 546.

[12] General Assembly Resolution 378 (v). The Resolution does not define the term "aggression." However, it provides a pragmatic method for quickly determining who is the aggressor. The basic postulate is that every nation involved in an armed conflict should immediately make a public declaration proclaiming its readiness to cease hostilities and withdraw its forces from the territory of another state. The Resolution was intended to preclude the possibility of concealing aggression under the guise of self-defense.

for adoption of other such resolutions. Constraint through consensual resolutions has become a Yugoslav trademark.

The role of international law in regulating the behavior of nation-states has absorbed the efforts of a significant segment of Yugoslav scholars dealing with international affairs; no subject is more extensively explored in the key journals devoted to the United Nations and its manifold activities.[13] According to Yugoslav scholars two trends were of crucial importance: first, the changed relationship between the Security Council and the General Assembly; second, the importance of General Assembly resolutions in the development of international law.[14] The lack of agreement among the permanent members of the Security Council resulted in the General Assembly's taking the initiative in recommending ways of maintaining international peace. The "Uniting for Peace" resolution, adopted on November 3, 1950, extended the authority of the small and medium countries in matters affecting peace and security. With this "democratization" the resolutions of the General Assembly, argued the Yugoslavs, assumed more than a recommendatory character; they ineluctably acquired the force of positive international law, and should so be regarded by all nations. Under these circumstances the voices of the small nations would acquire added cogency.

[13] The most important journals are *Medjunarodni Problemi* (International Problems), published by the Institute for International Politics and Economy; *Jugoslovenska Revija za Medjunarodno Pravo* (Yugoslav Review of International Law); *Review of International Affairs*.

[14] These points were treated during the early 1950's by several of Yugoslavia's most eminent scholars: Juraj Andrassy, "Common Actions for Peace," *Medjunarodni Problemi*, Vol. III, No. 4 (1951), pp. 24-53, and "The Relationship Between the Political Organs of the United Nations," *Medjunarodni Problemi*, Vol. V, No. 3 (July-September 1953), pp. 15-31; Milan Bartoš, "The Decision of International Bodies as a Source of Law," *Medjunarodni Problemi*, Vol. V, No. 4 (October-December 1953), pp. 12-27; and Aleksandar Magarašević, "The Progressive Development and Codification of International Law and the United Nations," *Arhiv za Pravne i Drustvene Nauke*, Vol. XXXVI, No. 3 (1949), pp. 475-485; and "The Problem of Legal Enforcement of Resolutions of the U.N. General Assembly," *Medjunarodni Problemi*, Vol. IX, No. 2 (1957), pp. 81-90.

At the 1952 session of the General Assembly, the Yugoslav delegation called for giving priority to the question of drafting a Convention on Diplomatic Intercourse and Immunities, which would protect diplomats from flagrant abuses at the hands of host governments. The resolution was passed, say the Yugoslavs, because the incessant mistreatment of Yugoslav diplomats by Soviet bloc countries lent urgency to Belgrade's advocacy.[15] Yugoslavia played a constructive part also in adoption by the United Nations of multilateral treaties designed to safeguard diplomatic personnel, e.g., the 1961 Vienna Convention on Diplomatic Relations and the 1963 Vienna Convention on Consular Relations.

With the resumption of Yugoslav-Soviet relations and with Tito's growing desire to act as intermediary and interpreter between the Soviet bloc and the nonaligned nations, Yugoslav officials lost interest in certain issues previously considered essential for easing international tensions. For example, they disapproved of agenda items directing attention to hostile propaganda disseminated by Soviet bloc countries against pro-Western, Afro-Asian governments. Thus, the Yugoslavs deplored the presentation before the U.N. by the Iraqi delegation in 1954 of instances of provocative broadcasts directed against Iraq by Radio Moscow and Radio Budapest, though two years earlier when they had considered themselves threatened, the item was regarded legitimate for inclusion on the agenda.[16] Its situation having improved, the threat to it from the Soviet Union having receded, Yugoslavia experienced a redirection of sympathies and interests. Believing that destalinization meant gradual desatellitization in the socialist camp, it counselled moderation and understanding in dealing with persistent but minor Soviet political irritants. The Yugoslavs were looking beyond the Cold War to ways of in-

[15] Milan Šahović, "Contemporary Aspects of the Codification of International Rules on Diplomatic Immunities," *Medjunarodni Problemi*, Vol. v, No. 2 (April-June 1953) , pp. 62-75.

[16] U.N., General Assembly, *Ad Hoc* Political Committee, *Official Records*, Ninth Session, p. 197.

stitutionalizing coexistence and improving their position in Eastern Europe.

The most ambitious Yugoslav juridical initiative has centered on attempts to codify the principles of peaceful coexistence. Under the stimulus of Dr. Milan Bartoš, Yugoslav jurists first offered a codification proposal at the 1956 Dubrovnik meeting of the International Law Association, a private, formally unofficial, but influential organization of jurists from all over the world. Prior to the meeting the matter had been discussed at the highest levels of the Yugoslav government. Full support was forthcoming after Bartoš apparently obtained the enthusiastic encouragement of President Tito. The Yugoslavs seek to elaborate the principles of peaceful coexistence, e.g., sovereign equality of nations, noninterference in the internal affairs of countries, self-determination for all peoples, mutual respect, duty to settle disputes by peaceful means, and the prohibition of threat or use of force. By relating these principles to relevant provisions of the U.N. Charter, they seek acceptance for them as norms of behavior in international relations. The special commission established within the International Law Association initially could not agree on the need for codifying the principles of peaceful coexistence. It stalled over the question of interpretation and the opposition of Western jurists who saw in the proposal discomforting similarities to Soviet formulations. Yugoslav scholars, however, persisted. Some did postulate the gradual development of "socialist international law,"[17] the essentials of which rest for them on the principles of active and peaceful coexistence, which are presumed to be accepted by the socialist camp and many of the new nations of Afro-Asia. But for all Yugoslavs peaceful coexistence is universally valid, irrespective of differences in social systems. Unlike their Soviet counterparts, they see the principles of peaceful coexistence as the core, not the casement, for binding norms for international behavior. Also, as Professor Bartoš has reiterated, the Yugo-

[17] Milan Šahović, "International Law in Contemporary Conditions," *Medjunarodni Problemi*, Vol. XI, No. 3 (1959), pp. 85-91.

slav conception of coexistence assumes not merely a *passive* tolerance of different social systems, but an *active* quest for cooperation among all countries, and not merely between social systems:[18]

> While passive coexistence as a doctrine was useful in a time of tension, it cannot be allowed to be the ideal of the United Nations, nor can it be defined in terms satisfying the minimum legal responsibilities of member nations toward their Organization. Passive coexistence is only a point of departure. The United Nations was not created for states to exist and vegetate, but in order to develop in mutually harmonious cooperation. The United Nations must be the center of that harmony.[19]

To effectuate the goal of peaceful *and* active coexistence, there must be a codification of the elaborated norms by which states are to shape their behavior, and these must be made part of international law.

Starting in the fall of 1957, when the General Assembly approved a joint Yugoslav-Indian-Swedish Declaration on Peaceful Coexistence, the issue became a perennial on the Yugoslav agenda of priorities. After six years of wrangling in the International Law Association and the U.N., the General Assembly established a Special Committee on Principles of International Law Concerning Friendly Relations and Cooperation Among States. The absence of the term "coexistence" is deliberate—the compromise result of several years of bitter discussion in the Sixth Committee. To gain consensus in the General Assembly, the formula "friendly relations and cooperation among states" was substituted for "peaceful coexistence," which to non-Marxists held an excessively Marxist connotation. One might assume that the Yugoslavs would be satisfied with having gained recognition by the United Nations for the *substance* of the effort at codification, but the *form* is clearly as crucial; Bel-

---

[18] Milan Bartoš, *Pravni Aspekti Mirne Aktivne Koegzistencije* (Belgrade: Yugoslav Association for International Law, 1956), p. 7.

[19] *Ibid.*, p. 47.

grade wants to establish its paternity. In Yugoslav publications scholars invariably refer to the work of the Special Committee, not by the official U.N. name, but by the appellation Special Committee for Codification of the Principles of Peaceful Coexistence.[20]

The process of negotiating a codification convention in the U.N. will be protracted at best. If retention of the term "peaceful coexistence" is so important for the Yugoslavs ideologically, politically, and psychologically, how much more intensely will they resist acceptance of definitions of coexistence that are congenial to non-Marxists and could gain universal acceptance? If acceptable to Marxist-Leninist and non-Marxist alike, is it probable that the definitions will have significant substantive content? Perhaps, as one American who is a close and judicious observer of the field of international law has suggested, "even if no code emerges, the effort expended in attempting to draft one can be educational":

> It will disclose that there is no simple formula for peace. It will also indicate the issues on which even independent scholars of good will can feel so strongly that they are willing to risk being misunderstood rather than to accept proposals in the name of peaceful coexistence that seem to them to threaten the continued existence of the values they cherish. If scholars in the newly emerging states can, through the codification process, come to realize that resistance to proposals that seem simple and sound at first glance is not necessarily motivated by a desire to preserve a position from which war may be waged, it will be time well spent.[21]

No firm agreement has yet been reached on the specific components of the principles of peaceful coexistence; preliminary deliberations have yielded draft texts of a general

---

20 *Borba*, March 17, 1966; Milan Šahović, "Establishing the Legal Substance of the Principles of Coexistence," *Review of International Affairs*, Vol. XVII, No. 388 (June 5, 1966), pp. 21-23.

21 John N. Hazard, "Codifying Peaceful Coexistence," *American Journal of International Law*, Vol. 55, No. 1 (January 1961), p. 120.

character only. Relevant resolutions passed by the General Assembly are broadly worded to enlist support of both the Soviet Union and the United States, with the result that specificity is relinquished for consensus, e.g., Resolution A/6220 of December 21, 1965, on "The Inadmissibility of Intervention in the Domestic Affairs of States and the Protection of Their Independence and Sovereignty." However, neither the special groups working on codification nor the resolutions themselves need concern us here. What is of interest are the reasons and expectations underlying the Yugoslav effort, and the effect of the effort on the nonaligned countries.

Many pragmatic and declamatory goals underlie the Yugoslav quest for codification. First, there is the desire of a small country for enhanced security. Yugoslav officials believe that the effort expended on codification will have been justified if, in moments of peril, the mobilization of opinion in the United Nations under the rubric of international law can provide even a modest increment in diplomatic support for the threatened party. From their own experience with the Soviet Union in 1951, from the Middle East crises of 1956 and 1967, and from U.N. intercessions in the Congo, South Africa, and Southern Rhodesia, the Yugoslavs know that the Great Powers are not insensitive to internationally generated pressures in situations where their immediate national security is not at stake. It is easier to bring pressure when an overwhelming majority of nations can be rallied behind a principle whose import is clearly related to their own long-term survival as a nation. As an instrument to restrict the behavior of nations, international law aims at forestalling changes in the status quo by force, though would-be reformers want guarantees that it will not bar further decolonization or "progressive" change. The greater the degree of universal acceptance of the norms of constraint, the greater the margin of protection of small and medium-sized powers.

Second, the Yugoslavs contend that "classical international law," which is inferentially linked to the pre-1945 period, must be superseded. For international law to be truly universal and to reflect the contemporary near-universality of the international community with its numerous new sovereign nations, it needs to be redrafted with the participation of all states.[22] International law must approximate universality in its origins as in its application. As Communists, the Yugoslavs see no reason to accept as binding on them, or on the new nations, international law that was formulated by a few capitalist countries at a time when they dominated international relations. They do not reject outright all pre-Charter international law; but they insist that elaboration and codification of the principles of peaceful coexistence based on the provisions of the U.N. Charter is consonant with the general feeling of the United Nations as expressed, for example, in the international conferences on the law of the sea in 1958 and 1960, and in the Vienna treaties of 1961 and 1963 on diplomats and consular officials. With more than half of the U.N.'s membership having become independent since 1945, the resulting new political groupings in the world look to a revision of the capitalist-created norms of international law.

Third, the revisionist appeal derives strongly from the liquidation of colonialism and the Yugoslav desire to be in the forefront of the new nations. Yugoslav scholars link the opposition to codification with last ditch efforts "of certain Western countries" who have shown "no genuine readiness to abandon the policy of pressure and force in their international practices"[23] and who seek to arrest the process of

[22] A condensed transcript of a conference, organized in 1961 by the influential Institute for International Politics and Economy (Belgrade), on new trends in international law was the subject of an issue of a leading journal of Yugoslav jurists: *The New Yugoslav Law*, Vol. xii, No. 1-3 (January-September 1961). The papers stressed the need for expanding the authority of international law and for permitting all nations to share in the redrafting and creating of a new international law. There is an extensive Yugoslav literature on this theme.

[23] Milan Šahović, "The Twentieth U.N. Session and Codification of the Principles of Coexistence," *Review of International Affairs*, Vol. xviii, No. 379 (January 20, 1966), p. 14. See also Obrad Račić, "Considerations on the Codification of the Principles of Coexistence at the

decolonization. They pay special attention to the right of self-determination. Where the Charter is evasive, the Yugoslavs are direct; where it is imbued with gradualism, they call for speed: all colonial areas must be granted independence. A revamped international law can peacefully advance political change and promote the cause of sovereign equality for all nations.

Fourth, the Yugoslav preoccupation with codification owes much to the chance combination of one man's insight and another's policy outlook. The idea of pressing for the codification of the principles of peaceful coexistence originated with Dr. Milan Bartoš. A prolific writer and an original mind, he has dominated the field of international public law in postwar Yugoslavia and shaped the views of a generation of Yugoslav scholars.

His proposal was philosophically consonant with the outlook of most Yugoslav social scientists dealing with international affairs, the majority of whom were trained as jurists. The study of international relations in Yugoslavia is heavily legalistic, and writings on the United Nations reflect this inclination. Bartoš has also had a long and close relationship with key decisionmakers in the League of Yugoslav Communists and the State Secretariat for Foreign Affairs. Prior to the 1956 Dubrovnik meeting of the International Law Association, he persuaded President Tito to embrace codification as a major policy objective. Codification coincided with Tito's intensified interest in developing the closest possible ties with the nonaligned nations.

For many former colonies codification was a welcome method of increasing national influence. They shared objections to adhering to international norms which dated from their colonial period. According to some observers many new nations are uncertain of the implications of the Yugoslav proposal, but they agree with the criticisms which underlie it and have joined fully in the taxing venture of

Twentieth Session of the General Assembly of the United Nations," *Medjunarodni Problemi*, No. 1 (1966), pp. 123-130.

lawmaking by the Special Committee. Whatever may be the juridical difficulties of the moment in gaining Western support for contemporary formulations by nonaligned countries of traditional international law, "it is to be remembered," observed an Australian official, "that propaganda can create pressure; that pressure can create practice; and that practice can create law. The process is valuable in proportion as it is understood."[24]

Peacekeeping

The Yugoslav attitude toward the development of a U.N. peace-preserving capability has been conditioned by three interrelated considerations: (a) the needs of national security; (b) the commitment to nonalignment; (c) the belief that strengthening the General Assembly will afford the small nations added leverage to cope with and restrain the ambitions of the Great Powers. During the period of confrontation with the Cominform, self-interest understandably predominated; Belgrade sought every additional margin of support. Since 1955 the growing centrality of nonalignment for Yugoslav decisionmakers has meant avoidance of any position on questions relating to the creation, maintenance, and operation of peacekeeping operations that are at variance with the prevailing views among the leading nonaligned countries.

Early in the postwar period Yugoslavia echoed Soviet suspicions of Western proposals to provide the U.N. with a modest police-patrolling capability. At the third session of the General Assembly in April 1949—almost a year after Yugoslavia had been expelled from the Cominform, but five months before it was publicly to denounce Soviet aggressive pressures in the U.N.—the Yugoslav delegation supported the Soviet Government and opposed efforts to create a United Nations Guard, deeming it illegal and apt to result in even more flagrant interference by U.N.

24 Sir Kenneth Bailey, "Making International Law in the United Nations," *Proceedings* of the American Society of International Law (1967), p. 239.

missions in the internal affairs of countries where they carried on their activities.[25] The Yugoslav delegate cited the Special Committee on the Balkans, established in 1947 over Yugoslav and Soviet opposition, as an example of a U.N. body whose functioning had been retarded and not advanced by the presence of an armed guard. Furthermore, the Yugoslavs argued that a U.N. Guard could not be used for enforcement purposes unless in response to actions approved by the Security Council[26]—a position the Soviet Union was to adopt toward the U.N. Operation in the Congo (ONUC) more than a decade later.

By October 1949, however, the Yugoslavs shifted from opposition to acceptance, in principle, of the Secretary-General's proposal for establishing a U.N. Field Service, subject to the proviso that appropriate safeguards ensure that "its relations with the authorities of the State in whose territory it would be called upon to operate should be defined as clearly as possible."[27] The danger from the East had heightened Yugoslav anxieties and occasioned a reassessment of the potential ways in which the U.N. could contribute to Yugoslav security. The insistence on adequate safeguards to reassure the benefiting country against attempts to use a U.N.-presence to meddle in the domestic affairs of that country reflected Yugoslavia's continuing sensitiveness to the propensity of Great Powers, however well-intentioned initially, to exploit weakness to maximize influence. Perceptions of threat, however, overshadowed ideologically conditioned suspicions, and Yugoslavia accepted the rationale for U.N. involvement in crisis situations, but preferred that the machinery be kept to a minimum, that each problem be approached in *ad hoc* fashion. On this basis it opposed the establishment of a panel of field observers, contending that "the problem of observers should be solved in

[25] U.N., General Assembly, *Official Records*, Third Session (Part II), p. 218.
[26] U.N., General Assembly, *Ad Hoc* Political Committee, *Official Records*, Third Session (Part II), p. 33.
[27] U.N., General Assembly, *Ad Hoc* Political Committee, *Official Records*, Fourth Session, p. 104.

accordance with the needs of the moment, by agreement between the parties concerned and the United Nations in such a way as to offer all possible guarantees of their impartiality."[28] The combination of Balkan astuteness, inherent caution, and uncertainty about the U.N.'s effectiveness made the Yugoslavs wary and pragmatic.

On September 25, 1950, with the Korean War and Cold War tensions monopolizing U.N. concerns, Dr. Edvard Kardelj, then Yugoslav Foreign Minister, deplored the inability of the small and medium-sized states to undertake independent initiatives for peace, and their tendency to follow blindly the lead of one Great Power or another. He proposed the establishment of a permanent international commission of good offices, which would be composed of the six nonpermanent members of the Security Council and six members of the General Assembly (other than the five permanent members of the Security Council), and which would examine "without undue publicity all existing international disputes, not from the point of view of substance but of possibility and desirability of direct negotiations and mediation between the parties to the dispute or between the largest number of states involved."[29] Kardelj's proposal was not adopted, but it marked the beginning of a diligent search by Yugoslav diplomats to gain acceptance for the small nations in the management of international conflict resolution.

1. *Korea*

Korea was the first challenge faced by the U.N. in the field of collective security. Yugoslavia supported the "Uniting for Peace" Resolution, which provides that "if the Security Council, because of lack of unanimity of the permanent members, fails to exercise its primary responsibility for the maintenance of international peace and security," the Gen-

[28] *Ibid.*, p. 105.
[29] U.N., General Assembly, *Official Records*, Fifth Session, p. 70. See U.N. Document A/1401.

eral Assembly may consider the matter and make recommendations to member nations for collective measures, including the use of armed force. The Resolution was adopted on the initiative of the United States to forestall any attempt by the Soviet Union, which had been absent from the Security Council in June 1950 when the decision was made to resist North Korean aggression, to cripple the U.N. operation in Korea. After submitting several amendments to ensure against the application of the resolution to situations of a colonial people struggling for independence, the Yugoslavs approved the Resolution and the military measures to repel the North Koreans; but later they disapproved of the decision to cross north of the 38th parallel.

The following year they supported the creation of the Collective Measures Committee, which was supposed to give teeth to the "Uniting for Peace" Resolution. Faced with a crescendo of "incidents" engineered from the East, and momentarily expecting a Soviet attack, they urged implementation of collective military measures in response to any breach of the peace that was found to exist. These they regarded as consonant with their proposal on "The Duties of States in The Event of Conflict."[30] Yugoslavia emerged as an ardent advocate of U.N. involvement in cases of aggression:

> We consider that the path for the search for peace leads directly to a strengthening of the U.N., to a strengthening of its democratic character, to a strengthening of the common struggle of all countries against the dangers of a new war, and, consequently, to a strengthening also of the system of collective security against violations of all states, large and small.[31]

By late 1954 the international climate changed with remarkable and unanticipated speed, and Yugoslav leaders

[30] U.N., General Assembly, Political and Security Committee, *Official Records*, Sixth Session, p. 151.
[31] *Borba*, January 8, 1952.

lost interest in military assurances: Stalin was dead; a truce had been concluded in Korea; the Geneva accords brought an end to French colonial rule in Indo-China; détente between the United States and the Soviet Union seemed in the offing. Belgrade tolerated the continued existence of the Collective Measures Committee as a standby measure, but held that the Committee had served its function and now further improvements would be made through diplomatic negotiations.[32] 1956 started as a year heralding peaceful change, but by autumn repression and war dominated events. In Eastern Europe destalinization hastened decompression, which in turn escalated demands for democratization, which Muscovite proxies were not willing to accept; revolutions broke out in Poland and Hungary in October 1956. Of more immediate concern for the Afro-Asian world was the eruption of aggression against Egypt. Yugoslavia became involved in a new conflict situation whose resolution is nowhere in sight.

2. *The Middle East*

On October 29, 1956, Israel attacked Egypt, and was joined the next day by Britain and France. Each felt possessed by imperatives of self-interest; each had reasons to topple Nasser, whose nationalization of the Suez Canal in July had triggered the chain of events that led to war. The Security Council was immediately convened. The United States called for a halt to hostilities, but France and Great Britain exercised their veto power. A hurried series of consultations between Secretary-General Dag Hammarskjöld, the United States, and various Afro-Asian states resulted in Yugoslavia's proposing the invocation of the "Uniting for Peace" Resolution. A member of the Security Council for the second time in six years, it was in a position to play a constructive role for a nonaligned colleague. Though adopted at the time of the Korean crisis, the resolution had not been applied on that occasion. It was applied for the

[32] U.N., General Assembly, Political and Security Committee, *Official Records*, Ninth Session, p. 277.

first time during the Suez crisis, at the initiative of the General Assembly, which convened in emergency session on October 31.

The United Nations Emergency Force (UNEF), an imaginative improvisation, kept the peace between Egypt and Israel until May 1967. Throughout UNEF's existence Yugoslavia behaved in exemplary fashion. The only Communist country to participate in a U.N. peacekeeping operation, it contributed a sizeable contingent (approximately 10 percent of the troops) and paid its assessed share of the costs—one of the few countries to do so. As long as UNEF's presence on Egyptian soil was welcomed by the U.A.R. government and did not exceed its stated purpose, to interpose a U.N. force between warring parties, Yugoslavia gave it full support.

In May 1967 the demise of UNEF came with tragic suddenness. Tensions mounted between Israel and its Arab neighbors, allegedly because of Israel's threatening activity toward Syria. In mid-May, two days before making an official request of the Secretary-General, Cairo informed the Yugoslav government of its desire to have the UNEF contingent removed from Gaza. Yugoslavia honored the U.A.R. request without question: the ties of nonalignment and the prerogatives of the nation-state prevailed over the tenuous internationalism that Yugoslavia had striven to engender within a U.N. framework. The hand of U Thant was weakened, hastening the Arab-Israeli war in June and bringing to an ignominious end what had up to then been the U.N.'s most successful venture in peacekeeping, an effort to which Yugoslavia had contributed generously and in which it had played a vital part.

The alacrity with which Yugoslavia (and, as it turned out, India also) pulled its contingent out of a U.N. operation should not have come as a surprise. A prominent Yugoslav diplomat and respected specialist on U.N. affairs, Djura Ninčić, authoritatively expressed the Yugoslav view of UNEF in 1960: UNEF was not, nor had it ever been, regarded by the Yugoslav government as a combatant force.[33]

> Its assignment was not to subdue aggression and restore peace and security in the area; its role was to ensure that the conditions of peace that had been brought about through the moral weight of General Assembly resolutions were in fact observed. . . . It had been called an "interposition force," because it was placed between formerly or potentially hostile forces, not so much as a physical—because as such it would have been inadequate—but as a moral and political barrier, and as such it has proved highly effective. *It is founded on consent: on the consent of the States participating in the forces and on the consent of the State within whose territory it was to carry out its function (i.e., the host state).*[34] (emphasis added)

For the Yugoslavs, UNEF was not a supranational force, nor was it envisaged as a prototype for future contingencies. It had been created in response to particular conditions and for a specific purpose. When these conditions no longer appertained to UNEF's stated task, the operation was terminated.

Advocates of a stronger peacekeeping role for the U.N. were disappointed not only with UNEF's failure to maintain the peace but in the untoward and unforeseen way UNEF died: the abruptness of its end; the seeming reluctance of the Secretary-General to throw the full weight of his office and influence into a determined attempt at least to delay dissolution in a moment of perilously mounting tension; the moral faltering of the nonaligned participants. The what-might-have-been school should not be criticized unduly for dwelling on the normative rather than the political. Conceivably, a golden opportunity was lost.

On the other hand, not by dreams alone do national lead-

---

[33] Djura Ninčić, "The Question of a United Nations Force," *Jugoslovenska Revija za Medjunarodno Pravo*, Vol. VII, No. 2 (1960), p. 232.
[34] *Ibid.*

ers protect national interests. Tito was not prepared to jeopardize his unique relationship with Nasser by equivocating at a crucial moment. Nor is there any evidence that the other nonaligned countries would have either. Had the contingents not been withdrawn as and when requested by the host government, it is unlikely that any country would have ever again voluntarily agreed to the stationing of a U.N. peacekeeping force on its soil. For its part the Yugoslav Government had on numerous occasions made amply clear its readiness to comply with a request for the withdrawal of its contingent by the U.A.R.[35] It has never conceived of U.N. peacekeeping activities as stepping-stones, however small, to world government.

3. *Congo*

Yugoslavia supported the U.N. intervention in the Congo in July 1960. It responded promptly to Hammarskjöld's request for technical personnel, contributing pilots and mechanics to the United Nations Operation in the Congo (ONUC). By late August – early September, however, Yugoslavia (along with the Soviet bloc and a number of nonaligned countries) criticized the U.N. Command for not actively assisting the legal government in Leopoldville to establish authority over the entire Congo and, in particular, to force secessionist Katanga back into line. After the deposal of Patrice Lumumba in September, dissatisfaction among the critics mounted. On December 7, 1960, the Yugoslav Government informed the Secretary-General that it did not wish to "bear or share, in any way, the responsibility for what is taking place at present in the Congo, in

[35] U.N., General Assembly, Special Political Committee, *Official Records*, Thirteenth Session, p. 55. "Yugoslavia had provided a contingent, with the consent of the country in which the Force [UNEF] was stationed, because it was anxious for the settlement of a crisis which at the time had presented an immediate danger to peace. Yugoslavia was therefore willing to continue to collaborate in maintaining the Force until it had accomplished the task assigned to it at its establishment, and as long as the government on whose territory it was based thought it useful."

the presence of the United Nations Force. . . ."[36] It withdrew its personnel from ONUC and for a time withheld financial support, accusing the Western powers of reducing the situation in the Congo to "legalistic trickery."[37]

As the cost of the Congo operation ballooned, and as the bitterness among the militants of nonalignment intensified, the Yugoslav Government experienced a period of indecision. Though disturbed by the ONUC's lack of partisan support for the central Congolese Government, it understood that the shortcomings of the operation were in important measure the result of imprecise Security Council and General Assembly resolutions. Reputable Yugoslav scholars gave the U.N.'s predicament critical but sympathetic treatment.[38] On October 10, 1963, Belgrade announced that it would pay its assessed share of the costs for ONUC for the November 1, 1961 – June 30, 1963 period, but reiterated that ONUC was not carrying out the purposes for which it had originally been established.[39] Furthermore, to help the U.N. surmount the financial crisis that threatened the future viability of the organization, the Yugoslav Government joined with eight other nations in sponsoring the resolution giving the U.N. authority to issue 200 million dollars in bonds to help finance the mounting costs of the Congo and prevent a paralyzing bankruptcy; it also gave a voluntary contribution of 100,000 dollars after the nineteenth session of the General Assembly in order to alleviate the crisis that arose when the United States sought to invoke the punitive provisions of Article 19.

In terms of the future of U.N. peacekeeping activities,

[36] U.N., General Assembly, Administrative and Budgetary Committee, *Official Records*, Fifteenth Session, p. 316.

[37] "How Yugoslavia Views the Worsening Situation in the Congo," *Yugoslav Survey*, Vol. II, No. 4 (January-March 1961), p. 563.

[38] Miodrag Sukijasović, "The Nature of the UN Intervention in the Congo," *Medjunarodni Problemi*, Vol. XIV, No. 2-3 (1962), pp. 65-86.

[39] For political reasons the Yugoslav government refuses to pay for the Congo operation for the September 1960-September 1961 period. The death of Hammarskjöld, and the concern over the crisis of electing a new Secretary-General no doubt were decisive considerations in its decision to pay its assessed share of post-September 1961 expenses.

the salient feature of Yugoslav behavior has been the willingness of the Yugoslav Government to uphold and accept
a financial obligation for the continuation of a U.N. operation with which it disagreed. Unlike the Soviet Union,
France, and some of the leading nonaligned countries, Yugoslavia did not seek to cripple the U.N. with acrimonious
debate, nor was it prepared to accept the view that *only* the
Security Council could play a role in determining peacekeeping operations. It paid its assessed share even though
disagreeing with the way in which the operation was carried out.

4. *Lebanon*

The Lebanese crisis of 1958 originated in the attempt by
incumbent President Camille Chamoun to amend the constitution of Lebanon to allow his reelection, and in the consequent reaction of his opponents. Actually, there were two
crises: the first in May and June led to the dispatch of a
U.N. observation group, an action the Yugoslavs approved;
the second, which arose out of developments in Iraq, involved the landing of U.S. troops in Lebanon and encountered bitter criticism by a number of countries, including
Yugoslavia. While not a peacekeeping operation of the
extent of UNEF or ONUC, the corps of U.N. observers sent
by Hammarskjöld to determine whether the United Arab
Republic was extending clandestine aid to opponents of
the legal government, as alleged by Lebanese officials, did
contribute to the subsequent resolution of the crisis.

Chamoun's ambitions triggered near-civil war. Fearful of
Nasser's popularity, especially in the wake of the union of
Egypt and Syria on February 1, 1958, Chamoun appealed
simultaneously to the Arab League and the Security Council
on May 22, 1958, for support against alleged interference by the U.A.R. in Lebanese affairs. On June 11 the
Security Council passed a Swedish resolution calling for the
dispatch to Lebanon of an observation group "to ensure
that there is no illegal infiltration of personnel or supply
of arms or other material across the Lebanese borders." By

July 1, 1958, the U.N. Observer Group in Lebanon made its first report, which concluded that little infiltration was occurring. The crisis atmosphere subsided: the Security Council was quiet; Chamoun agreed to step down at the end of his term; the Sixth Fleet left Lebanese waters; Nasser vacationed in Yugoslavia.

A new crisis erupted on July 14 with the toppling of the pro-Western government in Iraq, the murder of the King and his Prime Minister, and the seizing of power by a seemingly pro-Nasser military group. Nasserite elements stirred expectantly in Lebanon and Jordan. Perceiving a direct threat to its independence from UAR-financed groups, the Lebanese Government invoked Article 51 of the U.N. Charter and requested military protection from the United States. Inter-Arab feuds and Cold War rivalries rekindled Middle East tensions.

The Yugoslavs denied the relevance of Article 51 to the Lebanese situation and held "the landing of United States armed forces in Lebanon and of United Kingdom armed forces in Jordan an inadmissible act of armed intervention in the domestic affairs of those two countries."[40] In so doing, they presumed to second-guess another country's judgment concerning the precariousness of its domestic situation. For them the "manifestly progressive" Arab nationalism under the leadership of Nasser was seeking to eliminate the vestiges of colonialism from the Middle East. In such circumstances the invoking of Article 51 by an unpopular regime in order to secure military props under the guise of a threat to its independence was not to be condoned but rather condemned as an unwarranted and dangerous precedent—the encouragement of Great Power intervention to suppress national-liberation movements.[41]

Thus, the Yugoslav Government did not object to the injection of a U.N. "presence" into the confused and volatile political situation in Lebanon in June, though not irrele-

---

[40] U.N., General Assembly, *Official Records*, Third Emergency Special Session, p. 97.
[41] *Ibid.*, p. 98.

vantly neither did the U.A.R. It accepted the appropriateness of the Secretary-General's initiative, insisting only that the U.N. observers not interfere "directly or indirectly" in the internal affairs of the country. Indeed, Yugoslav scholars were in time to laud the skill with which Hammarskjöld "carried out one of the most delicate diplomatic actions of his career":[42] by avoiding taking sides in Lebanon's turbulent political election or accepting at face value the charges of the Chamoun Government, by convincing Nasser of the objectivity of the observer group and steering clear of association with the American troops, he skillfully discharged the mission assigned by the Security Council.

But the Yugoslavs moved into a political quagmire in disputing the pertinency of Lebanon's call, under the terms of Article 51, for assistance from a friendly government. They in effect substituted their judgment of what constituted a grave and legitimate threat within the intent of Article 51 for that of the government seeking to invoke its protective provisions. Partisan considerations moved them to disregard their own assertions of an earlier period that the U.N. was the last refuge of small nations, and raised doubts as to the character of their commitment to the principles of the Charter.

The Lebanese crisis highlighted two important strands of Yugoslav behavior in the United Nations: a readiness to support peace-preserving initiatives through the U.N. and a partisan alignment with nationalist, "progressive," anti-Western leaders of nonaligned countries. In this instance the two were interwoven, but had the U.A.R. not acquiesced in the dispatch of observers in mid-June, the Yugoslav position would very likely have been shaped more by pragmatic political considerations than by any *a priori* support for a U.N. presence in a troubled area. Thus, for example, out of consideration for the U.A.R., which had between forty and seventy-five thousand troops engaged in the civil war,

[42] Olga Šuković, *Polozaj i Uloga Generalnog Sekretara Ujedinjenih Nacija* (Belgrade: Institute for International Politics and Economy, 1967), p. 129.

Yugoslavia opposed efforts to intrude a "U.N. presence" into Yemen during the 1964-1967 period.

5. Observations

The Yugoslavs do not believe that any general agreement on peacekeeping that requires revision of the Charter is possible. Though peacekeeping remains *primarily* the responsibility of the Security Council, the General Assembly should assume a decision-making function in the event of paralysis there. Yugoslav officials do not favor any drastic alteration in the current constitutional relationship between the Security Council and the General Assembly, believing that such an approach would be both unwise and unrealistic. They do hold that each situation should be handled on its own merits, that there are no central underlying principles which should control the response of the organization to a threat to the peace. ONUC engendered reservations about the excessive political role of the Secretary-General. The Yugoslavs thought the Secretary-General should be somewhat less political-minded and should maintain a more restricted interpretation of his responsibility for intervening in international crises. On the other hand, they do not want to deprive him of all authority to undertake peace-promoting initiatives, even though they may sometimes disagree with them. For example, Yugoslav experts acknowledged candidly that their government's positions toward the Secretary-General's efforts to arrange for a U.N. "presence" in Lebanon in 1958 and in Yemen in 1964-1967 were dictated by "political circumstance," i.e., the attitude of the U.A.R., and not by the Secretary-General's assessment of the situation.[43] Nonetheless, as a member of the Special Committee on Peacekeeping Operations (known as the Committee of Thirty-three),[44] Yugoslavia is very much

[43] Interviews conducted in Belgrade at the State Secretariat for Foreign Affairs and the Institute for International Politics and Economy, March 10-22, 1968.

[44] The Special Committee on Peacekeeping Operations was established, at the suggestion of the Secretary-General, by the General Assembly on February 18, 1965, and charged with making "a compre-

involved in the continuing effort to devise a flexible format under which a variety of operations might be organized and implemented in the future. But ambivalence, unresolved and unresolvable, hampers Yugoslavia: it pleads for normative international law but accepts the sovereign-oriented character of peacekeeping functions; it argues for universalism but acts on the basis of political pragmatism. Lacking power, Yugoslavia seeks influence, but the very partisanship that makes possible such influence throws into question the goals underlying its internationalism.

Housekeeping Problems

1. *Membership*

Yugoslavia's reputation as an advocate of independence for colonial areas was earned early in the postwar period before the theme became fashionable. Having decided in 1945 that the United Nations should provide small nations the opportunity for expressing their views and should treat them on a plane of equality "especially as regards the free taking of decisions,"[45] and being committed to the proposition that the small nations can help clarify international problems and promote cooperation, Yugoslavia pressed for universality of membership, though it did oppose the admission of Spain in 1945-1946, on the grounds of Franco's previous ties to the Axis powers. In the case of the former Italian colonies, Yugoslavia supported independence for a united Libya and opposed the assignment of Somalia (Somaliland) as a trusteeship for Italy. In 1949 it favored admission of Romania, Hungary, and Bulgaria, even though they were promoting unrest and a warlike atmosphere along their borders with Yugoslavia. Later in the year Yugoslavia recognized the People's Republic of China and strongly supported its right to a seat on the Security Council, despite Peking's adherence to the Cominform line. This Yugoslav

---

hensive review of the whole question of peacekeeping operations in all their aspects, including ways of overcoming the present financial difficulties of the Organization."

[45] U.N., General Assembly, *Official Records*, First Session, p. 191.

position ironically reinforced Western suspicions of the genuineness of the Soviet-Yugoslav split. In February 1950 Yugoslavia acceded to the demand of the Democratic Republic of Vietnam and recognized the Ho Chi Minh Government, then in rebellion against French rule. Tito felt compelled to air publicly the Western pressure being exerted on him to forestall recognition.[46] According to Tito's biographer, Ho Chi Minh asked for recognition, "probably on Moscow's orders,"[47] in order to place Yugoslavia in a difficult situation with France and the United States; for once recognition was granted, the clandestine Vietnamese radio leveled vituperative attacks against Yugoslavia, echoing the Cominform line.

The Yugoslavs regard the implementation of the principle of universality as essential for the successful accomplishment of the basic purposes of the U.N. They maintain that all states, irrespective of size or social structure, should be admitted, in order to advance the democratization of the U.N.[48] On an earlier occasion the Yugoslav delegation had cited approvingly Hammarskjöld's eloquent call for universality:

> The idea of the United Nations as a club to which only the likeminded will be admitted, in which membership is a privilege and expulsion is the retribution for wrongdoing, is totally unrealistic and self-defeating.

By repeatedly inveighing against Great Power bargaining based on *quid pro quo* rather than on acceptance of universality, Yugoslavia has placed itself in the vanguard of the small nations, which see in an expanding membership a broadened basis for democratization of the world organization and a strengthened lever for wielding influence.

[46] Vladimir Dedijer, *Tito* (New York: Simon and Schuster, 1953), p. 435.

[47] *Ibid.*

[48] Djura Ninčić, "Yugoslavia and the United Nations," *Arhiv za Pravne i Društvene Nauke*, Vol. XLVIII, No. 1-2 (January-June 1961), p. 116.

2. *The Secretariat and the Secretary-General*

Long before resentment had jelled among the nonaligned and African states over Hammarskjöld's handling of the Congo crisis, it was expressed in dissatisfaction with various facets of the U.N.'s administrative and structural makeup. One source of discontent related to the staffing of the Secretariat. The Charter recommends that recruitment be based "on as wide a geographical basis as possible." With membership mushrooming after 1955, the new nations coveted posts for their nationals to satisfy their prerogatives as sovereign states and to train their able young men for future assignments in the home office. The Yugoslav delegation, too, called upon the Secretary-General to recruit qualified personnel from the new nations for professional-grade posts. Realizing the dearth of trained nationals from many of these countries and the importance of ensuring that they did not become denationalized, it suggested shortening the term of employment and introducing a system of rotation.[49] It also proposed allocating a minimum of five posts to each member state. At all times the Yugoslav delegation was alert to the problem and to the importance attributed to it by the new nations, and contributed constructive ideas.

Another vexatious issue was the unrepresentative composition of the U.N.'s leading bodies. By 1960 Yugoslavia was in the forefront of efforts, subsequently successful in 1964, to expand the membership of the Security Council and the Economic and Social Council. Not only did it contend that historical and geographical equity warranted revision of the U.N.'s organizational structure, but, more important, it linked the need for greater political influence for the developing countries to the necessity of narrowing the widening economic gap that divided the have and the have-not nations. Yugoslavia saw greater representativeness as a

[49] U.N., General Assembly, Administrative and Budgetary Committee, *Official Records*, Thirteenth Session, p. 110.

prerequisite for the consolidation of international ties and for world peace.[50]

If the imbroglio over the Congo aggravated political alignments and hostility toward the Secretary-General, Premier Khrushchev's "troika" proposal of October 3, 1960, brought the discontents to a head, threatening in the process to undermine the structural viability of the U.N. Apparently intended to give Moscow a veto over the operation of the Office of the Secretary-General, the "troika" proposal played on opposition to Hammarskjöld and held out the prospect of an enhanced role in the Secretariat for the African and Asian countries. Khrushchev proposed that the Secretary-General be replaced by a three-man directorate, representing the three political blocs, Western, Communist, and nonaligned. He expected to attract nonaligned support by artfully calling for more rigorous application in international secretariats of the principle of equitable geographical distribution of professional posts, particularly at policy-making levels.[51]

Tito was sympathetic, but not to be corralled. He acknowledged a need to reorganize the Secretariat, to make it more representative and responsive to the wishes of the General Assembly. At the same time he held that "since questions of far-reaching implications are at stake, their settlement should be approached in a most constructive manner and in accordance with the long-term needs of the Organization itself and of the entire international community."[52] Yugoslav officials not only doubted the constitutionality of the Soviet proposal but questioned its political wisdom, noting that "the veto of only one member . . .

[50] U.N., General Assembly, Special Political Committee, *Official Records*, Fifteenth Session, p. 55.

[51] For a thorough discussion of the Soviet position see the author's *The Soviets in International Organizations: Changing Policy Toward Developing Areas, 1953-1963* (Princeton: Princeton University Press, 1964), pp. 254-288.

[52] "Yugoslavia's Attitude Regarding Events in the Congo," *Yugoslav Survey*, Vol. II, No. 5 (April-June 1961), p. 750.

might paralyze the functioning of the whole executive apparatus of the United Nations."[53] They sensed political
pitfalls in Khrushchev's strategy and counselled care. When
Hammarskjöld died tragically in an air crash in the Congo
in September 1961, the Yugoslav Government was active
with other members of the nonaligned group in helping to
reach a compromise settlement, which led to U Thant's
investiture. Yugoslavia upholds the authority *and* duty of
the Secretary-General under the Charter to undertake diplomatic initiatives in the interest of international peace,
though reserving the right to disagree with the wisdom of
his chosen policy in specific cases.[54]

The Human Factor: Yugoslav Diplomats

Diplomacy is the art of the possible; and diplomats find
their potential for achievement circumscribed by the general design drafted by their superiors, by the resources they
command, and by the possibilities of the period. Nevertheless, they can elicit among otherwise openly critical delegations a sympathetic hearing and keep lines of communication open;[55] they can assure the respectful attention of a
rival delegation, draw confidently on the support of a
friendly one, or neutralize an undecided one; they can maximize the possibilities of persuasion by small nations who
cannot compete with Great Powers in the exercise of coer-
cion or high pressure salesmanship.

[53] Milan Bartoš, "Position and Function of The UNO Secretary-
General," *Review of International Affairs*, Vol. XI, No. 253 (October
20, 1960), p. 7. For a balanced Yugoslav overview, reflecting a thorough
familiarity with Western literature on the subject, see Olga Šuković,
"Political Functions of the Secretary-General of the United Nations,"
Jugoslovenska Revija za Medjunarodno Pravo, Vol. IX, No. 2 (1962),
pp. 211-221.

[54] Šuković, *op.cit.*, pp. 175-176; 192-193; 224-226.

[55] One American diplomat observed that "the ability and friendly
attitude of Yugoslav diplomats in the United Nations . . . have undoubtedly influenced the views of many other delegates about Yugoslavia." Richard F. Pedersen, "National Representation in the United
Nations," *International Organization*, Vol. XV, No. 2 (Spring 1961),
pp. 264-265.

Good diplomats are scarce. One reason for the prestige enjoyed by the Yugoslav Government among the non-aligned nations in the U.N. is the quality of its diplomats. The U.N. is the main focus for Yugoslav diplomatic initiatives, and the personnel assigned there have generally been distinguished by their ability, diligence, and discreetness. Yugoslavia has consistently sent uniformly competent diplomats to international organizations. Whether in the political organs or in the economic bodies and specialized agencies, Yugoslav diplomats have a deservedly high reputation for being well briefed and prepared. They have demonstrated astuteness in the intricacies of procedural strategies and sensitivity to the parameters of possible agreement. According to a distinguished former British Ambassador, the postwar Yugoslav representatives, in contrast to the prewar ones, are "uniformly charming and intelligent."[56] They are gregarious and enjoy the game of politics, a national pastime in which all Yugoslavs long to excel. At international conferences Yugoslav diplomats invariably demonstrate skill at drafting compromise proposals and reconciling divergent approaches. Their initiatives are often timely, reflecting a thorough understanding of the positions of all the interested parties. In the preparation of this study the author interviewed diplomats from more than twenty countries: never once did he hear a critical or derogatory comment about the performance of Yugoslav diplomats. Even though many diplomats disagreed with various facets of Yugoslav policy, they had nothing but praise for their Yugoslav colleagues. What makes this enviable record even more impressive is the absence of any noteworthy diplomatic tradition: Tito did not inherit a cadre of eminent diplomats; nor is there even now an established foreign service academy for training diplomatic personnel. Yugoslavia has been fortunate in the availability of able men who have contributed in no small measure to the realization of national goals.

[56] Sir William Hayter, *The Diplomacy of the Great Powers* (New York: The Macmillan Company, 1961), p. 65.

Observations

More than any other nonaligned country Yugoslavia considers the United Nations significant for the advancement of nonalignment and the democratization of international relations. It seeks to gain for the nonaligned and small nations a greater voice in the formulation of policies by enhancing the importance of the United Nations. If Yugoslavia has spoken passionately and often on behalf of human rights, anti-colonialism, and the end of racial discrimination, it has also acted pragmatically with prudence and skill to advance these causes. If its proposals have often been militant, its behavior has invariably been responsible and realistic.

Nonalignment has contributed to a lessening of Cold War polemics in the U.N. It has forced the international community to confront the major issues of our age and direct increasing attention toward their solution. The nonaligned countries have played active and constructive roles in the melioration of major crises such as those of Korea and Suez. Yugoslav officials contend, though the memoirs of American officials do not agree, that the nonaligned countries facilitated the solution of the Cuban missile crisis by encouraging direct contacts between the United States and the Soviet Union.[57] They also assert that it has not been the Great Powers which have acted "to bring about reconciliation among the smaller states, but rather the smaller nonaligned

---

[57] Aleksandar Božović, "The Eighteenth Session of the General Assembly of the United Nations," *Medjunarodni Problemi*, Vol. xvi, No. 1 (1964), p. 87. An even more assertive claim was made by A. B. [Aleš Bebler?]: "Although the question of Cuba and of the crisis in the Caribbean were formally not included in the agenda, the XVII session played, both directly and through the Security Council, a very active role in the solving of this crisis. A significant role in this respect was also played by the action of over 50 nonaligned countries, including Yugoslavia, which not only supported but also imparted an appropriate force and moral weight to the mediatory role played by the Secretary-General, U Thant. . . .", "Yugoslavia's Participation in the Work of the XVIIth Regular Session of the General Assembly of the United Nations," *Yugoslav Survey*, Vol. iv, No. 12 (January-March 1963), p. 1788.

states" which have helped settle disputes between the Great Powers,[58] thereby overlooking the conciliatory efforts of the United States in the Turkish-Greek crisis over Cyprus and the Soviet Union in the Indo-Pakistani war of September 1965. What is indisputable is the impetus that Yugoslavia has given to the coming of age of the Third World.

[58] Leo Mates, "United Nations Crisis," *Socialist Thought and Practice*, No. 17 (January-March 1965) , p. 126.

CHAPTER V

Yugoslavia and International Economic Cooperation: Focus on the U.N.

IN THE 1950's nonalignment came of age politically; in the 1960's its presence was felt economically as it generated pressures through international organizations to redress the disproportion between the developed and the less-developed nations.

As Marxists, the Yugoslavs attributed primary importance to overcoming the economic gap that they believed to be at the root of international tensions. They pressed for a re-ordering of international economic ties on the assumption that nonalignment could not reach its full potential for promoting international peace and security for small nations if its adherents were relegated to a dependent, underdeveloped, technologically inferior economic status in the world at large. As long as neocolonialism dominated relationships between the former colonial powers and the new nations, then genuine independence, and with it a strengthening of nonalignment, was deemed impossible. Economic redistribution was prerequisite for political democratization.

Economic issues loomed large in early Yugoslav perceptions and problems. War had ravaged the country. Devastation and backwardness beset a Communist leadership intent on building a socialist society. The assistance of the United Nations Relief and Rehabilitation Agency (UNRRA) to Yugoslavia had forestalled starvation in 1945 and 1946, and the decision of the United States to terminate support for this international program was bitterly received. In the polarizing alignments of 1946-1948, Yugoslavia was second only to the Soviet Union among the Communist states in its criticisms of American policy and the Marshall Plan, which it saw as an attempt "to create a Western bloc dependent on America and aimed against the USSR and the new democracies."[1] In the fall of 1948, in addition to repeated denunciations of the United States for the demise of UNRRA, Yugoslav spokesmen deplored the American tendency to "substitute unilateral action for international and multilateral cooperation, which, according to the Charter, ought to take place within the framework of the United Nations."[2] They also charged the World Bank with being "a subsidiary of the Marshall Plan." Newcomers to power and responsibility and burdened with staggering internal problems, the Yugoslav leaders focused on their own situation; their horizons were understandably European, their political outlook, militantly Stalinistic.

In 1946, 1947, and 1948 Chile, India, Burma, Lebanon, Brazil, and Egypt were the champions of assistance to economically underdeveloped areas. In particular, Hernan Santa Cruz of Chile and V.K.R.V. Rao of India called for international financial assistance and technical aid to the developing countries. Though Yugoslav diplomats sympathized, they were limited by their own economic difficulties and by bloc restraints from giving much more than support in principle. Thus, at a time when the Egyptian delegates stressed the urgent need for economic development in the underdeveloped areas, the Yugoslavs had not yet begun to link their economic problems with those of the underdeveloped countries. 1948 was to change this.

The SUNFED Idea

The alternative of aid through the United Nations—what was to emerge in 1951 as the SUNFED proposal—matured slowly, the result of constant discussions and exchanges, both among the Yugoslavs and the few developing countries who had originated the idea, and within the Yugoslav delegation to the U.N. and the State Secretariat for Foreign Affairs in Belgrade. The very small program of regular technical assistance, started in late 1948 and financed

[1] U.N., General Assembly, *Official Records*, Second Session, p. 236.
[2] U.N., General Assembly, Committee on Economic and Financial Questions, *Official Records*, Third Session, pp. 34-35.

out of the regular U.N. budget, and the Truman Point Four proposal of January 1949 were catalytic developments, stimulating Yugoslav thinking on the type of aid that was desirable and feasible.

Of key importance was the proposal put forth on March 30, 1949, by V.K.R.V. Rao, an Indian economist and for a number of years the Chairman of the U.N. Subcommission on Economic Development of the Economic and Employment Commission of the Economic and Social Council (ECOSOC).[3] Dr. Rao observed that the profit motive was not enough to attract capital to developing countries, that private investment had certain limitations, because it was as much influenced by noneconomic considerations such as racial and political affinities, imperial ties, geographic proximity, and tradition, as it was by economic. Further, "the very nature of private foreign investments made it impossible to plan their volume, their timing, their regional distribution or their functional distribution, i.e., the types of development they should stimulate and promote." Lauding the view expressed in President Truman's inaugural address of January 20, 1949, that assistance to underdeveloped countries "should be a cooperative enterprise in which all nations work together through the United Nations and its specialized agencies," he recommended the establishment of a new international agency that would provide both technical assistance and capital investment. But Rao's call for a U.N. Economic Development Administration to finance basic developmental projects which could not be expected to yield immediate returns adequate to support such projects commercially was not well received by Western countries, nor by the Soviet Union. Nonetheless, his proposal, which was to bear some fruit a decade later, entitles him to recognition as "the father of SUNFED."

At the fourth session of the General Assembly in Septem-

[3] E/CN.1/Sub.3/SR.60, pp. 4-9. For a detailed examination of Rao's proposal see James Patrick Sewell, *Functionalism and World Politics: A Study Based on United Nations Programs Financing Economic Development* (Princeton: Princeton University Press, 1966), pp. 94-102.

ber 1949, Edvard Kardelj, then Foreign Minister, for the first time linked equality of rights and independence of small nations with the problem of their economic development.[4] Having brought Yugoslavia's rift with the Soviet Union into the open, he sought to end his country's diplomatic isolation by making common cause with the new Asian nations. Economic issues proved a strong cement. The search for economic cooperation thus antedated the crystallization of nonalignment, which, in part, grew from the feeling of rapport engendered by the former. Yugoslavia supported the proposals of Chile, India, Egypt, Burma, Lebanon, and Cuba for promoting economic development; it seconded Hernan Santa Cruz's call for implementation of Dr. Rao's concept of public financial assistance. Dr. Vilfan, the Yugoslav delegate to the Second Committee, cited examples of his country's unfortunate experiences with private capital before the war and with government to government loans from the Soviet Union and concluded that "foreign aid must be rendered especially, if not exclusively, through international loans."[5] With the conviction that the United Nations should be in charge of financing economic development, Yugoslav preference and Afro-Asian need converged.

The following year Kardelj spoke strongly on behalf of international financing of economic projects in underdeveloped countries and urged the creation of a fund of several billion dollars, as recommended by the Chilean delegation. Concern that the war in Korea was a prelude to war in Europe intensified the interaction between Yugoslavia and the nonbloc Asian and Arab states in their common search for an end to the fighting. The discussions on Korea, the search for a broad base of support against Soviet pressure, and the desire for congenial diplomatic friends drew Yugoslavia increasingly into strategy sessions designed to establish a Special United Nations Fund for Economic De-

[4] U.N., General Assembly, *Official Records*, Fourth Session, p. 67.
[5] U.N., General Assembly, Committee on Economic and Financial Questions, *Official Records*, Fourth Session, p. 42.

velopment (SUNFED). Though Korea held the center of attention, Vilfan admonished the Assembly not to neglect Rao's proposal.[6]

In early 1951 ECOSOC's Subcommittee on Economic Development requested member governments to submit detailed ideas for economic development. In Belgrade the problem was studied in the Secretariat for Foreign Affairs and a paper drawn up which initially recommended that *all* financing be channeled through the U.N. However, this was rejected as unrealistic, and a more moderate proposal was drafted, largely by Dr. Rikard Lang, a distinguished economist at the University of Zagreb. The ideas were presented to ECOSOC's July meeting and then to the General Assembly in the fall.

The Politics of SUNFED

The SUNFED issue was a watershed for Yugoslavia. Belgrade's attitude on this question presaged its endeavors in the international economic field in the 1960's, and helps explain its continued leading role among the nonaligned nations and oft trying relations with the United States. SUNFED brought Yugoslavia to the forefront of efforts by the nonaligned to break the stifling pattern of underdevelopment, technological inferiority, and political debility that characterize so much of the Third World.

In 1951 the General Assembly convened in Paris. At the November 20 meeting of the Second Committee the Yugoslav delegate, Leo Mates, eloquently pleaded for organizing the financing of economic development primarily within the U.N. "in order to ensure the democratic nature of the entire program and its use for the economic development of the underdeveloped countries themselves."[7] He laid bare the weaknesses in the position of the underdeveloped countries, which remain, in their essentials, prevalent to

[6] U.N., General Assembly, Committee on Economic and Financial Questions, *Official Records*, Fifth Session, pp. 16-17.

[7] U.N., General Assembly, Committee on Economic and Financial Questions, *Official Records*, Sixth Session, p. 18.

this day.[8] In early December a working group of developing countries met in the Yugoslav Embassy to draft a proposal they hoped would be acceptable to the Western powers. On December 10 the delegations of Burma, Chile, Cuba, Egypt, and Yugoslavia submitted a joint resolution,[9] which was adopted by the General Assembly on January 12, 1952, despite the opposition of the United States. The Secretary-General appointed a Committee of Nine (of which Yugoslavia was a member) to draft the proposal that was to be known as SUNFED. Yugoslavia's role was important and earned it the goodwill and confidence of the developing countries. Thus, even before nonalignment became a conscious political factor in international politics, Yugoslavia was already an intimate of the new nations. It came via the economic route into close and continual association with the small and new nations.

The election of Yugoslavia to the Economic and Social Council on October 27, 1952, marked its transition in three years from a country preoccupied with political issues in the Security Council to one concerned with the development problems facing ECOSOC; it exemplified Yugoslavia's new relationship with, and interest in, the nations of Asia and Africa. Even more than before Yugoslavia lavished praise on the Expanded Program of Technical As-

---

[8] Mates noted that: "a) the increase in the financial resources of the underdeveloped countries would not reach the level some predicted; b) the increase in income was extremely unequal; c) it was impossible to plan vast development schemes on the basis of the increase in income as the income was highly precarious; d) the capital goods required were either in extremely short supply on the world market or were offered at inflated prices; e) the prices of the industrial products imported by the underdeveloped countries had also increased as a whole, in some cases more than the prices of the raw material exports; f) the difficulties of the underdeveloped countries were also being aggravated by a strong inflationary pressure." *Ibid.*

[9] The resolution requested the Economic and Social Council to submit to the General Assembly at its 1952 session "a detailed plan for establishing, as soon as circumstances permit, a special fund for grants-in-aid and for low-interest, long-term loans to underdeveloped countries for the purpose of helping them, at their request, to accelerate their economic development and to finance nonself-liquidating projects which are basic for their economic development."

sistance, defended as a prerogative of state sovereignty the right of the new nations to nationalize industries, and, in contrast to the Soviet position, supported the principle of balanced economic development.

The Yugoslav delegation believed that industrial development should evolve concurrently with the development of agriculture and of non-agricultural raw materials. In view of the fact that underdeveloped countries were mainly agricultural and that their population was usually high and had a low productivity, it was important to ensure that the objective of development plans should be not only to increase productivity by means of new investments and by modernizing cultivation methods, but also to create new possibilities for the employment of the surplus rural population. . . .[10]

In clear allusion to the Soviet approach to economic development, the Yugoslavs emphasized their opposition "to any tendency towards autarky in connection with the industrialization of underdeveloped countries." This difference in economic outlook reflects fundamentally antithetical political attitudes toward nonalignment, socialism, and the role of small nations in world affairs, a distinction too often overlooked by the West in its prepossession with transitional Cold War issues.

SUNFED was the most intensely debated proposal in the Second Committee during the 1952-1957 period, until the establishment of the Special Fund (which was a compromise substitute for, and not to be confused with, SUNFED itself). The United States and Great Britain were the main opponents. According to one former Yugoslav representative in ECOSOC, this had the effect of curbing "the enthusiasm of the underdeveloped countries which were not then prepared to risk a possible rupture with the United States over the SUNFED issue, because they all, in varying degrees, relied upon American assistance, and this included,

[10] U.N., Economic and Social Council, *Official Records*, Fifteenth Session, p. 149.

of course, Yugoslavia as well. The underdeveloped countries did not show enough determination at the time, possibly because they were still unsure of themselves diplomatically, and because the Cold War still preempted the center of the international stage." Another Yugoslav, a brilliant economist-diplomat, attributed the failure of SUNFED "to the excessive moral idealism that surrounded the proposal." Both agreed that beyond its impact on Yugoslav attitudes and policy the SUNFED idea had a number of beneficial repercussions: first, it enhanced the sense of community among the developing countries and added impetus to cooperation and consultation; second, it profoundly affected American thinking and policies, stimulating greater interest in the economic problems of the developing countries; third, it initiated closer ties between the Afro-Asian countries and the small developed nations of Western Europe, e.g., the Netherlands, and Norway; finally, it sharpened the Third World's appreciation of the possibilities of cooperation with the moderates in the West, thus strengthening Yugoslavia's commitment to the moderate path in world affairs.

Throughout the protracted discussions on SUNFED, Yugoslav attitudes toward the methods of promoting development altered, adapted, and matured. From skepticism in 1953 about the proposal to establish the International Finance Corporation (IFC) as a subsidiary of the World Bank to extend "soft" loans for projects which could not easily be financed on a commercial basis, Yugoslavia moved to full support by late 1954. Unlike those of the Soviet Union, Yugoslavia's criticisms of the limitations of private investment for promoting economic growth in developing countries were reasoned and persuasive, and not primarily ideological. It favored expanded contributions to existing programs. The Yugoslav delegation approved the establishment of the Special Fund in 1957, regarding it "as a practical step towards the organization of a system of capital financing through the United Nations,"[11] but

11 U.N., General Assembly, Committee on Economic and Financial Questions, *Official Records*, Thirteenth Session, p. 6.

promptly co-sponsored a resolution calling for the creation of a U.N. Capital Development Fund. As its conception of what was needed for economic development broadened, so, too, did its perceptions of the interrelationship between economic development and international security. Increasingly, Yugoslavia contended that sovereign equality was impossible under conditions of extreme economic inequality and differences in social standards and cultural levels. Those functions of the United Nations that promised improvement of material conditions were therefore invested with a special political significance.[12]

Broadening Developmental Perspectives

By 1957 many delegations sensed that the economic problems of the developing countries could not be solved by loans and credits: in more basic fashion, prospects for economic development were inextricably linked to the problem of foreign trade. That the latter was at the heart of the former was a significant insight elaborated by Janez Stanovnik, a leading Yugoslav economist and, since January 1968, the Executive Secretary of the U.N. Economic Commission for Europe. He drew attention to the division of the world along a north-south axis, to the enormous gap between the developed nations of the northern hemisphere and the impoverished ones of the southern hemisphere. By implication, the east-west rift was a pale and passing phase of world history. The message was unmistakable: unless economic inequities were alleviated, instability would intensify great power rivalries and heighten the danger of war. Stanovnik lauded the Special Fund and EPTA. But he perceived that inherent in the parsimonious contributions of the developed countries were unresolved doubts and national ambitions: contributing countries were skeptical of the operating efficiency of the U.N.; they expected, though never saying so openly, a modicum of political dividends, at least indirectly; and the Western countries feared that "financing economic development through the United Nations would

---

[12] Ljubomir Radovanović, "The Charter and Practice of the UN," *Medjunarodni Problemi*, Vol. VII, No. 3-4 (1955), p. 32.

shake the faith in private capital and private enterprise in the world."[13] Further, Stanovnik said that notwithstanding the important differences between the Soviet Union and the United States in their approaches to economic development, a narrowness of vision stigmatized the two global antagonists who viewed world development solely in terms of whether it strengthened their respective blocs; assistance to developing countries was but another instrument in the quest for new adherents to bloc membership.[14]

In searching for a solution to their own foreign trade problems, Yugoslav officials experienced first-hand the problems which beset the developing countries even more direly. They felt that this familiarity with common problems, the sharing of socialist ideals, and Yugoslavia's active espousal of far-reaching programs for promoting economic development fostered friendship between Yugoslavia and the new nations.[15] No doubt foreign policy considerations moved Yugoslav leaders to espouse a better deal for developing countries. However, domestic factors were at least as important. By the mid-1950's Yugoslavia had instituted major internal reforms designed to accelerate decentralization, self-management, and deetatization. Haltingly and often over bitter opposition from entrenched or unsympathetic elements in the Party, these reforms were pushed to make the Yugoslav economy productive and efficient enough to stand on its feet. Yugoslav leaders realized that the country could not indefinitely rely on foreign assistance, nor continue to run a heavy deficit in its international balance of payments.

The Yugoslavs argue that since autarky is impossible for all but a few countries, the developing countries "will inevitably be linked to the world market and in a very inten-

[13] Janez Stanovnik, "A Remarkable Achievement," *Review of International Affairs*, Vol. IX, No. 187 (January 16, 1958), p. 9.

[14] Janez Stanovnik, "International Assistance to Underdeveloped Countries in the Light of World Economic Development," *Medjunarodni Problemi*, Vol. IX, No. 4 (1957), pp. 3-15.

[15] Marijan Barišić, "Yugoslavia and West Africa's Countries," *Review of International Affairs*, Vol. XI, No. 238 (March 1, 1960), p. 5.

sive way."[16] To avoid the political servitude which inheres in excessive economic dependence on one crop or one market, developing countries must diversify their economies, raise productivity levels, and initiate internal reforms. Reliance on foreign aid for too long a period is dangerous because of the capriciousness of such assistance and because indebtedness reaches such a level that further borrowing "serves only to enable repayment of former loans."[17] The Yugoslavs say that it vitiates the capacity for genuine economic integration on a "free and voluntary" basis and leads to dependence on one of the exclusive market systems managed by one of the blocs, thus undermining nonalignment; to the extent that regional integration becomes "an instrument for preserving blocs" and institutionalizing semidependence of developing countries, it represents a regressive phenomenon.[18] Implicit also in their attitude is fear of being left out of the regional economic groupings which dominate world trade, or of being forced, out of necessity, to so link up with one as to jeopardize their policy of political nonalignment.

Economic development required a multifaceted approach, in which bilateral cooperation was deemed important for a long time to come. However, within the U.N. Yugoslavia pressed for the establishment of a U.N. Capital Development Fund and a Commission on Industrial Development, the expansion of existing programs, and greater attention to the plight of the Third World. On the controversial question of permanent sovereignty over natural resources, it upheld the view that every state may nationalize its natural wealth in accordance with local laws, and that compensation is a prerogative of national independence and not a practice guaranteed by international law.[19] But in-

[16] Janez Stanovnik, "The Impact of Industrialization on the International Economic Relations of Yugoslavia," *Medjunarodni Problemi*, Vol. XIII, No. 1 (1961), p. 25.

[17] *Ibid.*

[18] *The Program of the League of Yugoslav Communists* (Belgrade: Jugoslavija, 1958), pp. 85-86.

[19] Milan Bulajić, "Sovereignty over Natural Wealth and Resources,"

creasingly Yugoslav attention turned to the expansion of world trade. Extrapolating from their own experience, the Yugoslavs stressed trade, not aid. This aspiration was not new. Soviet delegates had often called for an international conference to discuss world trade problems, but their reasons had only marginally related to the development prospects of developing countries; from the late 1950's on, they sought basically to retard West European economic integration. By contrast, Yugoslavia pressed for changes in the structure of world trade that would benefit the developing countries and Yugoslavia.

Prelude to UNCTAD

At the Belgrade Conference of nonaligned states President Tito gave expression to the uneasiness prevailing among the new nations over the exclusiveness of regional economic groupings clustering along bloc lines. He noted that nonaligned countries outside the Western [European Economic Community (EEC) and the Organization for Economic Cooperation (OECD)] and Soviet [Council for Mutual Economic Assistance (CMEA)] economic organizations were subjected to grave discrimination, which in the future "could be even further aggravated, and could affect even more adversely the economic development of nonaligned as well as all other countries."[20] Tito made two far-reaching proposals. First, he called for systematic exploration of ways of expanding economic cooperation among the less-developed countries, which "should include all the nonaligned countries as well as all the other less-developed countries which are ready for such cooperation."

> This cooperation would not have a merely regional economic character, but also a broader, in a certain sense, universal one; at the same time, it would be, in addition

[20] *Tito: Selected Speeches and Articles, 1941-1961* (Zagreb: Naprijed, 1963), p. 400.

to its economic importance, of considerable general political significance.[21]

Second, he proposed the establishment of a "universal economic organization" to promote international trade on a nondiscriminatory basis and advance the development of the new nations:

> I feel that a world conference, at which all the most important economic questions would be considered, could facilitate a more effective approach to the solving of these problems. Perhaps the most suitable place for the convening of such a meeting would be the United Nations.[22]

The Belgrade Declaration invited all countries "to cooperate effectively in the economic and commercial fields so as to face the policies of pressure in the economic sphere as well as the harmful results which may be created by the economic blocs of the industrial countries." It played a leading part in setting in motion developments that culminated in the convening of the first United Nations Conference on Trade and Development (UNCTAD) in Geneva in March 1964, though there are Western scholars who would apparently disagree sharply with this assessment of the importance of Yugoslavia's role.[23] The road to Geneva went through New York and Cairo, and repeated obstacles placed along the way by the Western powers had to be surmounted.

On November 19, 1961, at a meeting in Cairo, Tito persuaded Nehru and Nasser to sign a joint communiqué urging the developing countries to examine the dangers threatening their vital economic interests. This course of action was a response to economic pressure exerted by the United States against Yugoslavia for its unwillingness at the Bel-

[21] *Ibid.*

[22] *Ibid.*, p. 401.

[23] For example, there is no mention at all of Yugoslavia, the Belgrade Conference, or the Cairo Economic Conference in the section devoted to "The Origins of UNCTAD" in the article by Richard N. Gardner, "The United Nations Conference on Trade and Development," *International Organization*, Vol. XXII, No. 1 (Winter 1968), pp. 100-106.

grade Conference to criticize the Soviet Union for having unilaterally broken the informal nuclear test ban moratorium that had been in effect since 1958. One month later the General Assembly adopted a resolution on international trade which called on the economically developed countries to bear in mind the interests of the developing countries when implementing their trade and economic policies, and requested the Secretary-General to consult with member nations and the specialized agencies about the possibility of convening an international conference on world trade. In February 1962 Tito and Nasser again discussed, *inter alia*, ways of eliminating barriers to international trade. Tito stated, in an interview with *The Observer* (London), that the nonaligned countries would have to act to protect themselves from the prejudicial economic tendencies manifested by the closed regional economic groupings. Koča Popović, the Foreign Minister, visited Cairo to discuss plans for an economic conference. On June 11, 1962, invitations were issued in the name of six countries—Yugoslavia, the U.A.R., Ethiopia, Ghana, Sudan, and Guinea—asking developing countries to come to Cairo the following month to discuss a variety of common economic concerns. Though India attended, its absence from the list of sponsoring countries (later expanded to eleven) was noticeable —another instance of Nehru's skepticism of large conferences of Afro-Asian states.

The Cairo Economic Conference, held from July 9 to 18, 1962, declared itself "resolutely in favor" of a world trade conference which should deal with such vital issues as the expansion of trade, primary commodity trade, and relations between developing and developed countries. At Yugoslav urging, it also called upon the developing countries to break out of the capital accumulation vise in which they found themselves by expanding mutual trade among themselves and by promoting various other forms of mutual economic cooperation.[24] On August 3, 1962, ECOSOC

[24] According to Janez Stanovnik underdeveloped countries obtain capital for investment largely from their export earnings. Since the

went on record in favor of convening the first UNCTAD after the Western countries dropped their negative attitude. The General Assembly gave its final approval on December 8, 1962.

From the first session of the Preparatory Committee in January-February 1963 through the third session a year later, Yugoslavia was a diligent participant.[25] Classified as a developing country, it was unprecedentedly linked with the African and Asian countries, and not with the other East European nations, and assigned as a member of the General Committee of the Conference with the Afro-Asian bloc.

Belgrade's Role at the First UNCTAD Conference

The First UNCTAD Conference was held from March 23 to June 16, 1964. It has been voluminously documented, and there is no need here to recapitulate well-known events. What is less known and noteworthy for this study is an account of Yugoslavia's behavior and impact.

One major success of Yugoslavia was gaining acceptance in the Afro-Asian group as an "Asian" country and inclusion as one of the LDC's (Less Developed Countries). Such recognition contravened geography and economics: Yugoslavia was the only European country included among the "77" LDC's, and economically it was far more developed than others in the group; socially and politically, it possessed a stable and effectively functioning system in contrast to the instability and haplessness of many of the

---

possibilities of increasing exports of traditional goods to developed countries are limited because of the restrictive policies of the latter, the underdeveloped countries must find new sources of capital, based on diversification, industrialization, and self-help. "Some Problems of Theory and Policy of Economic Development in the Light of the Declaration of the Cairo Conference," *Medjunarodni Problemi,* Vol. XIV, No. 2-3 (1962) , p. 43.

25 B. P., "Preparations for the United Nations Conference on Trade and Development," *Yugoslav Survey,* Vol. V, No. 16 (January-March 1964) , pp. 2354-2362.

LDC's. Its acceptance in the Asian group was a tribute to its role at the Belgrade and Cairo conferences and to its championing of UNCTAD in the United Nations. Undoubtedly, Tito's friendship with Nasser and Nehru contributed immeasurably as well.

The Yugoslavs believe, and most of the foreign diplomats interviewed agreed, that their main contribution was fostering acceptance among the developing countries of firm but responsible negotiating positions. In the words of one Yugoslav: "Yugoslavia had to fight against those who wanted to go too far and were too extremist in their demands, on the one hand, and against those in the group who were ready to give in too soon, to settle for too little." For example, it opposed the radicals among the "77" who, with Soviet bloc encouragement, pressed for the abolition of GATT (General Agreement on Tariffs and Trade) and the establishment of a new international organization devoted to trade matters. After more than a month of intensive, daily conferences, the Yugoslavs persuaded the group that such a task would have a polarizing effect and would jeopardize prospects for success. According to one of the Yugoslav participants, agreement on this point was obtained only in return for his delegation's acceptance of a more radical wording of the Declaration issued by the "77," which ironically led the American delegation to see the Yugoslavs as more radical than they really were. Realists that they are, the Yugoslavs see as inevitable the surfacing of extremist, unworkable views, but regard this as a necessary part of the process of the "77" learning to cooperate, maturity being as much a process as a function of experience.

Yugoslav diplomats strove for acceptance of consensual rather than confrontation politics. They counselled against marshalling numerical majorities to outvote the developed countries who, after all, could not be forced to make trade and tariff concessions; the effect, therefore, would only have been to embitter the negotiating atmosphere. By mitigating the extremis of some of the LDC's, they helped forge a degree of solidarity which greatly surprised the developed countries; by deploring steamroller tactics based on coalitions with Soviet bloc countries, they drew attention to the community-building role which international organizations could play for the LDC's.

That the Yugoslavs attributed enormous importance to the Conference is evident from the quality of their delegation, which many observers considered the equal of the best sent by the developed countries, and from their willingness to incur the ire of their closest colleagues among the nonaligned nations. Thus, when Algeria wanted to expel South Africa on the apartheid issue, Vladimir Popović, the chief Yugoslav delegate, publicly took exception, saying that the purposes of the UNCTAD conference were sufficiently vital not to be jeopardized by intruding other issues, which though important were not relevant to the considerations at hand.[26] On another occasion Dr. Janez Stanovnik, the Chairman of the Financial Committee, refused to be pressured by Arab delegations into denying the Head of the Israeli delegation, David Horowitz, the opportunity to submit a far-reaching proposal for establishing an interest equalization fund, designed to make investment in developing countries more attractive to private capital markets. Stanovnik cooperated in drawing up the draft resolution and submitting it to UNCTAD, despite the abstentions of Arab delegates. Israeli officials acknowledge that it was "an act of courage for a Yugoslav to submit and sponsor a proposal initially suggested by Israel, in view of possible Arab reactions." By adopting principled stands on is-

[26] By contrast, at the second UNCTAD conference, held in New Delhi four years later, political and partisan dissonances jarred the proceedings to a degree unknown at the 1964 conference. Frustration among the LDC's over the lack of progress may have exacerbated political differences and given the radicals a command over the strategy adopted by the LDC's.

"The procedural wrangles over South Africa alone delayed the plenary session for three days and finally culminated in the most successful walkout. When the South African delegate, Dr. William Naude, rose to address the conference, all except the delegates of 28 countries left the hall." *The New York Times*, March 8, 1968.

sues that could have become political liabilities, the Yugoslavs demonstrated the seriousness with which they approached the conference. They also showed their independence and courage, traits that further enhanced their international prestige.

Not even the Soviet Union escaped criticism. Yugoslav delegates lumped the narrowness of the integration efforts of the Common Market with that of CMEA, occasioning strong Soviet protests to Belgrade; and Yugoslav writers spotlighted the discrepancy between Soviet statements of intention to increase the consumption of tropical products and actual trade levels. Stanovnik wrote:

> The tendency of the East European economic bloc to produce as much as possible within its own economic region limits its readiness to achieve a broader division of labor with the nonaligned countries and deprives the underdeveloped countries of the income they could earn under conditions of general economic progress as a result of their natural advantage. . . .
>
> As there is obviously no systematic effort [by the Soviet Bloc] to include the underdeveloped countries in the division of labour, and hence assure continuity for the sale of their products, trade between the "socialist world market" and the nonaligned countries is developing in a haphazard manner as it depends primarily on the temporary shortages of certain raw materials or the readiness of the planning authorities to permit such luxuries as increased consumption of tropical fruits and beverages. Owing to its extreme instability such trade cannot provide a reliable source of export earnings to the underdeveloped countries nor a basis for drawing up their investment programmes.[27]

Other Yugoslavs have observed that despite Soviet assertions of "a readiness to expand their economic-trade rela-

[27] Janez Stanovnik, *World Economic Blocs: The Nonaligned Countries and Economic Integration* (Belgrade: Jugoslavija, 1962) , pp. 42-43.

tions and meet as many justified demands by the developing countries as possible," the fact is that "the activity and initiative of the socialist countries within UNCTAD has proved below the expectations."[28] One high-ranking official wrote that "socialist countries should be more active as a factor in international trade and economy . . . because their economic capacities are greater than their economic needs."[29] Such commentaries cannot make for easy relations between Moscow and Belgrade.

Stanovnik's role as chairman of the Committee on Financial Problems was outstanding. More than any of his counterparts he brought his Committee to early and reasonable agreement on specific problems. Many diplomats, recognizing his pioneering and persistent efforts on behalf of developing countries, thought he deserved the appellation, "the father of UNCTAD." A brilliant economist, he has written and worked indefatigably to arouse the international community to the urgency for prompt, bold actions to counter the disequilibrating dangers that are inherent in the changes in world demand and trade and that are intensified by the technological revolution:

> The weight of the argument favoring an increase in the international financing of economic development lies neither in restitution nor in charity but in the sound economic logic of developing a new integrated world economy.[30]

The Yugoslav delegation was more moderate in approach than one might infer from a reading of official Yugoslav speeches. While American officials tend to disagree with this evaluation, Asian and African diplomats tend to confirm

[28] Josip Kulišić, "Economic Cooperation Between the East European Socialist States and the Developing Countries," *Review of International Affairs*, Vol. XVIII, No. 425 (December 20, 1967), p. 14.

[29] Anton Vratuša, "Decolonization and Yugoslavia," *Teorija in Praksa*, Vol. III, No. 3 (March 1966), p. 493.

[30] Janez Stanovnik, "1/1000 or 1/100?", *Review of International Affairs*, Vol. XVIII, No. 423 (November 20, 1967), p. 15.

it. Here, in capsule, is manifest the complex relationship between perceptions and policies.

A discerning foreign diplomat, then resident in Rangoon, told this writer that "the United States has the most comprehensive intelligence information of any government, and an unfailing penchant for drawing the wrong conclusions." American assessments of Yugoslav behavior too often suffer from an incapacity to transcend the seeming reality in order to reach an understanding of what is. The addiction to "hard" data lends itself to oversimplified and distorted analyses of international phenomena.

The Yugoslavs consider themselves both moderators and mobilizers. They believe their own difficulties have required them to struggle for concrete solutions to economic problems, which in turn disposed them in practice toward compromise and adaptation to reality. Notwithstanding the official commitment to an ideology that often is neither scientific, realistic, nor logical, Yugoslav leaders have had their outlook and attitudes modified by the intractability of economic problems. In grappling with reality, they have excised much from day-to-day practice that was doctrinaire and dogmatic. Within the inner councils of the LDC's, theirs is a voice for pragmatism and cooperation.

Yugoslavia is a member of the fifty-five-man UNCTAD Board, one of the thirty-one LDC's involved in the continual work of the organization. Its election as a member of the Asian group is testament to the esteem in which it is held. One Asian diplomat said this was deserved because the Yugoslavs were energetic, constructive and "full of ideas."

Observations

The broad outlook underlying the Yugoslav approach may be described in the following manner: Yugoslavia has found from its own experience that the United Nations and international organizations advance the long-term independence and viability of small nations. If one wants to change the world, then it comes down to a matter of give-and-take, of mixing reason with purpose. One cannot change the attitudes of the small countries by telling them what to do, but they can and do learn from exposure and experience. One cannot tell them outright that they are wrong in their radicalism, but one can show that there are other ways to accomplish desired objectives. The indirect method, education through participation, holds out the best hope for transforming the international environment and for inducing those changes of attitude and policy that are preconditions for domestic development. Few of the new nations are now aware of what national sacrifice or national discipline means. All too often they think that they can get some money, draw up plans, and achieve development. A process of evolution is necessary, and this can be promoted most beneficially through international organizations.

Yugoslav leaders do not always agree among themselves on the priorities to be followed. There are no guidelines for strengthening the U.N. and improving the condition of the nonaligned nations. Since the 1967 Middle East war the Yugoslavs have undertaken studies intended to advance the peace-making activity of the U.N., not just in the political-military context but in the economic as well. While endeavoring to find political solutions acceptable to their nonaligned colleagues in the Middle East and south of the Sahara, they are at the same time paying ever greater attention to the widening gap between the industrially advanced and the less-developed nations. They fear the contagion of crises bred by economic inequality. The sterility of the second UNCTAD was a bitter disappointment. The developed countries had, in the words of one observer, brought nothing but "a basket of rubber bones."[31] The worst fears of Stanovnik that the conference would turn into "a dialogue of the deaf" rather than "a dialogue of continents" were regrettably justified.

New organizations have sprouted, but the yield is little improved. In November 1965, EPTA and the Special Fund were merged and the United Nations Development Program (UNDP) established. But dissatisfied because there

[31] *The New York Times*, April 15, 1968.

is no provision for international public financing of large-scale projects in developing countries, Yugoslavia continues to propose the creation of a U.N. Capital Development Fund.[32] In November 1966 a U.N. Industrial Development Organization (UNIDO) was set up "to promote industrial development," but the Western countries adamantly opposed giving the organization the financial wherewithal to generate specific industrial projects. Investigations and infrastructure overshadow investment and industrialization. Yugoslavia is involved in the executive activities of both organizations. The U.N. Decade of Development, of which so much was expected after it was sparked by President Kennedy in 1961, has not come close to attaining the goals of a 5 percent annual growth rate for developing countries and an overall investment by the developed countries in the Third World of a minimum of 1 percent of their national incomes.

Yugoslav analysts urge action. After more than a decade of praise for the principle of multilateral aid through the United Nations and the establishment of new organizations to help less-developed countries, the LDC's are still mired in backwardness, confined to the periphery of international decisionmaking, and unable to generate real power for development. There is an apt Serbian saying: "One praises the village, but lives in the town." Refusal by the developed countries to introduce a major restructuring of international economic relationships will, the Yugoslavs argue, feed radicalism and instability, and heighten the dangers of war. They hold that, like Yugoslavia, most nations of the Third World share a reserved attitude toward the West but, though progressive, are not now wedded to a radical course. The Yugoslavs believe that Western political decisionmakers became interested in the economic problems of the LDC's because of the Soviet challenge that has materialized there since 1954, as well as because they observed that the quest for change in the Third World did not pose a fundamental challenge to the Western order or

[32] *Borba*, November 18, 1965.

to Western interests and that the East could not, for the moment, dictate the prevailing trend. But the Yugoslavs caution that parsimony and indifference could change this situation.

Yugoslavia originally became involved in economic matters for a political reason: to find a way out of the diplomatic isolation in which excommunication from the Cominform had placed it. The SUNFED issue brought it into broadened consultations with the developing countries. This served to identify common areas of interest, which in turn led to awareness of common attitudes and aims, and to the formulation of common positions. Thus SUNFED initiated a continual dialogue with countries such as India, Egypt, Mexico, Burma, and Indonesia, out of which came nonalignment. UNCTAD is the lineal consequence of SUNFED. The continuing discussion of a variety of issues soon transcended the narrow and specific confines of economic matters to include broader questions affecting international relations and security and the role that the new nations sought to play to preserve their independence between blocs.

By the late 1950's Yugoslavia's quest for solutions to international economic problems was increasingly dictated by its own economic considerations. Its internal political and economic liberalization depended on the country's ability to compete in world markets. Thus the attention to economic issues since the Belgrade Conference is not just a response to the needs of the LDC's but a realization by Yugoslav leaders that there is an integral relationship between the economic viability of other countries and their own, and between their own economic viability and their ability to remain in the vanguard of nonalignment.[33]

[33] Two Yugoslav officials of the Secretariat for Foreign Affairs described the premises on which Yugoslavia bases its conception of international economic cooperation as follows: "One, that member nations shall have the same and equal rights and that the sovereignty of each nation to determine its own general policy for governing its own internal affairs shall be upheld; two, that socialist Yugoslavia is itself a developing country, and that since the end of the war she has been

The motivation to remain in the forefront of nonalignment keeps the Yugoslavs working hard, but there is an unprecedented and paradoxical situation: Yugoslavia espouses open trade and an end to blocs, but is forced by its economic weakness doggedly to seek privileged access to the major economic blocs, especially the Western one. It enjoyed observer status with the OEEC, and has representatives at OECD, the successor organization; it was a member of the European Payments Union. Through these organizations it has cooperated closely with Western economic measures. Yugoslavia is also the only nonaligned country that is both a full member of GATT and an associate member of COMECON. Though strenuously opposing the exclusivity of EEC and COMECON, it lobbies for preferential treatment not available to other nonaligned countries. Sensitive to this anomalous behavior, the Yugoslavs contend that as a full member of GATT they will now be in a position to exert efforts on behalf of the developing countries, to prevail upon industrial countries to grant far-reaching concessions to the new nations.[34] The foregoing cogently spotlights what they, for political reasons, prefer to pass quickly over: that though working on behalf of the LDC's and interested in expanding economic relations with these countries insofar as is possible, in the main their "most important [economic] ties are with the Western nations."[35]

---

concentrating her efforts to eliminate economic backwardness and its social consequences; and three, that international economic cooperation is a dynamic process in which every nation, to the limits of its ability, assists in solving the problems of other countries and thereby contributes to a speedier elimination of imbalances in world trade and accordingly to the consolidation of world peace." Mirčeta Čvorović and Milan Ristić, *Yugoslavia in the System of Multilateral International Economic Cooperation* (Belgrade: Medjunarodna Štampa, 1967), p. 12. See also Alvin Z. Rubinstein, "Reforms, Nonalignment, and Pluralism," *Problems of Communism*, Vol. XVII, No. 2 (March-April 1968), pp. 31-41.

[34] "Yugoslavia and GATT," *Yugoslav Survey*, Vol. VIII, No. 1 (February 1967), p. 128.

[35] John C. Campbell, *Tito's Separate Road* (New York: Harper and Row, 1967), p. 160. Dr. Campbell notes: "The West has been the

In the totality of ambitious policies pursued by the Yugoslav Government toward the developing countries there is fused the quest for a position of leadership among the nonaligned nations and the pursuit of concrete national aims. These policies it diligently and skillfully promotes within international organizations and on a bilateral basis as well.

---

source of essential credits. It produces what Yugoslavia needs to import. It has the markets where Yugoslavia can earn hard currencies. The world economy, not the Soviet bloc, offers the international division of labor in which the Yugoslav economy can find its place. The Western European countries, not the Soviet Union or Eastern Europe, provide large numbers of Yugoslav workers with jobs and training. The West has the advanced technology. Reform of customs duties, devaluation of the dinar, membership in the General Agreement on Tariffs and Trade, and the whole series of economic reforms undertaken by Yugoslavia in the past few years fortify this tendency of economic association with the West and the world trading system. It is a turn to the West of enormous potential significance, although Yugoslav public statements do not say so."

CHAPTER VI

Influencebuilding in the Third World

ALL NATIONS engage in influencebuilding. Success in influencebuilding is mistakenly associated with the possession of power, variously defined in political, economic, and military terms. This assumption of a basically arithmetic relationship between power and influence distorts our understanding of the arcane character of international politics. If it were correct, international relations would be highly predictable: the wealthiest and most powerful nations would with ease accomplish their aims and rarely experience frustration; influence would appertain to such governments, controlling the behavior of the weaker members of the international community. To paraphrase Trotsky, the weaker nations would merely read the proclamations issued by the stronger, and respond accordingly.

But the relationship between power and influence is complex. The mere possession of enormous power is no guarantee of the realization of goals, either by the individual, the group, or the nation-state. Power has both preventive and programmatic functions. It is subject to inherent restraints in periods of rivalry and competition. Its utility is at maximum in deterring war and in war itself. Power is easier to manage and manifest than influence is, because the essentials on which it rests are less frequently put to the test—and are more readily apparent.

Influencebuilding, on the other hand, is the principal occupation of nations in the protracted lulls between wars. Like power, influence is multidimensional but its components are different. For example, capability, the principal component of power, is not an absolute prerequisite for influencebuilding, though of course it can be useful. Instead, in influencebuilding the premiums are placed on opportuneness, relevance, and dependability. Influence may accrue to countries with little power because of their ability to fulfill needs at a crucial period.

Yugoslavia engaged in influencebuilding both to promote national security and to further its vision of international relations; it succeeded because its policies accorded with the basic needs of the nations it courted. The requirements of Yugoslav security and the prescriptions of Yugoslav leaders for new international relationships anticipated those of the new nations. By providing assistance, ideas, a sense of direction, and an adept diplomatic style, Yugoslavia drew close to, and was embraced by, the nonaligned nations. With minimal power, it advanced the fulfillment of their common aims, and in the process established unblemished credentials among the new nations. To solidify the influential position that it had obtained in the United Nations, Yugoslavia embarked on an ambitious and many faceted program aimed at developing firm ties on a bilateral basis with the Afro-Asian states. These bilateral efforts comprise the substance of this chapter.

Diplomatic Instruments

The diplomatic dimension of Yugoslav influencebuilding on a multilateral level has already been discussed: the penchant for conferences; the activism; the flair for programmatic initiatives; and the felicitous combination of preparation, persistence, and prudence that epitomizes the behavior of Yugoslav diplomats. A significant amount of energy is concentrated on the United Nations, which is suited to multilateral interactions and which initially provided the forum for the rapport Yugoslavia established with the new nations. But their rapport also stems from the sound and extensive bilateral relations they enjoy with one another. Certainly, friendship at one level reinforces cooperation at the other.

Influencebuilding presupposes prestige. Belgrade has understood that new governments, hypersensitive to slights to the sovereign equality of nations, regard their levels of accreditation as tangible indicators of the esteem with which they are held abroad and as symbols of their own self-images. Aware also of the status redounding to it from the presence in Belgrade of as many embassies as possible, the Yugoslav Government has pressed unceasingly in its relations with Afro-Asian nations for accreditation at the ambassadorial level. There are about sixty foreign ambassadors (a large number for a small country) permanently stationed in Belgrade. Almost half are from Afro-Asian countries. There are not more because few nations can afford the expense. Instead, many small countries locate their ambassadors in a major capital, e.g., Rome or Paris, but accredit them to several countries, *inter alia*, Yugoslavia.

In 1968 Yugoslavia maintained sixty-five embassies and ninety-nine diplomatic and consular missions.[1] Few medium-sized countries approach this number. Belgrade believes the maintenance abroad of so many embassies is a necessary luxury. Several purposes are served simultaneously: to make friends and achieve an easier rapport with national leaders; to facilitate Tito's personal diplomacy; and to promote economic ties (in the 1950's especially, Belgrade thought embassies would be better able to encourage African states to accept Yugoslav credits and purchase Yugoslav goods, which were experiencing difficulty in competing in Western markets). Many diplomats consider it the mark of an ambitious foreign policy; others say that it derives from Yugoslavia's anxiety over political isolation. Both considerations are pertinent. To play an important role in world affairs, a vast network of diplomatic missions is necessary. Not only does it keep Belgrade abreast of pressing problems in these countries, but, in the words of a former Greek Counsellor in Belgrade, "it also gives Belgrade a reason to express a view on every major international issue, from Vietnam to Rhodesia to South Africa to the Middle East, even though its vital interests are not affected."

Having many embassies abroad makes Yugoslavia seem important. A number of nonaligned diplomats noted that Washington and Moscow, for example, tend to see Tito as more important than he really is because of Yugoslavia's important role among the nonaligned countries: "Great

[1] *Politika*, March 3, 1968.

Powers tend to evaluate Tito in the light of how Africa sees him, and vice versa." A Sudanese official related that his country had agreed to raise its mission in Belgrade to the level of an embassy after the Belgrade Conference. Tito also persuaded President Abboud to assign a separate ambassador to Belgrade, not merely one who was accredited to Yugoslavia while based in Greece. On his return Abboud was criticized, since there was no real reason in terms of importance to the Sudan for an embassy in Belgrade. However, he argued that he had given his word, and an embassy was finally established in 1965. International conferences, personal visits, exchanges of notes between Heads of State, goodwill missions, and a network of embassies worthy of a great power are all essential components of Yugoslavia's diplomacy. Supplementing, but by no means subordinate to, these influencebuilding activities are the extensive links generated along bilateral lines through nondiplomatic channels.

Political-Organizational Links

The Yugoslavs are inveterate travelers. The visits of top officials are unrivalled by any other national leadership. Carried on at all levels by Party, government, trade union, scientific, and cultural personnel, they are the lifeblood of Yugoslav diplomacy, the protoplasmic substance of which influencebuilding is made. It is as if Belgrade considers Africa, Asia, and Europe a vital constituency to be nurtured in expectation of tangible political return. In the interest of operational effectiveness, contacts with elites in various countries are apportioned along functional lines. The principal organizations used are the League of Yugoslav Communists, the Chambers of the Federal Assembly, the Socialist Alliance, and the Yugoslav Trade Union Federation.

1. *The League of Yugoslav Communists (LYC)*

The League of Yugoslav Communists is responsible for promoting close ties with Party leaders in Communist countries and with Communist Parties in other countries. The

LYC casts a wide net. It conducts exchanges with Communist Parties in the Soviet Union and the nations of Eastern Europe; with Communist Parties in Western countries, e.g., Italy, France, and Scandinavia; with Communist Parties in developing countries where they are legal but out of power, e.g., India, Cyprus, and Indonesia (before the crackdown following the abortive coup of September 1965); with Communist Parties operating clandestinely in countries with which Yugoslavia does not enjoy cordial relations, e.g., Portugal and Spain; and with "progressive" one-Party states in which the Communist Parties do not function legally but are subsumed in broadly based national-liberation fronts, e.g., Algeria and Guinea. In dealing with the one-Party states in the Third World, the Yugoslavs will often send joint Party-state delegations headed, however, by leading Party officials who also hold government positions. The Yugoslav delegations sent to Algeria in recent years have usually been so constituted.[2] The group sent to Algeria in late October 1967, for example, was headed by Lazar Koliševski, a member of the Presidium of the Central Committee of the LYC and influential in the Socialist Alliance. It held high level discussions with members of the Secretariat of the National Liberation Front (FLN), which agreed to establish a joint committee that would meet every three months alternately in Algiers and Belgrade. Though such Party exchanges discuss important policy questions, the communiqués issued are couched in nonspecific, broad terms. An important adjunct of the LYC is the Institute for the Study of the Workers' Movement, housed in the old Central Committee Building in Belgrade.

Diplomacy by compartmentalization is characteristic of Communist states and is sometimes carried to ludicrous lengths. At an international seminar in Dubrovnik attended by the author the Yugoslavs, who are gracious hosts, arranged a series of intimate dinners for the delegates who were feted according to the bloc affiliations of their countries of origin, even though they had not all come as official

[2] *Borba*, November 4, 1965.

representatives of their governments: the Americans and West Europeans were entertained in one group, as were the delegates from the Soviet bloc countries, and those from the Afro-Asian states. As hosts of a country committed to the weakening of blocs, the Yugoslavs seemed determined by their behavior paradoxically to perpetuate them.

2. *Governmental Delegations*

When governmental ties supersede Party ones, delegations from the Federal Assembly and/or the Federal Executive Council (FEC) are sent. These parliamentary groups may serve a number of purposes. First, they fulfill ceremonial functions like representing the President at independence celebrations or inaugurations. For example, in January 1960, an FEC delegation attended the festivities proclaiming independence in the Cameroons and the reelection of President Tubman in Liberia. Second, parliamentary missions are sent on goodwill visits, often to determine whether the scene is ripe for a state visit by Tito. Thus, goodwill visits in 1953, 1958, and 1960, preceded subsequent state visits by President Tito in 1954, 1963, and 1961 to India, Latin America, and West Africa, respectively. Third, they establish contacts, explore possibilities for expanding ties on the governmental and Party levels, and gather information and impressions for their colleagues in Belgrade. In early 1965 Vladimir Popović, then chairman of the Foreign Affairs Committee of the Federal Assembly, headed a delegation that toured Tanzania, Zambia, Uganda, Kenya, and Sudan; in February 1967 Dr. Edvard Kardelj, then President of the Federal Assembly, visited Mali to discuss that country's internal situation with members of the ruling Party, the Union Soudanaise, and to consider the possibilities of closer ties between them and leaders of the LYC and Socialist Alliance. Similar visits have been made many times during the past two decades. Fourth, some parliamentary delegations concentrate on economic issues; for example, the one which visited Syria in October 1965 discussed the prospects for increased investments by

Yugoslav enterprises in Syria. Finally, all these visits are intended to convey Yugoslavia's interest and to give many of the mini-states a feeling of importance.

3. The Socialist Alliance (SAWPY)

The Socialist Alliance of Working People of Yugoslavia (SAWPY), the country's mass political organization, has the major responsibility for strengthening links with institutions and elites in non-Communist countries. Established in 1953 to replace the People's Front, it is the umbrella covering "just about everybody and everything: all organizations and groups, from sports societies to veterans associations, and all individuals who [are] willing to go along with the regime even part of the way."[3] Control is exercised by Party members who belong as individuals and who with the full weight of the LYC behind them shape policy and interact with courted foreign delegations. Thus when the General Secretary of the Chilean Communist Party visited, he met with members of the Central Committee of the LYC; but when members of the Executive Committee of the Chilean Socialist Party came, they were received by some of the same Yugoslavs who functioned, however, as members of the Federal Board of the SAWPY.

The principal functions and activities of the Socialist Alliance are internally-oriented, but its international tasks have steadily grown in response to the global requirements of Yugoslav foreign policy. SAWPY seeks to establish new connections and extend existing ones "with all movements, parties and organizations willing to cooperate . . . to strengthening the forces of peace"; to foster cooperation with "all progressive movements"; to study more intensively the national-liberation struggles and experiences of all nations.[4] At the fourth meeting of the Federal Conference of SAWPY on March 29, 1967, officials examined Yugoslavia's

[3] George Hoffman and Fred Warner Neal, *Yugoslavia and the New Communism* (New York: Twentieth Century Fund, 1962), p. 179.
[4] *Review of International Affairs*, Vol. xv, No. 278 (November 5, 1961), p. 20.

relations with the developing countries. They noted the importance of these countries as partners both "in Yugoslavia's international activity" and "in the field of economic, trade, scientific and technical, and social-political cooperation."[5] The Conference emphasized the need to devise "new forms" of economic cooperation which would take account of Yugoslavia's 1965 economic reforms and ensure that "economic relations between Yugoslavia and the newly liberated countries develop in accordance with actual possibilities and mutual needs." In revealing fashion, it also directed SAWPY "to acquaint the Yugoslav public with the efforts and achievements of the developing countries,"[6] an unusual step, perhaps indicative of the absorption of the rank-and-file with their own situation and their relative lack of interest in the leadership's foreign aid program.

Congresses of the Socialist Alliance have taken on the character of nonaligned conferences-in-the-making. Whereas delegates and observers from forty countries and movements attended the Fifth Congress in April 1960, representatives from sixty-four were present at the Sixth Congress in June 1966. Foreign policy resolutions are given prominence and reflect the views of the militants among the nonaligned countries and the unenfranchised radical movements. There has been a rapid expansion of delegations visiting Yugoslavia from national-liberation movements and other organizations with which the Socialist Alliance cooperates. In 1965 there were fifty-three such groups. Collaboration exists with more than eighty parties and movements. This is of course a reciprocal arrangement. A steady stream of SAWPY delegations is always visible abroad, e.g., in 1965 more than thirty were sent, generally

[5] "Conclusions of the Federal Conference of the Socialist Alliance," *Socialist Thought and Practice*, No. 26 (April-June 1967), p. 148.

[6] *Ibid.*, p. 151. On previous occasions, Tito had expressed satisfaction with SAWPY's "political activities," which "had favorable results because they enabled the people of other countries to become acquainted with the development of our social system." *Peace and Socialism* (Belgrade: Jugoslavija, 1960), p. 51.

headed by a leading political figure. The names include key members of the LYC's decision-making elite: Veljko Vlahović, Edvard Kardelj, Milentije Popović, Vladimir Popović, Petar Stambolić, Lazar Koliševski, and Josip Djerdja. Far from tapering off, the frequency of visits is rising, more than keeping abreast of the mushrooming number of new nations. This could indicate Belgrade's belief in their value, though it may also show that influencebuilding is a process requiring continual inputs of time, effort, and money;[7] and that once committed to a course and speed of action, any deviation or slackening could be interpreted unfavorably by the courted countries and could affect Yugoslavia's standing with them.

SAWPY delegations, too, have different aims: one delegation to Senegal sought to establish the first direct contacts with President Leopold Senghor and the ruling Union Progressiste Senegalaise (UPS); another attended the Congress of the Socialist Party of Chile to reinforce existing ties; still another acted as observers at congresses of the Moroccan Istiqlal Party and the Tunisian Neo-Destour, thus reciprocating previous visits to Yugoslavia; finally, observers attend conferences of organizations such as APSO (Afro-Asian Peoples' Solidarity Organization). In addition to this round robin of parties and organizations, the Socialist Alliance frequently hosts leaders of illegal movements that are seeking to gain independence from colonial rule or to overthrow dictatorship.[8]

[7] The growing expense of financing visits to Yugoslavia, coupled with the drastic curtailment of subsidies under the 1965 economic reforms, has led Yugoslav officials to find alternate sources of support. One ingenious and common practice is to tailor invitations to those extended by the Soviet bloc and West European countries which have budgeted more money for such purposes. When a trade union or scientific group is invited, let us say, to Moscow or Budapest, it will receive an invitation from the appropriate Yugoslav organization and be encouraged to stop off en route to or from the Soviet bloc capitals, thereby eliminating the expense of air tickets, which are usually the major item.

[8] For example, Louis d'Azevedo of the People's Movement for the Liberation of Angola (MPLA) spent several weeks in Yugoslavia discussing current problems in the Portuguese colonies with SAWPY officials. *Borba*, February 1, 1966.

4. *Yugoslav Trade Union Federation*

The Yugoslav Trade Union Federation is the other major institution completing the organizational network of influencebuilding activities.[9] Linked to the Socialist Alliance, it operates its programs independently and maintains a high level of interaction with trade union movements throughout the world. For reasons relating to the events of 1948, Yugoslavia is not a member of the Soviet-dominated WFTU (World Federation of Trade Unions) or the non-Communist ICFTU (International Confederation of Free Trade Unions). To overcome its exclusion from decision-making circles in these bloc-affiliated organizations, the Yugoslavs favored the creation of new regional trade union movements, e.g., the AATUF (All-African Trade Union Federation), "as a promising step toward breaking down the polarization of the international labor movement," a position that has brought them into dispute with the Soviet Union.[10]

> The Yugoslav activities represented a challenge not only to the WFTU's ideological monopoly and its ability to attract support from the unions of the underdeveloped world, but to Soviet policy in a broader sense.[11]

Though Yugoslav leaders deny seeking to extend nonalignment in the political arena to the international trade union

[9] A myriad of lesser institutional links exist. Federations of youth, women, scientists, and artists all function internationally, in part, to mobilize support among professional groups abroad for specific Yugoslav policies and attitudes. One of the more active is the Yugoslav League for Peace, Independence and Equality of Peoples, established by the Socialist Alliance on April 3, 1959, to replace the decade-worn Committee for the Defense of Peace. It seeks to link Yugoslavia with "anti-colonial, anti-war, and anti-nuclear organizations in Europe, Asia, and Africa," and is regarded by the Yugoslavs as effective. See "The 1961 International Activities of the Socialist Alliance of Working People of Yugoslavia," *Review of International Affairs*, Vol. XIII, No. 287 (March 20, 1962), p. 20.

[10] Donald L. M. Blackmer, *Unity in Diversity: Italian Communism and the Communist World* (Cambridge: The M.I.T. Press, 1968), p. 299. In this, the Yugoslavs have found an ally in the CGIL, the key union dominated by the Italian Communist Party.

[11] *Ibid.*, p. 300.

movement, this is the long-term implication of their initiatives, and has been so interpreted by an uneasy Moscow. Presumably this issue is the subject of continuing discussion between the Yugoslavs and trade union delegations from the Third World. The Yugoslav strategy is to overcome the division in the world trade union movement by lessening the WFTU's subordination to Soviet policy and by enlarging the front of "progressive and revolutionary" forces within a framework of voluntarism and equality. Short of attaining this goal, Belgrade works methodically at cultivating firm ties on a bilateral basis between its trade union movement and those in other countries.[12]

5. *On Utility*

Does the cumulative effect of these round robins contribute to the building of Yugoslav influence in the Third World? Officially the Yugoslavs say unequivocally, yes. In private, a few are less sanguine. One Ambassador to an African country said it is deeds and not discussions that count, shared concrete interests and not reiterations of programmatic goals that create an atmosphere within which influence can develop. Reservations or not, Belgrade acts as if it assumes that its multifaceted diplomacy does have an impact on the nations it courts.

Yugoslavia is limited in size, wealth, and power. Economically, it does not have the capability to affect significantly the developmental efforts of the new countries, though assistance is extended for economic and political reasons. But in foreign affairs Yugoslavia gave form and impetus to nonalignment and to the activism that brought greater recognition to small nations. For its efforts in this realm alone, it is accorded a leading position in the councils of the nonaligned and an ungrudging respect, which is prerequisite for influence exercised without the authoritative buttress of power.

[12] Svetozar Vukmanović, "Fifth Congress of the Yugoslav Trade Unions," *Review of International Affairs*, Vol. xv, No. 335 (March 20, 1964) , p. 18.

In addition to a conception of international affairs and a demonstrated ability to conduct a "pendulum policy" of swinging deftly from West to East and back again, there are elements of the Yugoslav experience with nation-building that some nations find relevant to their own internal evolution, and it is this that makes Yugoslavia doubly interesting to the developing countries. During the discussions that attend the exchange of Party, government, trade union, and professional delegations, pertinent aspects of the Yugoslav experience are without doubt related. If interest occasions emulation, then Belgrade may indeed consider this facet of its diplomacy well worth the investment.

The Yugoslav Model

Though Western specialists have written voluminously on the supposed relevance for the Third World of Soviet and Communist Chinese developmental experiences, little systematic attention has been paid to the Yugoslav. The powerful are not known for a readiness to borrow from the less powerful, whose lower stage of development they invariably regard as evidence of cultural inferiority. Soviet and American elites share an excessive admiration for scientism and technology, neither of which supplies the political and social wherewithal that will help the new nations manage their affairs with a measure of stability. Although deposed and discredited, Kwame Nkrumah expressed the urgency of this need when he said, "Seek ye first the political kingdom and all else shall follow."

1. State-building

The ruling elites in the new nations seek to create a sense of community which transcends particularism and tribalism. Though Nkrumah and Sukarno, the "playboys" of the Third World, are now discredited for their megalomania, ostentatious squandering of national wealth, authoritarianism, and pretensions to ideological originality,

195

they were driven, in part at least, by a desire to create unity and a sense of nationhood for their peoples.[13]

For many Afro-Asian leaders, Yugoslavia is an example of a relatively new nation that is nurturing national cohesion, maintaining its political independence, and making economic and social progress. They admire the Yugoslav success in forging the essentials of a modern state. They observe Yugoslavia's ability to balance ties between Great Power blocs, receive assistance from both, and still pursue an independent foreign policy. Unlike most developing countries, Yugoslavia has utilized its foreign loans without corruption and speculation (though it is possible to argue that the credits were not always used in the wisest manner). Stability has been preserved without sacrificing development or liberalization and with a diminution of bureaucratism.

Afro-Asians may misinterpret what is perceived and misperceive what is shown, but basically these would-be nationbuilders know that they must find their own road to socialism, that they cannot import markers from another country since the terrain and the obstacles differ dramatically. Yet, some environments are more familiar than others. The irrelevance of the Soviet and Chinese experiences with nation-building and modernization have generally been perceived. Yugoslavia's commitment to socialism and obvious empathy for the developing countries established a psychopolitical climate conducive to the leisurely communication of national experiences. In discussions with the new elites, Yugoslav leaders did not try to "sell" their model of socialism, but instead emphasized the multiplicity of paths and the need of each nation to discover for itself the most congenial route. To their credit, they recognized that for the new nations the road to hell might very well be paved with good intentions.

Models are simplified and artificial constructs of reality. Those of the Soviet Union and China have less applicabil-

13 For a favorable assessment of Nkrumah's efforts at nation-building see Immanuel Wallerstein, "Autopsy of Nkrumah's Ghana," *The New Leader* (March 14, 1966), pp. 3-5.

ity to the new nations than the Yugoslav model, which is more relevant because of its less complex character, its less formally structured mode of operation, and its componential similarities—political, economic, ethnic, and religious. Among the nonaligned countries, Algeria and the United Arab Republic, in particular, have maintained a continuing interest, but others, e.g., Tanzania, Ghana, Guinea, India, Indonesia, and Afghanistan, have also explored aspects of the Yugoslav approach.

One former Yugoslav ambassador to the United Nations describes the interaction in this way:

> Yugoslav leaders explain their position, ideas, and difficulties to officials from new nations. When asked, "What do we have to do?" the Yugoslavs say that all they can do is explain the Yugoslav experience to them, that they will have to find their own way, basing their development on their own experience, needs, and traditions. Whereas one might think the new nations would be "disappointed" in not receiving more reassuring and definitive answers, to the contrary, they are "delighted": their feeling of independence is *so strong,* so sensitive are they to any slight or interference, fancied or actual, to any exposure of inadequacy, that the Yugoslav posture is most attractive to them. Any other reply would have a negative effect. The Yugoslavs came to this position and insight as a result of their own experience and the recollection of how they felt in similar circumstances, and not through any inverse psychology.

A. THE ONE-PARTY SYSTEM

The appeal of Yugoslavia's one-Party system is threefold: first, like the LYC, the dominant political parties in Algeria, Guinea, Mali, and Tanzania took form during the period of revolution, preempting in the process governmental, as well as Party, functions; second, the LYC has successfully implemented economic and social reforms without relying on totalitarian type forms unsuited to developing societies not desirous or capable of emulating the Soviet or Chinese experience; third, the LYC has separated Party from State functions without divesting the Party of its essential political primacy in the system. It is also less cumbersome than the Soviet counterpart, and less chauvinistic than the Chinese one.

The ambiguity and overlapping of political authority is an asset in societies where personalities count more than bureaucracies and pressure groups. The "in-between" character of the Yugoslav political system is a source of its attractiveness. One Canadian diplomat described the Yugoslav phenomenon in the following manner: "There is no opposition, but one always talks as if there is; enterprises have independence, but the controlling levers invariably go back to the Workers' Council, and thence to the LYC; elections are held, many even with two candidates, but they in no way threaten the entrenched position of the elite: an enormously complicated and quite subtle system." Nothing is as it appears to be; everything has several aspects. And compared to the Soviet Union and China, control is less fractious, capricious, and pervasive.

Underlying the *modus operandi* of the LYC is a groping for feasible solutions to concrete problems within a remarkably malleable ideological framework. Pragmatism, not dogmatism, has been the trademark of Yugoslav nation-building. In their focus on the structure of the organizational-political apparatus of the LYC and its enviable record of maintaining power while promoting extensive reforms, African elites often do not realize the extent to which the Party has voluntarily relinquished effective control over large sectors of the economy and social life. As one Yugoslav noted, "The majority of them know too little about the specifics of Yugoslavia's experience to emulate it, but they don't realize how little they know." That they think Yugoslavia has something to offer them is more important than whether, in fact, it does.

The Algerian FLN has been interested in the operation of

the LYC and self-management since independence. The usual delegation is composed of Party and government officials, with the former being the real wielders of power. Boumedienne's visit of October 5-11, 1966, like Ben Bella's of March 5-13, 1964, was organized along Party-state lines. Even though Yugoslav-Algerian relations cooled noticeably after Ben Bella's deposal on June 19, 1965, the Algerians proclaimed Boumedienne's visit different from the usual diplomatic one: "This trip was as much political party as government."[14] Discussions of nonalignment, common socio-economic problems, and Party matters were reviewed. A year later, at the conclusion of another meeting of FLN and LYC officials, the official organ of the Algerian Party noted that "Some fruitful exchanges of views marked the meeting, notably the organization and functioning of intermediary structures of the Party and the implantation of Party cells in units of production"[15]—an indication that the FLN was still interested in the operation of the LYC.

Other one-Party states in Africa regard the Yugoslav experience as relevant and seek exchanges on problems involving the maintenance of effective controls by Party leaders over Party members working in governmental ministries, the mobilization of mass support, and the training of political cadres. In these areas the LYC appears to have developed techniques useful to these nations. The U.A.R., Algeria, Guinea, Mali, Tanzania, and Ghana (until the overthrow of Nkrumah in February 1966) have consulted frequently with Yugoslav Party officials. Ironically, all of them have outlawed the Communist Party, a policy which has not in the least forestalled active courtship by Yugoslavia, or for that matter by the Soviet Union or Communist China. Belgrade's willingness to disregard the Communist Party of Algeria (PCA) as of no significance and to accept the FLN, "first as the guiding force in the Algerian

14 "Algiers-Belgrade: The Escalation of Peace and Friendship," *Révolution africaine*, No. 193 (October 14-20, 1966), p. 13.
15 *Révolution africaine*, No. 247 (November 9-15, 1967), p. 7.

liberation struggle and later as a vanguard party capable of leading Algeria to socialism, has been a key feature of Yugoslav policy."[16]

Several countries have inquired into the operation of governmental institutions revamped under the 1963 Yugoslav constitution. The first Algerian parliamentary delegation to go abroad after independence went to Yugoslavia to learn about the Federal Assembly, an institutionally more complex, but functionally more representative and active parliament than its predecessor.[17] For a while Tanzania expressed interest in Yugoslavia's new constitution, but conditions there changed and nothing came of it. In the realm of elections one-Party states have begun to give their electorates a semblance of choice: two candidates, approved by the leadership, may vie for election in the same constituency. Though the Yugoslavs did not pioneer this innovation in the Communist world (the Poles did), they did introduce it slowly in the late 1950's and were probably the ones who first acquainted the Africans with its possibilities. In September 1965 Tanzania's TANU Party authorized such competition in the elections, with the startling result that more than half of the parliamentary incumbents were defeated; Algeria's FLN introduced the principle of contested seats into the elections for local Municipal People's Assemblies in January 1967.[18] Both have ventured far beyond Yugoslavia in this respect. The Yugoslavs are sometimes uneasy about the emulation of

[16] David L. Milbank, "Yugoslav Policy Toward Algeria in Perspective," *SAIS Review*, Vol. 12, No. 1 (Autumn 1967), p. 5. Milbank attributes the PCA's isolation from the mainstream of the nationalist movement and the liberation war to two factors. "The first of these was the PCA's close association with the Communist Party of France (PCF), an organization which placed the interests of Paris and Moscow above those of the Algerians. The second was the fact that the membership of the PCA, even after the 'Muslimization' effort made in 1935, was largely made up of skilled workers of European origin whose sympathies lay with their fellow 'colons.'"

[17] Anton Kolendić, "Yugoslavia in International Relations in 1963," *Godišnjak 1963* (Belgrade: Institute for International Politics and Economy, 1964), p. 26.

[18] *The New York Times*, February 5, 1967.

their practices. They tell of the Afghan ambassador who was told to become a specialist on Yugoslav elections, and when he returned home was made Minister of Elections, despite cautionary reminders that the experience of one country cannot be transposed to another. Nonetheless, they feel flattered.

B. THE COMMUNE

Yugoslavia aroused widespread interest in its system of local government quite early. The basic political-territorial unit of self-government and the "social organism in which relations in production, distribution, consumption, and other basic daily social relations between working people are established and promoted" is the commune. According to the 1958 Program of the League of Yugoslav Communists the commune "is the most prominent institution of direct socialist democracy":

> Increasingly assuming management of social affairs, and having the means to do so, the commune is neither merely nor primarily a school of democracy; rather, it is democracy itself; it is the basic cell of self-government of the citizens over common affairs.

Some Indian officials saw in the commune the medium for decentralizing political control over community development projects as one means of stimulating greater popular participation in economic development programs.[19] Among socialistically inclined Indian intellectuals those who think the commune can be adapted to the Indian scene are, however, still an uninfluential minority.

Another element in Yugoslavia's appeal is the belief that

[19] The report which recommended democratic decentralization (or *panchayati raj*) is: India, Committee on Plan Projects, *Report of the Team for the Study of Community Projects and National Extension Service*, Vol. I (New Delhi, 1957). Once this policy decision was taken, there was some examination of the Yugoslav experience: e.g., India, Ministry of Community Development and Cooperation, *Reports on Local Government in Yugoslavia* (New Delhi, 1960). I am indebted to Dr. Francine R. Frankel for this information.

she may have succeeded in developing a "higher" form of democracy, i.e., a participatory rather than a representative democracy. This appeals mostly to Gandhian intellectuals (and some socialists) who favor partyless or consensual political processes over competitive elections, because they fear the manipulations of well-financed elites standing behind the parties.[20] High-ranking missions from the U.A.R., Sudan, Nigeria, and Ceylon have spent periods of time in Yugoslavia under U.N. sponsorship, looking into the handling of local government problems. More recently, the Algerians enhanced the importance of the commune as part of their program of overall agrarian reform and revitalization of local government. Commenting that the commune is "designed to reconcile the citizen, the producer, and the consumer, " *Révolution africaine,* the organ of the FLN, also made clear that, as in Yugoslavia, the communal reforms were a reaction to excessive centralized power, an attempt to make government responsive to local needs.[21] Another interested observer was President Ayub Khan of Pakistan. In January 1961 he visited Yugoslavia, the first Head of State from a country linked to a Western alliance system to do so. The Yugoslavs believe that his program of "basic democracies" was implemented "not without some attention to the Yugoslav experience."

C. MULTINATIONAL FEDERALISM

Tito's most important contribution to the establishment of a viable political system in Yugoslavia may well be his defusing of the explosive nationality problem. The federal arrangement of six republics and two autonomous regions has kept the lid on the nationality cauldron. Without eliminating the inevitability and seriousness of present and

[20] The most articulate spokesman for partyless democracy based on some elements of the Yugoslav model is a Gandhian intellectual, Jaya Prakash Narayan, *Socialism, Sarvodaya and Democracy* (Bombay: Asia Publishing House, 1964) , pp. 106-107, 117, 246-259.

[21] "The Commune: The Framework of the Socio-Economic Base," *Révolution africaine,* No. 188 (September 9-16, 1966) .

future difficulties, it has made possible the forging of a nation. Postwar Yugoslavia surmounted the strains of a multinational, multilinguistic, multireligious, and multicultural society, burdened by historical animosities and oft hostile neighbors. It attracted attention as early as 1947 when, to the surprise of Yugoslav leaders who were barely aware of the country, a delegation came from Burma to study the handling of the nationality problem under the new Constitution. The one-Party system has made centralized control possible within a federal and decentralizing political framework. Indeed, a compelling argument for retaining the one-Party system in Yugoslavia can be made on the grounds of the nationality problem. This knowledge of the divisiveness inherent in demands by unsatisfied minorities for self-determination has, *inter alia,* moved Belgrade to uphold dictatorial and military efforts of elites in multinational nonaligned states to impose unity by force, e.g., in Indonesia, Nigeria, and Burma. Yugoslav federalism may not be appropriate for other nations beset by the threat of ethnic fragmentation, but it is an example of what can be accomplished in the building of a national community by a determined, adaptive, well-intentioned leadership.

Sensitivity to the importance of the nationality problem may have provided Yugoslav leaders with some insights relevant to the promotion of nonalignment. The wartime and postwar experience in dealing with hostile and diverse groups and regions impelled the LYC to discard unsuited formulations, to develop a heightened sensitivity to the persistence of historical and cultural continuities, and to allow that socialism could be reached by very different byways. Only by transcending the past animosities of its peoples could the LYC acquire power; and only by building positively for the future could it expect to galvanize continuing popular support and soothe present remembrances of past conflicts. The LYC leadership acquired a facility for mingling with peoples of different backgrounds, a trait that served it well in diplomacy. Furthermore, as the only

European country (excluding the Soviet Union) with a sizeable Moslem minority, Yugoslavia found an important element of communality with Arab and African countries. Many new nations have discerned in the Yugoslav one-Party, multinational, quasi-democratic model evidence of the stability and sustained growth that they seek to develop in their own societies; and also of the implantation, in a hitherto tradition-bound, ethnically particularistic society, of a future-oriented outlook, so essential for modernization.

A *caveat* is in order. The preceding argument is conjecture, offered tentatively because most Afro-Asian countries, in reality, know little about Yugoslavia's nationality problem and tend to perceive the situation as more harmonious than it really is. Their estimate of Yugoslav accomplishments in this area is exaggerated, for nationality divisions have, in the twilight of the Tito era, once again become a central political problem for the leadership.

2. *Building Socialism*

A notable feature of the Yugoslav road to socialism is the principle of self-management functioning institutionally through the Workers' Councils.[22] Introduced in 1950 to

[22] "The Workers' Councils are democratic, economic-political organs of social self-government through which the producers—within the framework of the unified social economic plan, and in conformance with the general interests of the community expressed in the unified economic system—manage the enterprises independently and take a decisive part in the development of the productive forces. The driving force behind the activity of the direct producers in the Workers' Councils, aimed at raising the productivity of labour and speeding up development of the productive forces to an increasing extent, is their determination to improve their own living conditions and the general material standards of the social community by means of improved individual labour, greater business efficiency in the enterprise as a whole, and rapid general economic progress in the social community; and their determination to develop freely their individual creative abilities and propensities, in accordance with the general interests of the working people.

"The Workers' Councils . . . manage the means of production on behalf of the community, being stimulated in their work by their own material and moral-political motives. This is precisely why they are the most suitable social-economic instrument of struggle against bureauc-

curtail abuse of power and bureaucratism, promote "direct and mass democracy," gain popular support against Cominform pressures, and stimulate labor productivity and discipline, self-management has become the faith on which Yugoslav leaders base their hopes for socialist democracy. Nowhere was this principle more enthusiastically embraced than in Algeria.

With independence, the French colons fled, leaving the vast commercial farms without trained managerial personnel. Not wanting to turn them over to private farming, and shying away from Soviet-style collectivization with its stringent bureaucratic controls, Ben Bella sought a solution which would permit a measure of state control, yet give the workers a sense of participation and commitment to the success of the collective or cooperative farms. He adopted the Yugoslav method of self-management, seeing in it a stress on the productive rather than the bureaucratic side of agriculture and an organ to provide the workers with the experience of direct democracy, thereby evoking an enthusiasm which was for him a political necessity. Self-management held out the promise of revolutionizing economic and social relationships, of bringing change to the peasants and gaining their loyalty to new institutional forms which could be used by the FLN to generate economic as well as political development. It also made more administrative sense to place a group of untrained peasants in charge than to appoint one of them Director.

Within six months the nationalized and expropriated industrial, agricultural, mining, and commercial sectors were functioning as self-management bodies, comparable to those in Yugoslavia; within a year, the Algerian government announced that the workers themselves had spontaneously set up self-management systems: " 'Spontaneously'

racy and selfish individualism." *The Programme of the League of Yugoslav Communists* (Belgrade: Jugoslavija, 1958) , pp. 179-180. See also Vojislav Vujović, "Some Actual Problems of the Development of Algeria in the Light of the Work of the National Liberation Front," *Socijalizam*, Vol. vii, No. 5 (May 1964) , pp. 680-684.

means to say without any sort of interference from outside forces or pressure from the top."[23] Ben Bella claimed that Algeria's achievement placed it in "the forefront of contemporary socialist movements"[24]—a claim he brashly made, belittling the Yugoslav experience, during his March 1964 visit, much to the annoyance of his hosts. The Boumedienne government has eschewed grandiose declarations, lauded Yugoslavia's pioneering of self-management,[25] and remained committed to self-management, though experiencing serious difficulties with its operation which has been beset by corruption, inefficiency, and production difficulties.[26]

The genuine interest in self-management should not obscure the lengthening shadow of the procentralization trend which is enveloping more and more of the new nations,[27] many of whom watch the Yugoslav economic reforms, but themselves move toward centralization and state control over the economy. They sense in the Yugoslav decentralization and deetatization the possible outline of their own future course; many realize that centralization breeds

[23] Documentation and Publications Department, Ministry of Information, Government of Algeria, *Documents on Self-Management* (Bone, Algeria, September 1963), p. 26.

[24] During a visit to a factory near Belgrade, Ben Bella addressed the Workers' Council. He expressed appreciation for Yugoslavia's assistance, outlined Algeria's difficulties, and then said: "You in Yugoslavia have been applying the system of self-management for the past few years, and we have only started this project. We did not waste a lot of time in discussing the matter, since the workers themselves made up their minds to do so. In fact, both the land and the various enterprises were abandoned by the colons, and the workers then spontaneously began to work on the land. And if it may appear necessary to provide evidence of self-management as the only road harmonizing socialism and democracy, in that event we too could serve as an example of it. . . ." Joint Translation Service (Belgrade) No. 3736 (March 7, 1964), p. 26.

[25] *Révolution africaine*, No. 250 (November 30-December 6, 1967), p. 36.

[26] *The New York Times*, July 16, 1966; October 23, 1966.

[27] At a meeting of African states in Dakar, Senegal, the delegates unanimously agreed "that the state must hold in its own hands the principal economic factors, secure a planned economy, and become the basic investor." Kiro Hadži-Vasilev, "African Ways to Socialism," *Review of International Affairs*, Vol. XIV, No. 307 (January 20, 1963), p. 5.

bureaucratism and is counterproductive to development, and that they may in time have recourse to a variant of self-management. However, as long as political instability threatens, centralization will preoccupy elites in developing countries. The growing divergence between the trend of economic development in Yugoslavia and that in most Third World countries is readily discernible in policies concerning agriculture, economic planning, and private foreign investment: whereas Yugoslavia abandoned forced collectivization in 1953, in Algeria, the U.A.R., and elsewhere collectivization and state cooperatives dominate official thinking; whereas Yugoslavia has weakened the central government's authority to legislate economic planning on the Workers' Councils, in the Third World planning is a byword, and excessive planning, endemic and constricting; whereas, to import Western technology and hard currency, Yugoslavia passed an extraordinary law (the first Communist country to do so) permitting enterprises to enter into joint investment projects with foreign private investment capital on the basis of equitable sharing of risks and profits, among other nonaligned countries there is still suspicion of private capital for political reasons and strong opposition to its return lest the flag follow the dollar. (Unlike many of the elites in nonaligned countries, the Yugoslavs feel sufficiently confident of remaining masters in their own house, but it remains to be seen whether the inducements to private capital are attractive enough to bring large-scale investment.)

The relevance of the Yugoslav model of development for Afro-Asian countries has been subject to other reservations. One longtime Ethiopian diplomat resident in Belgrade said that he admired Yugoslavia's achievements but was not sure what the Yugoslavs meant by "socialism," and preferred a free enterprise economy. "I have lived in Belgrade for several years," he said, "and I still find the Workers' Council and self-management incomprehensible. How then can anyone emulate them?" A key official at the Indonesian embassy acknowledged his government's initial interest but added that it soon became apparent the operation of Workers' Councils and self-management required a level of education and social consciousness still largely absent in Indonesia. In Algeria the Minister of Industry and Energy, Mr. Belaid Abdelsalam, prevents union meddling in the state enterprises under his jurisdiction because he believes "that the workers proved incompetent in running the 'self-managed' small industries they took over when the former French owners left the country following Algeria's independence in 1962."[28] There are skeptics even among Yugoslav officials. One influential social scientist observed that the vice of self-exaltation among certain of his countrymen had led to exaggerated evaluations concerning the influence of the Yugoslav experience for developing countries. Not only was self-management as practiced in Yugoslavia virtually impossible to describe to a foreigner but, he thought, it was now an impediment to further economic and social development, an innovation that had become an orthodoxy, with all that that implied. No less a personage than President Tito lent substance to criticism, for during an interview in Cairo in 1965 in which he noted the achievements of self-management he added:

> Of course, we are still faced with certain difficulties and weaknesses which are not always of an objective nature, but may be explained by the fact that these principles are not always consistently applied in the work of individual bodies or individual sectors of economic and social life, or because the activities of some bodies have not been adjusted to these principles to a sufficient degree.[29]

3. Observations

Causal relationships between the ideas, institutions, and practices of one country and those of another cannot be traced accurately in this age of sonic borrowings, but they do exist. What was overlooked by the American diplomat

[28] *The New York Times*, January 26, 1968.
[29] *Socialist Thought and Practice*, No. 18 (April-June 1965), p. 20.

who insinuated that if the developing countries were searching for a model to emulate they would do better with prosperous Sweden than pinched Yugoslavia was the oft demonstrated fact that political appeal in international affairs is more than an amalgam of national income and political respectability. We are not sure why an Algerian Minister says, "It is the Yugoslav model that inspires us";[30] why Tito earned so prominent a place in the councils of the nonaligned; why delegations from the Third World come to Belgrade; why intellectuals in nonaligned countries are interested in Yugoslavia's brand of socialist democracy. Perhaps the key lies in the trust and intimacy that Yugoslavia evokes among the new nations who do not fear aggrandizement from it or intervention in their domestic affairs; perhaps in the courage and determination that Yugoslavia demonstrated in helping to pioneer nonalignment; perhaps in the conviction that it communicates of belief in socialism; perhaps in the pragmatism, in the adaptation to changing circumstances, in the receptivity to improvisation wedded to shared aspirations. Chimerical? Exaggerated? Unrealistic? Yes. But there it is.

The Economics of Influencebuilding

In the totality of Yugoslav influencebuilding efforts in the Third World there remains one major unexamined component: the economic. Supplementing and reinforcing the institutional linkages and the psycho-political-organizational relevance of features of the Yugoslav political system are the trade, aid, technical assistance, and joint ventures composing the spectrum of functional economic cooperation.

1. Trade

Expanded trade has been a key goal of Yugoslav diplomacy toward the Third World since President Tito's first visit to South Asia in December 1954. Then beginning to in-

30 *The New York Times,* January 16, 1967.

dustrialize, Yugoslavia sought markets for its new manufactures and sources of raw materials. Glowing possibilities were foreseen for Yugoslav enterprises which were assumed capable of supplying many of the industrial products needed by the new nations.[31] Increased industrial production was dependent on foreign trade since it was impossible, given the limited potentialities of the Yugoslav internal market, to absorb all production. The major industries—metal processing, shipbuilding, and electronics—must compete in world markets. As the commodity structure of Yugoslav exports has altered, almost half of the exports of manufactured goods go to developing countries, leading many Yugoslav economists to regard the addition of new trade partners in Africa, Asia, and Latin America as vital to the placement of Yugoslav products and the further development of the economy.[32]

Though trade with developing countries has grown steadily, from less than 2 percent of total foreign trade in 1954 to about 15 to 16 percent in 1967, it has fallen short of early expectations and has not provided the answer to Yugoslav economic problems. Not only has the volume of trade remained below the level anticipated by Yugoslav planners, but "the fact was that for the most part the countries of the third world could provide neither the capital goods Yugoslavia wanted nor the free currencies with which these goods could be purchased elsewhere."[33] The major trading partners are generally countries with which Yugoslavia enjoys the closest political ties, i.e., India, the U.A.R., Algeria, the Sudan, Indonesia, Ethiopia, and Brazil. Trade with India, Yugoslavia's best customer among the developing countries, rose from less than one million dollars in

[31] For example, see V. Mesarić, "Yugoslavia's Economic Cooperation with Southeastern Asia," *Review of International Affairs*, Vol. VIII, No. 197 (June 16, 1957), p. 12.

[32] Vojislav Vlajić, *Jugoslavija u Svetskoj Razmeni* (Belgrade: Sedma Sila, 1965), pp. 47-48. See also Todora Dragomanović, "A Review of Yugoslavia's Relations with Developing Countries," *Medjunarodni Problemi*, Vol. XVI, No. 2 (1964), pp. 157-162.

[33] John C. Campbell, *Tito's Separate Road* (New York: Harper and Row, 1967), pp. 71-72.

1955 to about one hundred million in 1967. But despite the expansion of trade with these countries and the multiplicity of forms of economic cooperation, and apart from trade pacts of the classical variety, Yugoslavia is too small to be a major purchaser or supplier for any of them. To none does it represent more than 2 to 3 percent of their total foreign trade, and even these levels are seldom reached. Furthermore, Yugoslavia's trade with developing countries has been artificially stimulated by generous dinar credits.

2. *Credits*

Yugoslavia's ability to compete with Western firms depends on the quantity of long-term credits it can grant to developing countries. To sell machinery a country must give commercial credits. By 1967 Yugoslavia had extended credits for more than 650 million dollars, in nonconvertible dinars, including approximately 200 million to African countries. These credits involved deliveries of Yugoslav industrial goods and the construction by Yugoslav firms of more than 120 different projects: hydro-electric power stations in India, Cambodia, Guinea, Togo, Ethiopia, and Syria; cement works in the Sudan and Ethiopia; textile mills in Algeria; tractor plants in Ghana and the U.A.R.; ports in Syria, Tunisia, and Ghana; slaughterhouses in Mali, Tunisia, and Liberia; a leatherware factory and food processing plant in Algeria. These are a few of the projects constructed with Yugoslav funds, equipment, and technicians.

A small country with scarce reserves of convertible currencies, Yugoslavia is one of the few developing countries giving credits, though these are tied to the purchase of Yugoslav goods and services. Its purposes, like those of Israel, Taiwan, the U.A.R., and India, are political as well as economic; the credits are given on favorable commercial terms—generally 3 percent—not only to compete economically with Western and Soviet bloc countries, but to reap some of the uncertain harvest of "political goodwill." Since most of the recipients of Yugoslav foreign aid (i.e., credits) cannot repay in convertible currency and indeed insist that trade be organized on a barter basis, Yugoslavia must accept in payment goods or raw materials produced by these countries. Since few African countries have anything except fruits and other agricultural commodities to sell, Yugoslavia has had to accept fruits, and often second grade ones at that, because the prime fruits are sold in hard currency markets. Thus, as one Yugoslav wryly noted, "for its capital goods Yugoslavia receives second-rate bananas." Yet credits are necessary to attract buyers of Yugoslav manufactures, otherwise developing countries might purchase even more of their machinery and finished products with Soviet and Western credits than they do. Yugoslav enterprises had expected developing countries to find their technology and products congenial because of the greater similarity in level of development, only to find them obstinately acquiring the most sophisticated equipment from the West and the Soviet Union; even the poor want the latest models.

Credits are also the ante necessary to play at influence-building; since 1965, however, the government has had fewer available to dispense abroad. The economic reforms reduced the government's ability to offer subsidies; they also granted individual enterprises increased autonomy over resources. As a result, many African and Asian countries, who have established state trading corporations which they consider a progressive development, find the present decentralized and competitive Yugoslav arrangement quite alien for a socialist country; not fully understanding the extent of Yugoslav liberalization, they are frustrated, often irate, at the difficulties of doing business with Yugoslav firms in contrast to the bureaucratically familiar pattern of dealing with state corporations in other East European socialist countries.

3. Technical Assistance

Technical assistance is an adjunct of influencebuilding. It can enable a small country to have an impact greater than quantifiable data might suggest; and, being highly personalized, it can with modest expenditures make impressions that have more lasting effects than trade or aid on basic political attitudes.

The principal organization responsible for the implementation of technical assistance agreements is the Federal Institute for International Technical Cooperation. Originally established in 1952 under the title of Administration for Technical Assistance in order to handle technical aid from the United Nations, it was reorganized in late 1953 when it started to serve as a vehicle for extending Yugoslav assistance to developing countries. The first recipient was Ethiopia. In general the Institute is concerned with two types of technical assistance activities: (1) at the request of governments, it makes experts available in various fields such as public health, agriculture, and engineering; (2) it arranges for fellowships and training programs for foreign personnel who come to Yugoslavia, excluding the regular placement of students in universities, which is arranged through the Commission for Foreign Cultural Relations.

During the 1954-1960 period the scale of operation was modest. By the late 1950's and early 1960's, the tempo and scope grew, as Yugoslav involvement and the number of new nations ballooned. From 1954 to 1967 Yugoslavia placed about 2,500 experts at the disposal of the governments of thirty-two developing countries; approximately 2,400 citizens from seventy-five nations completed Yugoslav schools under scholarships given by the government; 900 students received specialized training and completed postgraduate courses; in 1968, a thousand or so Yugoslav experts were working in developing countries.[34] The bulk of these specialists have been sent to Africa, in particular, Algeria, the U.A.R., Tunisia, Ethiopia, Libya, and the Sudan. This type of technical assistance is financed either by the Yugoslav Government or by the requesting government which pays the technicians in local currencies, with

[34] Blagoje Bogavac, "Yugoslavia and International Technical Cooperation," *Review of International Affairs*, Vol. XIX, No. 430 (March 5, 1968), p. 24.

the Yugoslav Government contributing a special overseas allowance in hard currency. One of the Deputy-Directors of the Federal Institute for International Technical Co-operation emphasized that in all cases, "the specialists are placed at the disposal of the requesting government; the specialists are not subject to the authority of Yugoslav administration, that is to say, the Institute, which remains responsible only for recruitment but not for supervision of the experts in the field." The experts do not have any special diplomatic status, as have U.N., Soviet, and some American specialists. Yugoslav technicians in a foreign country are in the employ of that government and subject to its supervision. Belgrade adopted this approach because of its sensitivity to the manifold circumstances in which interference may be perceived by insecure elites, and its desire to reassure recipient governments using Yugoslav technicians.[35]

In addition to technicians recruited and dispatched by the government, several thousand experts have been sent by Yugoslav commercial enterprises operating abroad: e.g., "Naftaplin" specializes in oil drilling and has experts in India, Ethiopia, and Libya; "Ingra" is building transmission lines in the Sudan and Syria; "Prvomajska" and "Ivo Lola-Ribar" sell and install machinery in the U.A.R., Syria, and India.

Yugoslav technicians have compiled an enviable record of performance. Politically, they do not arouse suspicion. Coming from a small country with no residual economic interests in the new nations, they do not seek to leave behind a "presence" in the ministries or factories which could be interpreted by the host government as a possible lever for gaining a future foothold. Psychologically, they have proven highly adaptable and hardworking, often more so than at home. Not coming from a society with a high standard of living, they do not find the difficulties of adjustment to a society with a lower standard of living arduous,

---

[35] The details of technical assistance, the status of specialists, their salaries and expenses, are spelled out in advance. Many of the protocols are published in *Dodatak Službeni Lista SFR Jugoslavija.*

as do many from highly developed countries. Themselves heirs to a social revolution, they do not form closed or restrictive social circles; they mingle easily and widely. Economically, the Yugoslavs come relatively low-priced compared to the pay required to attract specialists from Western countries. At times this lower salary even spurs them on to prove that they are as capable as their higher paid Western counterparts. Professionally, they have done a good job in preparing native specialists to assume full responsibility. Empathetic, able, and conscientious, they come not as "missionaries" but to carry out a particular task, earn some hard currency, and return home. The three hospitals operated by Yugoslavs in Libya, for example, have received repeated plaudits from the authorities.

The Yugoslav government has responded generously to emergency requests. During the winter of 1962-1963, after the exodus of French settlers, Algerian officials faced a crisis in arranging the spring planting. A call was made to Belgrade for tractors and tractor maintenance personnel. Within four months Yugoslavia provided 400 tractors and trained more than 600 Algerians to handle the situation. On the eve of the African Summit in 1961, Emperor Haile Selassie wanted to have an exhibition of Ethiopia's industrial progress ready for the delegates. Several months of discussions in the Ministry of Industry and Commerce ended with the conclusion that a suitably impressive exhibition could not be organized in the time remaining. The Yugoslav specialists working in the Planning Office in Addis Ababa convinced the Ethiopians the job could be done in a month. Working round-the-clock, and with full cooperation of the Embassy, they sparked the enthusiasm of the Ethiopians and met their deadline. The record, however, is not one of unmixed success. When President de Gaulle capriciously withdrew all French officials and aid from Guinea in late 1958, Sekou Touré urgently requested 500 teachers for the primary schools. The Yugoslavs promptly sent several hundred, but these were soon withdrawn when the Guineans complained that the students knew French better than the teachers. There are other problems: too few technicians to meet the needs of most new nations, and an even smaller number who are linguistically competent. Notwithstanding wholehearted efforts to meet Algerian requests, Yugoslavia cannot match the 15,000 French technicians and teachers working in that country. Yugoslavia is, after all, itself small and developing. Some Yugoslavs believe the Africans are taking their assistance for granted: they sometimes pay irregularly, and when they do pay, they criticize the Yugoslavs for not being altruistic, for trying to profiteer. Despite these shortcomings, the overall record of technical assistance has been excellent. According to one Belgrade official, "the Yugoslavs are the most appreciated whites in Africa." Political bonds have been strengthened by the performance of Yugoslavs working on irrigation projects, roadbuilding, power plants, small factories, and public health. The availability, empathy, and ability of these technicians have greatly reinforced Yugoslavia's other economic efforts.

4. *Joint Ventures*

Since the Belgrade (1961) and Cairo (1962) Conferences, Yugoslav leaders have paid increasing attention to the creation of new forms of economic cooperation with developing countries. Disappointed by the apparent limits of commodity exchanges negotiated along traditional lines, anxious over the continued strong ties between the new nations and the former metropoles, and fearful lest they be left out of integration efforts generated by the European Economic Community, they give priority to new institutional arrangements. Hence their commitment to UNCTAD and to expanding bilateral economic relations.

In a number of instances the Yugoslavs pioneered the establishment of mixed companies with Morocco, the Sudan, and Nigeria. Though India and African countries have sought more such arrangements, Yugoslavia has been of two minds. Obviously Belgrade welcomes expanded economic ties. At the same time, it is troubled by ideological ambivalence: can a socialist country enter into international economic cooperation for the joint exploitation of economic resources in a foreign country? Should Yugoslav investment abroad be geared to making profit? Would this not open Belgrade to charges of "revisionism" and betrayal of socialism by Moscow and Peking? In the case of an agreement concluded with Morocco in early 1966 after nearly four years of negotiation, Belgrade allayed its uneasiness by insisting on a clause that states Morocco can, in the joint exploitation of the six nonferrous metal mines, "whenever it thinks necessary, take over the management of the mines, provided it pays its debts."[36]

A bold step was taken at the Tripartite Conference, held in New Delhi from October 21 to 24, 1966.[37] While the leaders of India, the U.A.R., and Yugoslavia gave considerable attention to international tensions—deploring the Vietnam war, neocolonialism and colonialism "in all their forms and manifestations," and the arms race, and reaffirming their commitment to nonalignment—in the economic realm they contributed something new. According to Prime Minister Indira Gandhi, "perhaps the most outstanding result of the meeting" was the collective approach "to the economic challenges to nonalignment and peaceful coexistence": they resolved to join in an effort "to expand the area of mutual cooperation, increase trade exchanges among themselves, pool technical and scientific experience, and undertake joint endeavors to develop mutually beneficial patterns of trade and development."[38] Representatives of the three countries met in New Delhi in December 1966 and established three *ad hoc* working groups: one to negotiate tariff preferences, payment procedures, and measures for

---

[36] *Politika*, February 2, 1966.

[37] The meeting was the third: the first had been at Brioni in 1956, the second, in Cairo in 1966. See Milan Draškić, "The Tripartite Meeting and the Asian Situation," *Socialist Thought and Practice*, No. 24 (October-December 1966), pp. 152-159.

[38] *Yugoslav Facts and Views*, No. 15 (October 26, 1966), p. 4.

expanding trade; another to consider possibilities for economic specialization; the third to investigate the establishment of a joint shipping company. Despite the setback to U.A.R. participation occasioned by the June 1967 war, the three countries proceeded with a major first step, implementing an agreement on tariff reduction in April 1968. The mutual concessions cover more than 500 products and are valid for five years.

Yugoslav officials say the principal difficulty will be finding means of compensation that are comparable for each country in terms of what each brings to the arrangement. For example, Yugoslavia, with a fairly well-developed ship-building industry, is prepared to concentrate in this area, provided that the U.A.R. and India can offer goods that are equally advantageous to Yugoslavia. Cotton from the U.A.R. for Yugoslav textile mills is one possibility. Both Yugoslavia and the U.A.R. have well advanced television industries and could presumably provide for India's needs. However, the Yugoslavs realize that for military purposes any modern country needs an advanced electronics industry, of which television is an offshoot, hence India's reluctance to be dependent on another country in so vital an area. Moreover, the structure of commodity exchange is changing under the impact of industrialization. India previously purchased railroad cars from Yugoslavia; today it produces its own. What can Yugoslavia purchase to its economic advantage from India in repayment for the 80 million dollar credit granted in 1966 and for which it has agreed to accept repayment in rupees? Talks continue.

In the past, the Yugoslav position on mixed companies was not really flexible; but enterprises are coming to accept the necessity of using their capital for the creation of new capital, as well as profit. The "Iskra" enterprise launched what could be a new course for commercial risk taking by Yugoslav firms by investing the sum of 300,000 dollars in the Asian Electronics Company of Bombay in return for half the profit earned from the venture.[39]

[39] *Politika*, January 14, 1966.

5. Domestic Dissonances

The wisdom of the foreign aid program is not universally accepted in decisionmaking circles. Critics argue several points: that Yugoslavia is not a rich country and can ill-afford to extend credits, the repayment of which is all too frequently in commodities unlikely to strengthen the economy; that expectations for these credits have been exaggerated—the new African nations have not redirected their trade from the former metropole to new sources of supply, nor indeed have they utilized the credits already extended; that Yugoslavia should not distribute its credits widely, but on the contrary should concentrate on a few countries which are reliable in repaying and with whom it has better long-term prospects for expanded and mutually beneficial economic cooperation. On occasion criticisms have even been aired publicly: one Bosnian delegate in the Federal Assembly asked, "Why does Yugoslavia offer technical assistance to some developing countries while such assistance is still needed in some underdeveloped areas of Yugoslavia itself?"[40]

Since 1966 the questioning of Yugoslav economic policy toward developing countries has become more overt. The acknowledgment over television by a high government official that Yugoslav claims against foreign countries, "mainly in the developing countries where our country has constructed a number of enterprises, sold equipment, or done other services," amounted to 272 million dollars,[41] apparently signalled the beginning of a series of such reevaluations.[42] The dispute is over the economic importance of the

[40] Belgrade, January 13, 1966. Cited in a mimeographed information bulletin circulated in the Institute for International Politics and Economy.

[41] *Borba*, January 28, 1966. The statement was made by Kiro Gligorov, a member of the Federal Executive Council.

[42] A number of conferences, attended by representatives from the government, Party, and academic community, have been held in recent years. One of the most comprehensive and informative presentations of Yugoslav economic relations with the Third World was offered at a two-day conference, sponsored by the Higher School of Political Science,

developing countries to Yugoslavia's future development. At a time of membership in GATT, of expanded trade with COMECON countries, and of far-reaching economic reforms designed to make Yugoslav enterprises more efficient and their wares competitive in Western markets, economic relations with developing countries have settled on a plateau with little likelihood of increasing beyond their present 13 to 16 percent of Yugoslavia's total foreign trade.

One consequence of the 1965 reforms is that the second echelon levels of the Party and government are less interested in foreign policy and more occupied with the implications for the political system of moving toward market socialism: aggravated unemployment; political confusion, particularly at the commune level, in the face of a precipitous decline in government subsidies; uncertainty over the Party's role in society; and rising nationality discord. In addition, with profitability replacing political loyalty as a criterion for material reward and advancement, there is a renewed interest in closer ties with Western Europe. Prior to August 21, 1968, there were also high hopes for expanded economic relations with an Eastern Europe less dominated by the Soviet Union, but the Soviet invasion of Czechoslovakia has exploded these for the time being. Looking to the future, internal economic and nationality problems, the urgent need to gain privileged access to Western European trade groupings, and the aggravated sense of insecurity engendered by the recent turnabout in Soviet policy, all could well draw the energies of Yugoslav leaders more and more to European affairs and away from the Third World.

The importance of nonalignment *politically* to Yugoslav

---

in Ljubljana (June 23-24, 1966). Among the topics developed were the nature and structure of Yugoslavia's foreign trade with developing countries, the pattern of investment, the experience of the major enterprises, the key organizational and institutional difficulties faced by Yugoslavia in its relations with developing countries, and the specifics of technical assistance. *Jugoslavija i privredni razvoj zemalja u razvoju: materijali simpozijuma* (Ljubljana, 1966), mimeographed edition, 371 pages.

national interest does not appear to be in question. The same cannot be said of the economic implications. Criticisms have impelled Tito to confront this sensitive topic in various speeches, especially in the less-developed regions of the country. Talking in Priština in Kosmet on March 26, 1967, he defended the grant of more than 650 million dollars in credits to African and Asian countries on the ground that "sooner or later, this assistance will be returned to us, and indeed this assistance will prove profitable for us."[43] Tito emphasized that this was one way in which Yugoslavia had built its prestige in the world, especially among the newly liberated nations of Africa and Asia: "Today our country is playing a role as if it had a hundred million rather than twenty million." He also made clear, in a mixture of moral and material imperatives, the reasons for helping these countries:

> It is of course clear that in trade relations these countries cannot be equal partners as would be possible for them if they were to have a highly developed national economy. However, we must not wait for them to develop, for if everybody were to wait for this to happen—they would never be able to develop. . . .
>
> It is therefore expected of us, of the socialist countries, to engage there more, and to extend them what assistance we can. Because, tomorrow, when they are a little more developed, these countries will be good partners for us, we shall be able to develop equal mutual trade with them.

On other occasions, Tito has urged expansion not contraction of economic commitments to developing countries so that Yugoslavia would be an exemplar of equality, dependability, and disinterested involvement in the strengthening of socialism and mutual ties between states and peoples. These views have been echoed by other Communists of Tito's generation and temperament. One prominent political writer dismisses the economic arguments against in-

[43] Joint Translation Service (Belgrade), No. 4669 (March 26-27, 1967), p. 50.

creasing help to the Third World, asserting that "Yugoslavs are not just merchants." He "would hate to see Yugoslavia become the Switzerland of the Balkans: prosperous, smug, insular." The dissonances within the leadership remain, however, compounded by the evident shortcomings of Yugoslav efforts and capabilities, and by differences over specific policies.

6. *Disappointments and Pitfalls*

Yugoslavia has encountered many problems in its economic relations with developing countries: some stem from conditions in the Third World, others inhere in the Yugoslav milieu itself. Its officials are reluctant for diplomatic reasons to specify the difficulties that inhibit efficiently organized exchanges. They will acknowledge the prevalence there of endemic weaknesses: widespread corruption; incessant manipulations for power that adversely affect commercial contacts; a preoccupation with social status that complicates negotiations; the relative backwardness of agents and agencies responsible for conducting foreign trade; the poor education of many of the officials; and a distorted picture of the Yugoslav economic system. Further, some developing countries, e.g., the U.A.R., set limits on the amount of their "cash" crops (those that can earn hard currency) that they will sell to countries like Yugoslavia. Given the limited supply of these crops, Yugoslavia is handicapped in what it can purchase. Quite frequently the new nations retain close economic links with the former metropole, which has experience, connections, and quality goods, making Yugoslav entry into these markets difficult. While disappointed with the constricting effect these conditions have on trade, many Yugoslav officials are more disconcerted by the shortcomings of their own people.

During the 1958-1968 period, Yugoslav enterprises compiled an impressive record in more than thirty developing countries. They built harbors, hydroelectric power stations and factories, roads and artesian wells. In general these were well-received. However, glaring weaknesses emerged which officials acknowledge and are prepared to discuss.[44]

First, officials lamented the lack of cooperation between enterprises seeking commercial orders abroad. All too often an enterprise is so engrossed in its own quest for business that it neglects to consider the advantages inherent in pooling resources with other firms to maximize its competitive posture abroad. In a discussion with members of the Federal Economic Chamber on December 24, 1965, President Tito, noting the paucity of integrated managerial overviews, criticized the indifference of firms cooperating on projects in developing countries to anything but their own particular responsibility:

> One of the chief negative phenomena is the well-known lack of care of our enterprises, not only of export-enterprises, but also of investor-enterprises who are building factories abroad. Such defective work harms our country's prestige and results in significant damage.[45]

Less than two years later he was caustic toward exporters who make a quick profit and move on to new pickings, and urged greater probity in dealing with new nations:

> The problem of a good reputation concerns not only quality . . . the soundness of the operation plays an enormous role. This is particularly true among the developing countries, among the African and Asian peoples, who have a great mistrust in general, since [everyone] robbed them in the past. Now, if we were to go to these countries

[44] The persistence of many of these faults must be discouraging to Yugoslav officials. In 1956, in an article listing "the subjective shortcomings" impeding efforts to make headway in Middle Eastern markets, a Yugoslav analyst wrote: "These shortcomings include: the still inadequate trade network on the market itself, frequent cases of unorganized appearance on the market and disloyal rivalry between the Yugoslav exporter and producer enterprises, failure to execute the deals concluded within the terms stipulated by contract, defective packing of the goods delivered, neglect of business contacts established, etc." A. Partonić, "Yugoslavia and the Near and Middle East Markets," *Review of International Affairs*, Vol. VII, No. 152-153 (August 1-15, 1956) , p. 18.

[45] *Politika*, January 18, 1966.

to take the greatest advantage and then leave, to let happen what may, we would lose our reputation and would have difficulties in selling in those countries.[46]

Second, Yugoslav businessmen too seldom critically appraise their capabilities, particularly in relation to the fulfillment of a contract. All too often they agree with alacrity to all requested conditions without reference to climatic, geographic, or institutional difficulties. Thus, they overlook the monsoon or the poor harbor facilities in agreeing to a particular delivery date. This incomplete knowledge of local conditions denotes a casualness toward the rigors of business performance and competition that costs heavily in reputation and in arbitration penalties.

Third, trained market analysts are in short supply. Enterprises agree to build the kinds of factories that do not even exist in Yugoslavia or for which they do not have the requisite technical know-how or equipment. In Ethiopia, for example, a joint-enterprise department store was set up. Yugoslav enterprises provided heavy Central European furniture, which could not be sold in Yugoslavia or the West. They were ignorant of the operations of Danish, Swedish, and Italian competitors in Ethiopia, and the venture failed dismally. Also, Yugoslav firms have inadequate inventories to draw on to meet stipulated delivery dates. In Burma, for example, Japanese salesmen arrive with many samples of textile goods, and can promise delivery within one month; Yugoslav salesmen have few samples, and cannot offer delivery before six to twelve months, and even then without full confidence in fulfillment.

Fourth, some of the mistakes which were made in Yugoslavia's own industrialization have been repeated abroad: improper investigation of plant sites; miscalculations as to the marketing possibilities for finished goods; outmoded technology that is utilized at considerable cost; a tendency to obtain a contract by offering the latest solutions or factories to a customer, knowing it would be wiser to propose

---

[46] Quoted in *East Europe*, Vol. 16, No. 10 (October 1967), p. 33.

a less advanced technique that would be more in accord with the client's capability.

Fifth, there is a growing realization that responsibility does not end with the construction of a plant, that it also involves supervision to ensure the proper functioning of the plant, the training of adequate staff, and the preparations for sale abroad of finished products.

Sixth, far-sighted officials say that to expand its trade materially with the Third World in the decades ahead, Yugoslavia will have to restructure the pattern of domestic commodity production. Thus, to expand trade with Burma, Yugoslavia should deemphasize its reliance on domestic production of rice and purchase it instead from Burma, which has a comparative advantage in this commodity. Some food product not available from a trading partner in the Third World should be planted in Macedonia instead of rice. However, at present, Yugoslav farmers are planting even more rice, thereby precluding expanded purchases of Yugoslav goods by Burma, Thailand, or Cambodia.

Seventh, because of the limited credits Yugoslavia can extend, its firms must plan for better cost accounting procedures, for financial adjustments to allow for inflation, and for avoiding resale in hard currency areas of goods purchased from developing countries, e.g., Indian jute and Egyptian cotton.

Eighth, credits should not be awarded in desultory fashion, but be used to stimulate the construction of factories whose products Yugoslavia would be willing to accept in repayment, thus establishing a sound basis for trade. Since Yugoslavia cannot aspire to self-sufficiency, why build factories at home which duplicate those built abroad? For example, why build leather factories, when some African countries intend to stress such industries, and when most of the hides must be imported from convertible currency areas, adding to the drain on Yugoslavia's balance of payments? Officials say candidly that Yugoslav credits should promote both the transformation of a developing country's economy and the development of an integrated pattern of foreign trade, but there is no agreement on what to stress.

Perhaps most critical is the necessity of modernizing Yugoslav attitudes toward business. Nowhere is this more poignantly evident than in the field of tourism, Yugoslavia's major source of hard currency earnings. "Why," I asked one official, "do you not simplify the procedures for permitting tourists to mail gifts home? Why don't Yugoslav stores catering to the tourist trade provide, at cost, a wrapping and mailing service to encourage purchases of local handicrafts, as is customary in Italy, Switzerland, or other countries?"

"If I were to explain," he answered resignedly, "I would require ten days of vacation to do so."

Before maximizing its economic capability for influence-building, Yugoslavia will first have to set its own house in order.

The Limits of Influencebuilding

The ultimate measure of influence is action: did the impact of Country A on countries B and C affect their responses to international problems? A definitive answer is unknowable. The variables are complex and do not lend themselves to comparability. The success in influence-building of country A upon country B may be perceived variously by A, B, and C, with each adopting policies based on its own perceptions and predicated on a level of influence which, in fact, does not exist. Tito's influence on Nasser may be marginal, but if the United States or the Soviet Union perceives it as being greater than it is, then the attitude of Washington or Moscow toward Belgrade will be different from what it would otherwise be. The calculations of policymakers in Washington and Moscow are based on certain assumptions about the influence wielded by different countries, and these assumptions are rarely based on empirical referents, perhaps because what can be measured with relative precision in international relations does not illumine policy purposes or the subjective evaluations on which they are formulated.

Several purposes underlie influencebuilding: to enhance national security through diplomatic support and the cultivation of close ties with governments to which one hopes to turn in crisis; to speak and be listened to in the councils of decisionmaking bodies, be they national, regional, or international; to affect the behavior of foreign elites in a manner conducive to the general advancement of one's own perceived interests; to promote ties resulting in a strengthening of one's socio-economic system; to gain adherents to one's vision of international community.

Influence waxes and wanes: *tout lasse, tout casse, tout passe*. It fluctuates according to the effectiveness and capability of the courting power, the receptivity of the courted to what is offered, and the conditions inhering in the international environment. Decisionmakers confront bitter policy dilemmas: e.g., despite Tito's relationship with Nasser, until June 1967 Yugoslavia not only maintained diplomatic relations with Israel, but Israel was its second best trading partner in the Middle East; Yugoslav criticisms of American policy in Vietnam were kept within limits tolerable to the United States because of Yugoslavia's desire for economic advantages.[47] In both cases Yugoslavia was criticized by more militant nonaligned countries and, as a consequence, found its capacity for influencebuilding there limited by its immediate national interests.

The criteria for determining success are imprecise and depend on the point of view of the beholder. In the absence of full disclosures by policymakers of the factors which impelled them to respond to Yugoslav policy and the phe-

---

[47] Yugoslavia was also restrained in its criticisms of Britain's Rhodesian policy. When the Ian Smith regime repudiated Whitehall and declared its independence in the fall of 1965, and the British Government failed to suppress the move, the African Ambassadors in Belgrade caucused and decided that a more vigorous presentation of the African case should be made to the Yugoslav public. They requested the assistance of the Secretariat for Foreign Affairs to obtain time over television and radio, and to obtain greater news coverage. The Secretariat moved cautiously because it did not want to jeopardize friendly relations with Britain. A talk was permitted over radio, but according to Africans the reports in the press were watered-down versions.

nomenon of nonalignment, assessments of what Yugo-slavia achieved must be individual. The Afro-Asian governments have accorded Yugoslavia a permanent seat in the councils of the nonaligned—the only European country so honored—because Yugoslav contributions have been continual, important, and consonant with their own aims. They have backed Yugoslav initiatives and activism because they agree with them. They have responded generously to Yugoslav efforts to broaden the base of economic relationships, even though Yugoslavia can never be of more than marginal value to their developmental efforts. Their present relationship with Yugoslavia connotes respect, perhaps more for remembrances of past services than for any expectation of future rewards. Unlike the Soviets, the Yugoslavs are not hampered in their dealings with developing countries by obsessive secretiveness or mistrust; unlike the Americans, they are socialists and advocates of fundamental changes in the international socio-economic order. There are no "ugly Yugoslavs."

There is in this record sufficient evidence to justify a favorable verdict on Yugoslav efforts at influencebuilding. Their endeavors have served them well. But the changing international environment is presenting the Yugoslav leadership with challenges for which their past endeavors may not be of more than passing value. Further insights into the systemic factors inexorably checking and placing a ceiling on Yugoslav attainments in influencebuilding can best be discerned in the concrete example of the evolution of Yugoslav-U.A.R. relations and in the larger context of developments in the nonaligned world since 1964.

CHAPTER VII

Yugoslavia and the United Arab Republic: A Study of the Evolution of Interdependence

FRIENDSHIP WITH the United Arab Republic is the cornerstone of Yugoslav diplomacy in the nonaligned world. The consequence of the vagaries of international politics, the diminution of the core of charismatic leaders among the nonaligned nations, a communality of strategic interests in the Mediterranean region, and the existence of shared problems and positions on foreign policy issues, it has been cemented by the mutual esteem and personal regard of Presidents Tito and Nasser. The Belgrade-Cairo entente conditions Yugoslavia's approach to the Arab world, to much of Africa south of the Sahara, and to endeavors to bring the nonaligned countries into a cooperating constellation.

While the departure of the other commanding figures of the nonaligned world contributed to the preeminent status of Tito and Nasser and brought the two even closer, their personal friendship had already become a major factor in their international relations. Since their first meeting on February 5, 1955, the two have developed a friendship unique among the leaders of the nonaligned world, and perhaps even in the international relations of the postwar period. During the 1955-1968 period they met more than twenty times, a frequency of personal contact not approached by the leaders of any other two countries. Continuity in power was a factor, but coalescing international outlooks and interests were of greater importance. The two senior statesmen of nonalignment share the realization that any initiative for strengthening it will most likely have to come from Belgrade or Cairo, though since June 5, 1967, Cairo's capacity for bold initiatives has been seriously limited; and since August 21, 1968, Belgrade has viewed the Soviet military buildup in the Mediterranean with undisguised concern.

Early Contacts

Prior to the second World War, Yugoslavia had no direct ties with the Afro-Asian world, then almost completely under European colonial rule. It had no experience with, or knowledge of, the Arab countries; its cotton and oil, the principal imports from the Middle East, were purchased via the Bourse in Paris and London. During the 1945-1948 period Yugoslav-Egyptian relations were restricted to the United Nations. There they became vaguely aware of one another, especially in the meetings of ECOSOC and its subsidiary bodies concerned with the general problem of economic development. But in Cairo, Yugoslavs were still suspect, even after the Cominform break.[1] As Slavs, they were not highly regarded by the Egyptians—especially the British-trained officer corps—who considered themselves Westerners.

Yugoslavia's awareness of Egypt heightened at the time of the Korean conflict. As members of the Security Council (Egypt started its two-year term on January 1, 1949; Yugoslavia, on January 1, 1950), both sought to avoid taking sides in the East-West cleavage in the U.N. Out of this shared search for an independent position vis-à-vis the Great Powers, Yugoslavia, Egypt, India, and several other countries initiated informal discussions in December 1950 that foreshadowed the emergence of nonalignment.[2] In

[1] *Borba*, April 21, 1949. The Egyptian Government banned the annual meeting of the Yugoslav Club, the society of Yugoslavs in Egypt, presumably because of suspicion of groups affiliated with Communist countries.

[2] Until the early 1960's Cairo preferred to use the term "positive neutrality." In 1951-1952 the term "nonalignment" was in the dictionaries, but not in the parlance of political discourse. The first term used was "neutrality," but this had the tradition behind it of reference to wartime conditions. "Neutralism" came increasingly into vogue, and was understood to mean a desire to remain aloof from Cold War blocs. However, after the revolution of July 1952, Egyptian leaders felt that "neutrality" and "neutralism" were too passive and started to use "positive neutralism," which connoted a more active role. Gradually the term "nonalignment" came to be considered an improvement, though Tito and Nasser both have expressed dissatisfaction with it and have sought a substitute more indicative of their true intent. To them

1951 the time was not yet ripe for greater intimacy between Belgrade and Cairo: for Yugoslavia, the Soviet Union was the main threat, and for Egypt, Great Britain; also, Yugoslavia was not in a position to defy the West when Israel brought before the Security Council the issue of the free passage of vessels through the Suez Canal. According to Egyptian diplomats Yugoslavia was predisposed toward Egypt. In the discussions leading up to its adoption, Turkey had at first been disinclined to vote for the Western approved resolution. Under Western pressure, however, it contributed its vote, thereby ensuring the required majority of seven. Seeing that Turkey's vote meant acceptance of the Western-approved resolution, and considering their own difficult position and heavy reliance on Western assistance, the Yugoslavs, too, voted for the resolution, making it eight votes. An Egyptian diplomat noted: "The Yugoslavs did try to offer some amendments which would have made the resolution less onerous to Egypt, but the hour was late and the effort was not successful." Yugoslavia found itself in agreement with Egypt on anti-colonialism, support for the seating in the United Nations of Communist China (whom Egypt recognized on May 18, 1956), and other issues. But it was the Egyptian revolution of July 23, 1952, that opened the way for intimate and extensive relations between them.

The July 1952 Revolution

On July 23, 1952, a group of Egyptian military officers, members of various political factions in the Egyptian army dating back to 1936, smarting from the humiliation of defeat by Israel in 1948, overthrew King Farouk, who abdicated and left for exile three days later. In Belgrade the initial reaction to the coup was one of skepticism, the prevailing opinion being that Naguib and Nasser were military dictators of the traditional type, a view incidentally

"nonalignment" seems to imply a quality of being impartial and nonpartisan; indeed, it can be interpreted as a protest against partisanship. Also, in the words of one Egyptian diplomat, it says more about "what you are not than what you are."

shared by the British, who fully expected to be able to make a suitable compromise arrangement with them over the Suez Canal Zone. There were few signs of the dynamism that drove the young colonels, led by Gamal Abdel Nasser. Most Yugoslav diplomats in Cairo believed, as did their Western counterparts, that the military junta expected to turn power back to the political leaders as soon as the necessary reforms of the army and the Wafd Party were introduced and then to "return to the barracks" in the best tradition of the British army. Only gradually did Nasser and his colleagues grasp the enormity of the task before them: in Nasser's words, "the full picture of a soldier's duty did not become clear until long after the Revolution."[3] At first (1952-1954) Nasser believed that what Egypt needed was a purge of the corrupt political parties. He soon discovered that this would not get at the root of Egypt's ailments. However, not until the adoption of the Arab Socialist Charter in 1961 did he begin systematically to make a social and economic revolution. In fact, between 1952 and 1957 he apparently believed in "guided capitalism" and encouraged private entrepreneurs.

One of the first Yugoslavs to perceive the revolutionary and nationalist character of the July revolution was Zdravko Pečar, the Tanyug Agency's correspondent in Cairo. As a Communist he was at first followed everywhere; his stories for *Borba* were delayed and scrutinized by the Egyptian security police. Pečar pressed his colleagues to acknowledge the broadly-based nature of the revolution. Just as the Egyptians gradually overcame their British-acquired prejudices that all Communists were conspirators and subversives, so, too, did the Yugoslavs alter their thinking about national revolutionaries in the Middle East who were neither Communists nor sympathetic to communism, but who were nonetheless "progressive," nationalist, and anti-imperialist, albeit military men. The period of mutual

---

[3] Gamal Abdel Nasser, *The Philosophy of the Revolution* (Cairo, 1954), as quoted in Keith Wheelock, *Nasser's New Egypt: A Critical Analysis* (New York: Frederick A. Praeger, 1960), p. 11.

reserve was short-lived. Optimistic reports from Cairo convinced Yugoslav leaders of the genuineness of the Egyptian revolution, i.e., that it was not British-engineered. For their part, the Egyptian leaders, impelled by a desire to avail themselves of Yugoslav offers of small arms, overcame their initial hesitancy.

Nasser sought modern weapons to reequip and retrain the Egyptian army. His attempts to purchase arms in the West failed; not even Sweden would sell because of strong pressures from Britain. That he did not then turn to the Soviet bloc was due to several inhibitory factors: absence of experience and contacts with the Soviet bloc; uncritical acceptance of the Western view that all Communists were intent on internal subversion and took orders from Moscow; and the prevailing belief among the Egyptian leaders that contacts with Communists were to be avoided lest they worsen relations with other Arab countries and precipitate violent opposition from the still powerful traditionalist forces in the country. However, Nasser's pragmatism and growing understanding of the independent policy of Yugoslavia, reinforced by reports of its behavior in the U.N., led him to explore the possibility of obtaining small arms from the Yugoslavs. In August 1953 the first Egyptian military mission visited Yugoslavia; in early 1954 Yugoslavia agreed to sell (for cotton) 10,000 modern rifles, several hundred machine guns, and ammunition, thus becoming the first country to help Nasser break out of the cycle of dependency on Western arms.

As it did with Burma, Yugoslavia first demonstrated its credibility as a friend by its readiness to sell small amounts of arms in defiance of Western pressure. According to Yugoslav officials strong pressure was brought against Yugoslavia by the British and American Ambassadors in Cairo: when the first Yugoslav ship bearing arms arrived in Alexandria, they warned that Belgrade was jeopardizing the continuation of wheat shipments from the United States. However, Tito remained firm, an act that perhaps impressed the Egyptians more than the sale of arms.

Cairo appreciated the arms assistance, but its needs exceeded Belgrade's capability. The implementation of the Western-contrived Baghdad Pact, with its military buildup of Iraq—Nasser's main rival in the Arab world—and the Israeli attack against the Fedayeen stronghold in the Gaza strip in late February 1955, made urgent Nasser's need to satisfy the army and to build up Egypt's military strength. As one specialist has noted:

> Nasser is a tactician rather than a strategist; he tends to react rather than to initiate. During the critical period under discussion, his policy was shaped by a variety of circumstances, among them his discussions with Nehru and Tito, the clash with Iraq over the Baghdad Pact, and the Israeli attack on Gaza.[4]

Soon after, Nasser negotiated an agreement with the Soviet bloc that culminated in the arms pact of September 1955.

Coalescing Interests

The sale of Yugoslav arms and the appreciation by Egyptian leaders of Belgrade's desire for friendly relations gradually overcame the inertia of political ignorance and indifference, thereby facilitating an atmosphere conducive to closer relations. But the ties between the two countries were dramatically strengthened because their national outlooks and interests coalesced, and because each saw in friendship with the other important benefits to itself.

First, conditions were ripe. By 1953-1954 the Yugoslav leadership had begun to discuss ways of cooperating with nations who desired to stay aloof from involvement in the Cold War and to work toward lessening international tensions. The alternative that Belgrade sought to guide it safely between the Scylla of Soviet hegemonic tendencies and the Charybdis of Western capitalism was on the verge

---

[4] *Ibid.*, p. 233. Another specialist argues that though Gaza was important in making Nasser receptive to the Soviet offer of arms, it did not initiate any new trend of events; that the prospects of an Egyptian-Israeli settlement broke down before not after the Gaza raid. Earl **Berger**, *The Covenant and The Sword: Arab-Israeli Relations 1948-1956* (London: Routledge and Kegan Paul, Ltd., 1965) , pp. 174-181.

of realization: nonalignment. As a country that had successfully withstood aggressive pressures from one Great Power and accepted assistance from another without relinquishing political independence, Yugoslavia held a particular attraction for Egyptian leaders, who saw remarkable similarities in their respective situations. Yugoslavia was without friendly states on its borders, as was Egypt; though ideologically akin to the Soviet Union, it craved the right to formulate its own domestic and foreign policy in the light of its own perceived national interests; and Yugoslavia resisted Soviet hegemony, just as Egypt was struggling against British domination. There were differences, to be sure, but at the time they did not bar close relations: unlike Yugoslavia, Egypt was intellectually the center of an enormous and vital region—the Arab world, and had played a key role in the Westernization of Arab countries; furthermore, whereas Yugoslavia knew that it had everything to lose from the Cold War and yearned to remain apart from it, Egyptian leaders sought to exploit the Cold War, viewing the Soviet Union not as a potential threat with competing strategic-political aims in the Middle East, but as a supplier of weapons against its mortal foe Israel.

The Yugoslav groping for an "unaligned" and independent position in international affairs touched a responsive nerve in Cairo, which was in 1954-1955 in search of a foreign policy for Egypt. The idea of "neutrality" or "neutralism" had attracted Egyptian nationalists even before the July revolution; it even antedated the era of Soviet-American "Cold War"; it had developed out of the circumstances of Egypt's abject position in the context of the Anglo-French "Cold War" of the nineteenth century and their rivalry in the Middle East. Ever since the Napoleonic period the Arab world had been the scene of European rivalries as the Western Powers carved out spheres of influence from the debilitated Ottoman Empire. The Anglo-French Entente of 1904[5] made clear to thoughtful Egyptians the need for a policy

[5] Under the agreement France relinquished all claims of influence in Egypt in return for Britain's recognition of France's hegemony in Morocco.

of neutralism, a policy that would free Egypt from British rule and keep her outside the sphere of European struggles and machinations. The Sykes-Picot Agreement of 1916, which divided the non-Turkish areas of the Ottoman Empire between Britain and France; the Balfour Declaration of 1917, which held out the promise of a homeland in Palestine for world Jewry; and the continued control by Britain and France over Arab countries after World War I, thus belying the wartime promises of independence, intensified Egyptian bitterness. Not only had Egypt not benefited from participation on the Allied side in World War I, but it remained very much a disdained dependency of Britain. No surprise then Egypt's unwillingness to fight on the Allied side during World War II; to Cairo, Berlin seemed to offer an alternative, but London, merely new promises to be broken. One of the founding members of the United Nations, it was still occupied by the British, the legal basis being the 1936 Treaty of Defense which gave Britain the right to defend the Suez Canal. According to officials in Cairo, Egypt voted against the intervention of the United Nations in the Korean war because it was opposed to any type of military intervention in the affairs of other countries by the U.N., seeing in the "police action" a possible forerunner of a similar action against Egypt by a Security Council and General Assembly dominated by the Western powers; and because it preferred to stay out of the wars of the West, which have never benefited it. (On the other hand, Egyptian officials lauded the U.N. role in preserving Cairo against the combined British-French-Israeli attack in 1956, and have favored the use of force against the Ian Smith government in Southern Rhodesia since 1966. They acknowledge the inconsistency, and now accept *in principle* the need for a permanent U.N. peacekeeping force, but admit that agreement is not likely to be reached soon on the financing, composition, competence, operation, and character of such a force. Since Cairo's dismissal of UNEF in May 1967, the issue has become more immediate and less tractable.) Cairo's goals, as enunciated by Nasser shortly after coming to power, were to gain complete independence, keep out of the Cold War, and follow a policy of positive neutralism.

A second factor making for friendship was the undisguised sympathy of Yugoslavia for Egypt's nationalist revolution and the willingness of Yugoslavia to provide military assistance, admittedly limited but nonetheless given within the limits of its capability, in defiance of pressure from the West and at possible risk to its own national interests. In 1953-1954 no other country went so far to demonstrate solidarity with Egypt. This early support and acceptance of the Egyptian revolution as a genuine nationalist movement enhanced Yugoslavia's stature in Cairo and eased the process of discourse.

A third factor—an important one for the Egyptians—was Yugoslavia's success in gaining acceptance of its independent and unaligned position, first by the West, and in 1955 by the Soviet Union: both Great Powers accepted Yugoslavia's unalignment, an objective that was at the heart of Egyptian foreign policy. Cairo sought for the key. The period of 1954-1955 was crucial for Egypt. The United States sought to extend its "containment" policy to the Middle East and induce Egypt to join the projected Middle East Defense Organization (MEDO), holding out the lure of a return of the Suez Canal Zone to Egyptian control. However, even the Wafd government of King Farouk had rejected such an arrangement in October 1951.[6] In the spring of 1953 Secretary of State John Foster Dulles visited Cairo to persuade the new government to participate in an agreement that led to the Baghdad Pact. According to one Egyptian official, Dulles tried to impress upon Nasser (in the only personal contact they were destined to have) the urgency of forming a military alliance to safeguard the Middle East against the enemy. Whether apocryphal or authentic, Nasser is supposed to have asked: "Who is the

---

[6] The Farouk regime also unilaterally abrogated the 1936 Anglo-Egyptian Treaty. This precipitated political unrest when the British refused to recognize the abrogation. Farouk's efforts to quell the nationalist feelings that he had unleashed eventually led to his undoing. Wheelock, *op.cit.*, pp. 208-209.

enemy?" To Dulles it was international communism; to Nasser it was the continued occupation of Egypt by Great Britain and the pervasive domination of the region by the West. Egyptian officials tell of Nasser's attempt to make Dulles understand that for Egypt, which had been occupied and dominated by Britain for more than seventy years, the primary goal was complete independence. Nasser acknowledged that the Soviet Union might be a threat to the area, as Dulles argued, but stressed that Egypt had not had any adverse experience with the USSR. Seen from Cairo, Moscow did not pose a problem. Nasser argued the difficulty, even the danger, of his government's moving dramatically from the status of a subordinate of Britain to that of an ally; he did not believe that popular support could be obtained for such a sudden political turnabout. Finally, Nasser contended that the main threat from communism, if one did exist, came from the direction of internal subversion to which the best antidote was a vigorous nationalism: a strong, stable, independent Egypt could cope with any attempted overthrow by indigenous Communists. If the Red Army attacked militarily, an eventuality he seriously doubted, Egypt could then turn to alliance with the West. These views of Nasser ran counter to the ideological and military cast of Dulles' thinking. Washington thought to forestall the intrusion of Soviet influence into the Middle East through an interlocking system of military pacts. In November 1954, with American and British blessings, Iraq and Turkey started negotiations which led to the signing of the Baghdad Pact in February 1955. But "pactitis" only magnified the ills of the area; it polarized the political alignments in the Middle East, accelerated the alienation of Nasser from the West, and provided the Soviet Union with a golden opportunity to become a major meddler in the diplomacy of the region.

This frustrating experience with America enhanced the attractiveness of the alternative that was emerging from Belgrade and Bandung. As talks between Yugoslav and

Egyptian officials broadened, Cairo's interest in Belgrade's outlook intensified.

A fourth consideration that made for friendship inhered in Yugoslavia's search for political allies. Despite the thaw in Yugoslav-Soviet relations in September 1954 when trade relations were resumed, Yugoslavia was still without an ally in a politically bipolar world. A return to closer ties with the Soviet bloc attracted a few Yugoslav leaders, but within the League of Yugoslav Communists opposition to such a policy was deep-rooted and not easily overcome. Only in the Afro-Asian world did Yugoslavia seem capable of finding allies whose political situation and aims resembled in important fashion its own and whose social outlook and aspirations made them ideologically compatible. Tito's visit to India and Burma in December 1954-January 1955 was undertaken in quest of such allies. While his travels and speeches claimed international attention and lent diplomatic momentum to incipient nonalignment, it was Tito's unplanned meeting with Nasser in the Suez Canal that had the important and lasting consequences for both.

A fifth bond was a common strategic interest in seeing that bloc politics did not make the Mediterranean a major Cold War arena. This aim was not generally articulated in the 1950's, but was nonetheless central to the foreign policy of both, at least until the Middle East war of 1967.

Finally, any analysis of the genesis and evolution of the Yugoslav-U.A.R. relationship must consider the friendship between Tito and Nasser. Their friendship is now an integral part of the history of our times. Its durability is testament to its mutually beneficial character. And its international significance derives from the role they have played individually and together in the shaping of nonalignment.

When Tito set out from Yugoslavia on December 2, 1954, for South Asia, he had no intention to meet with Nasser. During the passage of his ship the *Galeb* (Swan) through the Suez Canal, Egyptian officials informally made some overtures for a possible meeting between Tito and Nasser. According to one Yugoslav the staff of the President's party, mostly career foreign service officers, were unenthusiastic about the idea. Probably operative were the usual bureaucratic inertia against arranging a top level meeting on such notice, psychological factors, and considerations of protocol. However, several of the Yugoslav "Cairo hands" persuaded Tito and his aides of Nasser's interest and of the value of such a meeting. Arrangements were prepared and on his return Tito met Nasser for several hours. The date was February 5, 1955; the setting was Tito's yacht as it passed through the Canal; the incident indelibly marked the future of Yugoslav-Egyptian relations.

For leaders of nations, personality is the servant and not the arbiter of national interests. When two personalities are in harmony, that is helpful—but only as far as national interests and ideas are in harmony. Tito saw in Nasser, then still a little-known figure, a genuine national leader, a military man but one with political insight and determination. Nasser respected Tito as the leader of a small country which had successfully thwarted the giants and as a man of action and ideas whose conceptualizations and analyses of international affairs accorded with his own sentiments.[7] Respect ripened into a friendship that gave added impetus to the close relationship between the two countries and to the evolution of nonalignment.

Diplomatic Cooperation

In his speech to the National Assembly on March 7, 1955, Tito said of his meeting with Nasser in the Suez Canal:

[7] One biographer of Nasser quotes him as saying of his initial impression of Tito: "I was very much impressed with him. He was quite different than I had imagined. We quickly became good friends. He seemed to me to be a simple man and a reasonable one. He had no pretensions. He did not try to impress me that he was a more important person than I was, or a better soldier, or knew more than I did about anything. We got along well together." Robert St. John, *The Boss: The Story of Gamal Abdel Nasser* (New York: McGraw-Hill Book Company, 1960), p. 190.

"That conversation confirmed our conviction that there is an ever wider circle of countries which is prepared to take an active and constructive attitude on the basic problems of peace and international cooperation."[8] Encouraged by his reception in India and Burma, and by Nasser's readiness to strengthen Yugoslav-Egyptian ties, Tito studied the possibilities implicit in nonalignment, notwithstanding the developing rapprochement with Khrushchev. At the end of September both governments agreed to raise their Legations to Embassies. Eager to consolidate his relationship with Nasser, Tito made his first State Visit to Egypt from December 28, 1955, to January 6, 1956. He strongly upheld— the first national leader to do so—Egypt's opposition to the Baghdad Pact and Nasser's purchase of Soviet arms as a legitimate exercise of the right of self-defense. In the joint communiqué issued on January 5, 1956, the sinews of nonalignment stood out boldly. The two Presidents affirmed their commitment to the U.N. Charter, their opposition to military pacts and blocs which they blamed for creating international tensions, and their intention of pursuing a policy, designed to promote worldwide collective security, that was not passive but "positive, active, and constructive." They "noted with satisfaction" the steady development of Yugoslav-Egyptian relations, saying that this friendship rested on three essential areas of communality: their determination to defend their freedom and independence; their realization that "they are confronted by similar problems regarding their internal development"; and their identity of views on "the fundamental questions of foreign policy and economic cooperation." In an interview with Zdravko Pečar during his Cairo visit, Tito revealed the importance in his mind of the new relationship:

> I consider that Egypt, as a great and strong state on the African continent, and partially on the Asian one, represents a significant factor and can play a decisive role in the further development in this part of the world. I wish

[8] "Spoljna Politika," *Jugoslovenski Pregled* (1959), p. 1.

241

to emphasize here that I was impressed by this determination of the leadership of Egypt in regard to maintaining the independence of their country and by the same bold steps in bringing up the level of Egypt's economic and cultural development.[9]

Within less than a year after the first meeting with Nasser, Tito was clearly beginning to consider Cairo the prime focus of his intensified efforts in the nonaligned world. Proximity, political chance, and personality drew him to Cairo and laid the foundations for his closest tie to an Afro-Asian country. Cordial relations with Ethiopia, Burma, and India preceded those with Egypt, but they did not possess as many lasting ingredients for empathy and expansion. Increasingly, Yugoslavia linked itself to Nasser's star in the Arab world.

Nasser attended the Bandung Conference in April 1955 but was a minor figure in the assemblage dominated by Nehru, Chou En-lai, and Sukarno. It was at Brioni in July 1956 that he stepped into the limelight with the elders of nonalignment, Tito and Nehru. Tito had invited Nasser to meet with him several days before the arrival of Nehru, hoping to gain his approval for more active involvement in major international issues. Nehru did not come out of conviction, but to return Tito's State Visit. Nehru, a Brahmin aristocrat reared in the tradition of British parliamentary democracy and conscious of India's distinctive position in the world, viewed nonalignment very differently from Tito, the national Communist, and Nasser, the untested thirty-six-year-old military ruler. Indeed, at the conclusion of the tripartite talks at Brioni, he was reluctant to issue a formal communiqué. To an Egyptian correspondent who asked him whether a statement would be given, Nehru retorted irritably, "Whenever two or three people get together you [the press] call it a conference." In the official communiqué of July 19, 1956, the three leaders ex-

[9] Zdravko Pečar and Veda Zagorac, *Egipat: Zemlja, Narod, Revolucija* (Belgrade: Kultura, 1958), p. 321.

pressed their commitment to the principles of Bandung: respect for the U.N. Charter; noninterference in the internal affairs of other countries; renunciation of the use of force in international relations; peaceful settlement of disputes; and promotion of peaceful cooperation among all nations. They agreed on the need for economic development and independence for colonial areas. In response to a memorandum submitted by a four-man delegation from the Algerian National Liberation Movement through the intercession of the Yugoslav Foreign Ministry, they singled out the Algerian struggle and expressed "their sympathy for the desire of the people of Algeria for freedom." They also supported greater efforts to facilitate disarmament, the admission of Communist China to the U.N., and the establishment of the International Atomic Energy Agency and SUNFED, thus reaffirming positions that each had already espoused in the U.N. But Brioni is remembered not because of the expected accord of the "Little Three" but because it was there Nasser learned that Dulles had abruptly withdrawn the U.S. offer to help Egypt build the Aswan Dam.

1. *Suez to Cairo*

A week after Brioni, Nasser nationalized the Suez Canal and a major crisis erupted in the Middle East. A conference, to which Yugoslavia was not invited, was convened in London to resolve the Suez crisis. On August 11, 1956, Tito upheld Egypt's right to nationalize a company operating on its territory and asserted that no conference, i.e., the London Conference, had the authority to discuss the legality of Egypt's action.[10] In a note dated September 13, 1956, the Yugoslav Government expressed to the Government of Egypt its support for Egypt's handling of the situation and its confidence that the Egyptian Government would operate the Canal in the interest of the international community. Tension mounted as Anglo-French military preparations on Cyprus and Malta heightened the threat

---

[10] "Spoljna Politika," *Jugoslovenski Pregled* (1957), p. 7.

of intervention. The Security Council discussed the problem in September and October at the request of an Egypt fearful of attack. But neither it nor the independent efforts of Dulles and Nehru could find a formula satisfactory to London. In early October France entered (and later brought Britain) into a secret agreement with Israel concerning the timing and strategy to be adopted in a concerted attack against Egypt. The collusion aimed at toppling Nasser: Britain ostensibly to preserve its lifeline to the East;[11] France to end the Cairo-channeled flow of supplies to the FLN in Algeria; and Israel to thwart any Egyptian intention of using its newly acquired Soviet arms, stop the destructive Fedayeen raids, secure its lifeline through the Strait of Tiran, and force Egypt to talk peace.

As a result of the Security Council discussions, a meeting of the Foreign Ministers of Great Britain, France, and Egypt was scheduled for October 29 in Geneva to resume talks that had started early in the month in New York. But Britain had opted for war. On October 29 Israel launched its attack; the following day Britain and France issued an ultimatum to Egypt, which rejected the terms. Then British and French forces invaded Egypt.

The Security Council, convened on October 29 in response to the Israeli attack, was thwarted by the British and French veto. Egyptian diplomats at the U.N. were in constant communication with all governments and U.N. officials, and feelers were put out, with the objective of im-

---

[11] In retrospect, the British-inspired adventure appears the result of the pique of an Anthony Eden obsessed by the remembrance of Britain's former grandeur and the compulsion to show his domestic critics that he could act with Churchillian vigor and forcefulness. Also a strong factor was Eden's intense dislike for Nasser, whom he saw as threatening the vestiges of British influence in the Middle East. Notwithstanding Eden's claim to safeguarding British access to the Canal, there were no signs that Egypt intended to cut Britain's lifeline to the East; on the contrary, Nasser astutely did not interfere with British or French ships passing through the Canal, even though they paid their fees to the former Suez Canal Company in London or Paris, and not to Cairo. See Anthony Nutting, *No End of a Lesson* (New York: Clarkson N. Potter, 1967), and Hugh Thomas, *Suez* (New York: Harper and Row, 1966).

plementing the "Uniting for Peace" Resolution. They found a sympathetic audience among most of the small countries, who saw in the attack on Egypt the form of a possible threat to their own independence at some future date. With Soviet acquiescence the Yugoslav representative in the Security Council, Jože Brilej, proposed a resolution on October 31 for a special session of the General Assembly. In accordance with the provisions of the "Uniting for Peace" Resolution, the Yugoslav proposal was considered a procedural question, not susceptible to the veto. An emergency session of the General Assembly was convened on November 1. Throughout the next ten days the Yugoslavs, among others, played an active and constructive role. With Egyptian sanction Yugoslavia contributed a contingent to UNEF and participated in this peacekeeping operation until its demise in May 1967. Yugoslavia's undeviating support in the United Nations enhanced its prestige in Cairo. Nasser did not forget nor belittle the Yugoslav contribution. During his 1958 visit to the Soviet Union he went out of his way, at a time of Soviet-Yugoslav tension, to laud Yugoslavia as well as the Soviet Union as "the only countries which helped Egypt in the Security Council at the time of [the Suez] aggression."[12] While not a completely accurate statement, it was indicative of Nasser's special regard for Tito.

The next few years witnessed important realignments in the Middle East: the stabilization of Nasser's power in Egypt and his emergence as the leading figure in the Arab world, the consequence of his survival of Suez; the union of Egypt and Syria on February 28, 1958, establishing the United Arab Republic (the union was dissolved three years later, but Egypt retained the new name); the overthrow of the pro-Western monarchy in Iraq on July 14, 1958, the consequent dissolution of the Baghdad Pact, and Iraq's turn to nonalignment and Nasser. In Black Africa decolonization brought independence to most of the former colonies and resulted in greater attention being paid in

12 Quoted in "Spoljna Politika," *Jugoslovenski Pregled* (1959) , p. 2.

the U.N. to the problems and needs of the new nations; it lent impetus to proposals for African unity and regional cooperation; and "nonalignment with respect to all blocs" was affirmed as a policy at the Conference of African Unity, which drafted a Charter of African Unity at Addis Ababa in May 1963.

Tito and Nasser developed a pattern of consultation that has resulted in their meeting on an average of twice a year. Many of these meetings came at moments of critical developments and kept Tito and Nasser in the forefront of nonalignment as they sought to elicit support for their political initiatives. Thus, their meeting in July 1956 preceded the crisis over Suez; in July 1958 they met as the coup occurred in Iraq and the Lebanese crisis involved the United States; they met in mid-June 1960, a month after the collapse of the Paris Summit Conference over the U-2 incident. In the communiqué of June 20, 1960, Tito and Nasser called upon the "uncommitted" countries to assume a more active role in the United Nations for preserving world peace. In a move to expand the realms of their cooperation, they announced the establishment of a joint Ministerial Committee that would explore ways of increasing cooperation in the economic, technical, and scientific fields. At the Fifteenth Session of the General Assembly, held in the fall of 1960, they took the lead, together with Nehru, Nkrumah, and Sukarno, in calling upon the United States and the Soviet Union to resume discussions aimed at easing tensions. One Yugoslav commentator stressed the importance of this initiative, even though the draft resolution itself was withdrawn as a result of the objections of the Great Powers, because it represented a joint action of nonaligned countries which "for the first time assumed the form of active assertion on a general plan of international policy, intervening in interbloc relations in the interests of peace."[13] In April 1961, after his two-month African trip, Tito was in Cairo on an

[13] Ljubomir Radovanović, *From Bandung to Beograd* (Belgrade: Yugoslav Information Service, 1961) , p. 18.

unofficial visit to exchange views with Nasser when the abortive American-sponsored Bay of Pigs invasion seeking to overthrow Castro occurred. In their joint communiqué the two Presidents denounced U. S. machinations and agreed to convene a conference of nonaligned countries, the Belgrade Conference of Nonaligned States in September 1961. Less than two years later, in May 1963, Tito persuaded Nasser to join him in planning for a second nonaligned conference. Disturbed by the near showdown between the United States and the Soviet Union over the emplacement of missiles in Cuba in October 1962, Tito was eager to broaden the membership and functions of nonalignment; by January 1964, when the preliminary meeting of Ambassadors of the so-called Belgrade group convened in Colombo to fix the time, place, composition, and agenda for the conference, Tito had become increasingly concerned by the rising stridency of Sukarno, speaking the language of Peking and calling for a polarization of the Afro-Asian states along racial rather than political lines.

The Second Conference of Nonaligned States was held in Cairo in October 1964. That it accomplished little of significance need not concern us here. What was important was what it signified for Nasser: in eight years he had come from the brink of disaster and oblivion to host a vast assemblage of forty-seven Heads of State or Government from nonaligned countries and observers from ten other countries. Cairo, not New Delhi, Jakarta, or Addis Ababa, had become a Mecca for nonaligned and "progressive" countries.

Though the Yugoslavs insist that the Cairo Conference of Nonaligned States was useful, officials in Cairo state privately that it was a failure. One key confidant of President Nasser attributes this to several shortcomings. First, there were too many participants, most of whom were really not nonaligned. These states, primarily African, dominated the proceedings by sheer weight of numbers. Second, he noted, "Yugoslavia is willing to pretend that countries are nonaligned if they claim they are, in the expectation that in the future the country may become truly nonaligned. This may have merit as a long-term proposition, but it is scarcely designed to ensure the success of a particular conference." Finally, there was not a need for a Second Conference of Nonaligned States so soon after Belgrade. Cairo had agreed because of President Nasser's friendship for Tito.

Tito adheres to his belief in the utility of top-level conferences in periods of crisis. Though often settling for less than a whole loaf, he does manage consistently to come up with a solid enough chunk to warrant the ascription of "success" to his efforts. For example, he pressed for a "Little Summit" in March 1966 because of the deposal of Nkrumah, the ultramilitancy of the Chinese Communists at the Tri-Continental Conference in Havana two months earlier, and the disarray among the nonaligned. Cairo agreed reluctantly, knowing that it would incur the ire of Peking, which it did: Peking showed its displeasure by refusing an Egyptian invitation for Chou En-lai to stop in Cairo after his visits to Romania and Albania in June 1966. India refused because of the preoccupation of Indira Gandhi with domestic affairs (she had succeeded Shastri as Prime Minister upon his death in January). However, Mrs. Gandhi did respond favorably to the invitation of Tito and Nasser, issued during Tito's visit to the U.A.R. in early May, for a "Little Summit" in New Delhi in October. For fear of offending Washington, she would not agree to a brief meeting on her way home from the United States, where she had gone for economic assistance. Notwithstanding this stylized rigamarole, the three leaders did meet in New Delhi in October 1966, establishing a more institutionalized pattern of tripartite cooperation.

2. *Belgrade and the Third Arab-Israeli War*

Yugoslav relations with Israel have complicated but not impeded the development of Yugoslav-U.A.R. friendship. Yugoslavia recognized Israel in 1948, shortly after it came into existence as a new nation. It has upheld Israel's right to exist as a state,[14] despite the acrimonious intransigence of some Arab countries who deny the applicability of this proposition to Israel. Yugoslavia has carried on extensive economic relations with Israel, which, after the U.A.R., has consistently been its most important trading partner in the Middle East. However, it has deliberately restricted accreditation to the Legation level out of deference to the strong sentiments of the U.A.R. At times, e.g., at the Belgrade Conference, Yugoslavia has resisted Arab pressures for thorough condemnation of Israel, though in general it adheres to the Arab position on refugees and borders in U.N. debates. Because of its attachment to Cairo, Belgrade has minimized official manifestations of friendship for Israel:[15] no scientific or cultural agreements were negotiated; the normally peripatetic goodwill missions stayed clear of Israel; and contacts in Belgrade were restricted to the realm of trade. Sometimes irritations develop, a reminder of the incongruity of trying to compartmentalize diplomacy. On one occasion the Yugoslavs organized a festive flight to inaugurate the extension of JAT (the official Yugoslav airline) service to Beirut and other Arab cities. Many Arab officials were invited aboard the maiden flight. Underway, orange juice was served to the non-alcohol-drinking officials. An incident was barely avoided when it was discovered that the liquid refreshment came from Israel. Since the June 1967 war, the problem of Israel in Yugoslav-Arab relations has undoubtedly become more open and serious.

[14] For example, on October 5, 1967, at the Twenty-second Session of the U.N. General Assembly, Marko Nikezić, the Secretary of State for Foreign Affairs stated: "The right of all States to existence is for us a principle beyond dispute. It fully applies to the State of Israel, whose existence and equality of rights with other States we have never questioned."

[15] Though there are no formal scientific or cultural agreements between Yugoslavia and Israel, there is an active unofficial system of exchanges because these activities are largely decentralized, the responsibility of individual enterprises and university departments, and not of the central government.

Few Yugoslav officials uncritically support the behavior of the Arab states toward Israel. In 1965-1966 a number of high-ranking officials in the State Secretariat for Foreign Affairs privately expressed the fear that Nasser would provoke a war when he was sure that his Soviet-equipped army could win. What made these speculations notable at the time was that they were made almost exclusively by Yugoslavs; with one exception, none of the resident foreign diplomats voiced any reasons for concern. Whatever reservations individual Yugoslav officials may have concerning the wisdom of the government's policy toward Israel are of course curbed by higher considerations of national interest and by the personal predilections of President Tito.

The third Arab-Israeli war in June 1967 was the most significant recent event in the foreign policy of the U.A.R. and has had far-reaching consequences for relations between Cairo and Belgrade. Like a summer storm, the clouds gathered and the sky darkened almost before one realized what was happening; there was heavy thunder, a deluge—intense and brief—and then a new stasis. The situation in the Middle East has altered beyond our still incomplete comprehension, and a new synthesis, with profound consequences for Yugoslav-U.A.R. relations and nonalignment, is forming.

Yugoslavia's response to the May-June 1967 Middle East crisis was fashioned by Tito's perception of threat and political priorities. On April 30, 1967, the Belgrade newspaper, *Večernje novosti*, published an interview with Marko Nikezić, the State Secretary for Foreign Affairs, in which there was no hint of anxiety over the Middle East; within a fortnight it was the center of Tito's attention. Yugoslav leaders watched the Baathist regime in Syria, which had come to power in a military coup on February 23, 1966, adopt an increasingly strident stance toward Israel. Despite its self-proclaimed Marxist and socialist character, the El-Atassi government in its use of harsh, aggressive slogans set the Yugoslavs on edge. A sharp Israeli punitive raid exacerbated tensions along the Syrian-Israeli frontier. However, for the moment, Yugoslav leaders were more concerned over the military coup in Greece, which had resulted in a closing of the Yugoslav-Greek frontier. By early May they became uneasy over what was perceived as an attempt by "imperialism" to surround Yugoslavia and even aggravate its internal difficulties. From their perspective the rising tension in the Middle East in early May was placed in a pattern of unsettling developments which boded no good for Yugoslav security: (a) the Finlay amendment of late 1966 which precluded the extension of credits by the U.S. Government to Yugoslavia for the purchase of wheat; (b) the unwillingness of the U.S. to allow a carry-over of Yugoslav debts and a sudden hardening of demands regarding repayment; (c) the Greek coup of April 1967, which they believed to be masterminded by the C.I.A.; and (d) the meeting of NATO reservists in Trieste at a time of difficulty between Yugoslavia and Italy. All these factors heightened Tito's suspicions that the West was "tightening the noose around Yugoslavia"—a notion difficult to take seriously in view of past American support, yet one which was apparently believed unquestioningly by Tito.

By mid-May the fuses were set in the Middle East powderkeg. Syria inveighed against an alleged Israeli buildup. Despite the deeply antagonistic relationship between the U.A.R. and Syria, Nasser would not publicly question Syrian allegations about Israeli preparations. Already touchy because of criticisms from extremist Arab quarters that he was hiding behind the "blue helmets" (UNEF), and confident of Soviet diplomatic support, Nasser moved to calculated boldness. On May 16 he demanded the removal of U.N. forces; on May 18 Secretary-General U Thant ordered their removal from Gaza and Sinai. Yugoslav leaders had been apprised of Cairo's intention several days before. In his speech in the Federal Assembly on May 18, on the occasion of his reelection as President, Tito cited as "very dangerous" the pressure against Syria and the United Arab Republic, "pressure which, because of aggressive threats on the part of Israel, under the protection of imperialists of course, may bring about a military conflict at any time."[16] *Borba* echoed Nasser's charges of an impending Israeli attack against Syria and justified his request for the removal of UNEF forces.[17] Tito was apparently convinced that Nasser had no intention of precipitating a war since he had more than 50,000 of his best troops fighting in Yemen. Though surprised by the May 22 blockade of the Strait of Tiran at the neck of the Gulf of Aqaba, he viewed the action as part of Nasser's attempt to establish his leading position in the Arab world. As one important Yugoslav diplomat put the matter, "for Nasser not to have requested the withdrawal of the blue helmets in a moment of high tension and possible imminent war would have been political suicide." He indicated furthermore that he had heard that Cairo had given formal assurances it did not plan to start a war.

With two isolated exceptions the accounts and analyses of developments published in the Yugoslav press were uncritically pro-Nasser: only Jurij Gustinčić, the Political Editor of *Politika*, suggested that the U.A.R.'s demand for the removal of UNEF troops was "the move which contributed most to the creation of an impression of extremely dramatic tension" and expressed the hope that some U.N. presence could be retained in the area;[18] and Secretary of State for Foreign Affairs Nikezić emphasized, during a press conference given on June 2 and marking the end of his official visit to Scandinavia, "that Yugoslavia was opposed to bringing in question the existence of any country in the said [Middle East] area."[19] There was no mention in the Yugoslav press of Israel's offer to permit the U.N. to inspect its frontier area with Syria to determine that no buildup existed, no hint of anxiety over the possible consequences

[16] "Yugoslavia's Views and Actions in Connection with Israel's Aggression Against the Arab Countries," *Yugoslav Survey*, Vol. VIII, No. 4 (November 1967), p. 131.

[17] *Borba*, May 16, 1967; May 20, 1967.

[18] *Politika*, May 20, 1967.

[19] *Yugoslav Survey*, *op.cit.*, p. 132.

of the dramatic signing on May 30 of a Defense Pact between Jordan and the U.A.R.,[20] no uneasiness over the
crescendo of frenzied demands by Arab propagandists for
the extermination of Israel. Overwhelmingly the press reflected the policy of President Tito.

The third Arab-Israeli war erupted on June 5 and ended
on June 10. Within hours of the first reports of hostilities,
Tito threw his full support behind Nasser. In a statement
later broadcast over Radio Cairo, he unequivocally condemned "the Israeli aggression," laid the "full responsibility for the outbreak of the war" on Israel, and called on
the United Nations and all governments to "take urgent
steps to stop aggression and to ensure peace in the Near
East." Tito was determined to avoid the hesitation of October 1962, at the time of the Chinese attack on India, and to
demonstrate his friendship and the usefulness of nonalignment for a nation under duress. Overriding the reservations
of some of his colleagues in the LYC, he attended a meeting of the Warsaw Pact members, convened in Moscow
on June 9, to condemn Israel and discuss ways of helping
the Arabs. On June 13 Yugoslavia broke off diplomatic
relations with Israel. While this followed closely the lead
of the Soviet bloc countries (except for Romania), it was
motivated by Tito's felt need to show himself a partisan
friend of Nasser's, and not by any direct Soviet or Arab
pressures.[21] Belgrade could do no less than Moscow; yet,

[20] *Borba*'s correspondent in Cairo, Milutin Milenković, wrote somewhat euphorically that "Hussein has now practically surrendered to
Nasser. Urgently and directly, without announcements or soundings,
he came to seek protection. . . ." *Borba*, June 2, 1967.

[21] Tito's visit to Moscow raised questions among both Western and
nonaligned countries concerning the meaning of this move for Yugoslavia's policy of nonalignment. In Belgrade, Yugoslav officials went
out of their way to assure resident diplomats that Tito's trip was designed solely to discuss possible areas of assistance to the Arab countries,
and in no way signified any intention of establishing closer political
and military ties with the Warsaw Pact. The participation, in August
1967, of Yugoslav observers in WTO maneuvers in Bulgaria was intended by Belgrade as a signal to the United States that Yugoslavia
was not isolated and had powerful friends upon whom it could rely
in the event that "imperialism closed in."

in so doing, it sharply limited its capacity to assume a mediator's role.

That differences exist within the leadership of the League of Yugoslav Communists over President Tito's Middle East policy is clear;[22] that the dissidents are unwilling to challenge him openly on this issue is also manifest. Yugoslav press accounts during the period of fighting played down Arab losses, but avoided repeating Arab charges of American collusion in the Israeli attack; they also did not publicize Moscow's use for the first time of the "hot line" to Washington to ensure against an inadvertent and undesired confrontation with the United States. Party "hardliners" did, however, accept Cairo's allegations of American air and naval assistance to Israel,[23] allegations which Nasser himself retracted less than a year later.[24] Notwithstanding the lack of unanimity in the LYC, Tito remains adamant. For him, as for Nasser, Israel is a client-state of the United States, and would presumably obey Washington's every wish.

During the emergency session of the General Assembly in the summer of 1967, and in the U.N. since then, Yugoslavia

[22] In early 1968 one member of Tito's staff told this writer that in his personal opinion Israel could not have acted any other way once the U.A.R., Jordan, and Syria closed the ring around it and intensified their declarations of intent to destroy Israel. He acknowledged that there had been a difference of opinion among Yugoslav leaders about the Middle East situation and what to do about it.

In a series of well-documented reports Radio Free Europe (RFE) traced some of these cleavages in the Yugoslav leadership. See the following RFE Research Papers: "Tito's Anti-Israeli Policy an Effort to Restore Domestic Balance," 15 June 1967; "Some Yugoslav Papers Critical of Nasser's Attitudes," 22 June 1967; "After the Seventh Plenum of the Yugoslav Central Committee," 3 July 1967; "Yugoslav Foreign Minister Attacked in Parliament on Middle East Policy," 12 July 1967; "Middle East Crisis Provokes Political Controversies Among Yugoslav Leadership," 20 July 1967; "Former Yugoslav Ambassador to Israel Criticizes Anti-Israeli Press," 21 August 1967; and "Yugoslavia: Tito's Balancing Act Between Two Factions," 14 September 1967.

[23] Marko Morić, "An Attempt to Check National Emancipation," *Socialist Thought and Practice*, No. 26 (April-June 1967), p. 91. *Borba*, June 10, 1967.

[24] William Attwood, "Nasser Talks," *Look* (March 19, 1968), p. 63.

has been in the forefront of efforts to effect a withdrawal of all Israeli forces from occupied parts of the U.A.R., Jordan, and Syria, and to condemn Israel. Its draft resolutions came closest to obtaining the necessary two-thirds majority. In August 1967 Tito launched a peace offensive with visits to Cairo, Damascus, and Baghdad, and the dispatch of notes to the United States, the Soviet Union, Britain, France, and other interested parties in what was the first of several attempts to mobilize support for his peace plan. While disclaiming any intention to play the role of mediator, Yugoslav authorities had hoped that Tito's five-point proposal,[25] which Nasser worked hard to sell to the Arab states "simply because it came from Tito,"[26] would prove acceptable to Washington, which would pressure Israel to accept.

Tito has labored long and hard on Nasser's behalf, trying to mobilize support among the nonaligned and Communist countries. Frustration and disappointment have been his harvest. Nonaligned nations as a group have not rallied round Cairo; they have not shown any proclivity for disciplined, bloc voting in the United Nations. On the contrary, as one scholar has observed, the nonaligned states do not, except in the most general terms, "agree among themselves on most basic cold war issues," and "gen-

[25] The main points in Tito's plan were: 1) The withdrawal of all troops from the territories occupied by Israel after June 5, with appropriate supervision by U.N. observers; 2) Guarantees of security by the Security Council or the four big powers of the June 5 frontiers of all countries in the area until final solutions were found. This would include the possible stationing of U.N. troops on both sides of the frontier; 3) Freedom of passage for vessels through the Strait of Tiran pending a ruling of the International Court of Justice; 4) Restoration of the situation prevailing in the Suez Canal on the eve of the war; 5) As soon as all the above measures had been put into effect, the Security Council would, together with the parties immediately concerned, undertake steps for a settlement of the remaining disputes, particularly the problem of the Palestine refugees and the issue of passage through the Suez Canal for Israeli ships.

[26] Anthony Carthew, "There is No False Courage Left in Egypt," *The New York Times Magazine* (December 3, 1967).

eralizations about the foreign policies of the 'Third World' are dangerous and largely erroneous."[27] In particular, the African states have been reluctant to choose sides in the Arab-Israeli controversy, "or even to discuss it—during sessions of the Organization of African Unity, when the topic was inevitably introduced by one or another of the North African heads of state":

> Indeed, persistent Arab efforts to introduce the dispute with Israel into African organizations have aroused a good deal of resentment in countries that consider the conflict a Middle Eastern issue, not an African problem, and wish to keep good relations with both sides.[28]

Of the African states south of the Sahara, less than half (twelve out of thirty-two) voted consistently for the Yugoslav or Soviet-sponsored resolutions.[29]

In January-February 1968 Tito visited Cambodia, Pakistan, India, Ethiopia, and the U.A.R. in an effort to generate interest in another conference of nonaligned states and to promote Cairo's cause. An examination of the official communiqués reveals that there was less than unanimity on the Middle East problem: only in Moslem Pakistan and, of course, the U.A.R., was there specific reference to "Israel's aggression against the Arab states" and a call for its condemnation; in India, concern was expressed "that little has been done so far to settle the crisis in the Near East," an indication that Prime Minister Indira Gandhi preferred not to be identified as a partisan in the dispute; in Cambodia, the issue was not even touched on, no doubt reflecting Sihanouk's preoccupation with matters closer to home; in Ethiopia, Tito perhaps received his most unwelcome surprise when Emperor Haile Selassie would not agree to any criticism or mention of Israel or of aggression. Indeed, Tito heard unfamiliar criticism of U.A.R. policy

[27] Theodore L. Shay, "Nonalignment Si, Neutralism No," *The Review of Politics*, Vol. 30, No. 2 (April 1968), p. 230.

[28] Samuel Decalo, "Africa and the Mid-Eastern War," *Africa Report* (October 1967) p. 59.

[29] *Ibid.*, p. 60.

from a leading African country. First, the Ethiopians considered Cairo's closing of the Suez Canal to Israeli shipping disturbing and asked what would prevent the U.A.R. from doing the same thing to Ethiopia sometime in the future in the event that relations between them were to deteriorate. Second, the Emperor informed Tito of the seriousness with which he viewed Arab support of Somali (a Moslem country) guerrillas against Ethiopia.[30] Clearly, nonalignment still means different things to different countries. The Black African countries see in nonalignment priorities other than those considered important by the Arab countries.

Throughout the summer and fall of 1968 Yugoslav diplomats worked hard at generating interest among the nonaligned, with little success. In an interview with Yugoslav and Austrian journalists on October 5, 1968, President Tito commented on the preparations for the conference:

> When the nonaligned countries meet at the summit conference, I believe they will discuss the questions on which most countries agree. We shall not include in the agenda any questions likely to lead to a split among the nonaligned countries. Questions will be discussed on which it is possible to reach agreement, such as, in the first place, noninterference in the internal affairs of other countries, second, the policy of peaceful and active coexistence, third, disarmament, and fourth, economic assistance to and growth of the developing countries.[31]

[30] Ethiopian authorities claim to have crushed the Arab-supported guerrilla movement known as the Eritrean Liberation Front. They attribute their success to the effectiveness of the Ethiopian army and the sharp drop in arms and supplies from Arab countries since the Middle East war of June 1967. *The New York Times*, September 26, 1968.

Ethiopia's suspicions of Arab intentions have no doubt intensified as a result of the attack by two Syrian Arabs on a passenger plane of the Royal Ethiopian Airlines in Frankfurt am Main (Germany) on March 12, 1969, an incident which curiously enough was unreported by American newspapers, including *The New York Times*. When questioned, the terrorists said their act was intended to help free Eritrea from Ethiopian rule.

[31] *Yugoslav News Bulletin*, No. 432 (October 11, 1968).

If questions "likely to lead to a split among the nonaligned countries" are to be excluded from the agenda, then few would have reason to support Tito's initiative, and certainly none of the Arab belligerents.

At a major press conference at Jajce on November 30, 1968, Tito acknowledged that "the preparations [for a nonaligned conference] are more or less at a standstill, not because we think the conference is unnecessary, but because the present situation is such that there is no need to accelerate the preparations. It would be better to delay them a little until we see where the world is headed, and what the situation will be in the coming months." A few weeks later, Dimče Belovski, Assistant Secretary of State for Foreign Affairs, reiterated the discouraging note, "that the present situation does not offer the most favorable conditions for the immediate convening of such a conference."[32] Nonetheless, in late January 1969 he left for visits to Ethiopia, India, Indonesia, and the U.A.R., presumably in connection with Yugoslavia's year-long efforts to organize a new conference of nonaligned nations.

Lacking the military and economic wherewithal, Tito contributes where he can, which is primarily in the diplomatic realm. Toward a region steeped in a history not noted for its propensity for reasonableness or compromise, Tito persists in his efforts to aid Nasser and in the process to promote the internationalization of nonalignment. Besides his bitter disappointment over the protracted failure to convene a nonaligned conference, Tito was deeply troubled by the Soviet intervention in Czechoslovakia. He also views with less than equanimity the U.A.R.'s growing dependence on the Soviet Union, not only for what it means for his friend and for the future of nonalignment, but for his own country as well.

Soviet policy in Czechoslovakia and Moscow's enunciation of the "Brezhnev Doctrine" (which Soviet leaders for-

[32] Dimče Belovski, "Current Activities by Nonaligned Countries," *Review of International Affairs*, Vol. XIX, No. 449 (December 20, 1968), p. 1.

mulated to justify imperial interventions) forced Yugoslav officials to reassess their previously benevolent evaluation of the expanded Soviet military presence in the Middle East since mid-1967. Contrary to Yugoslav expectations, the buildup of Soviet naval power, a consequence of the June war originally welcomed by Belgrade as a counter to American dominance in the area, has sharpened, not diminished, bloc antagonisms and made the Mediterranean more than ever an area of imminent confrontation; and more than any development since Dulles' misguided Baghdad Pact it has institutionalized the Cold War in the Middle East.

In the months prior to June 1967 Yugoslav analysts inveighed against the alleged American strategy of collecting " 'tactical points' in favor of the 'free world' through coups d'état, local wars (interventions) and various other means and methods of pressure, power and violence."[33] To them U.S. policy sought to overthrow all the "bastions" of nonalignment in the Middle East, especially Nasser. Accordingly, Belgrade egregiously blamed Israel for the June war and hailed the movement of Soviet naval power into the Mediterranean, not only as a shield for the Arabs, but also as a restraint on "the anti-Yugoslav aspect of NATO activities."[34] The noted military analyst General Andro Gabelić (Ret.) lauded the new Soviet strategic doctrine of breaking out of the "continental Eurasian geostrategic shell without relying directly on nuclear missiles of intercontinental calibre."[35] Gabelić noted that the Soviet Union had developed a merchant marine that is outstripping in size the American fleet, a navy now indisputably ranked as second in the world, and a submarine fleet that is numerically twice the size of the American submarine force. "Unless all the logical assumptions deceive," he ob-

[33] Andro Gabelić, "Greece, NATO and the Middle East," *Review of International Affairs*, Vol. xviii, No. 412 (June 5, 1967), p. 18.

[34] Andro Gabelić, "NATO Shift," *Review of International Affairs*, Vol. xviii, No. 419 (September 20, 1967), pp. 7-8.

[35] Andro Gabelić, "The USSR: New Accent in Strategy," *Review of International Affairs*, Vol. xviii, No. 423 (November 20, 1967), p. 16.

served, the Soviet buildup is defensive, designed to counter or oppose the interventionist activities of the U.S. Sixth Fleet, whose effectiveness as "an instrument of intervention, blackmail and pressure on countries bordering the Mediterranean" has as a consequence been significantly neutralized.

A year later Gabelić returned to his subject, but in changed circumstances: the intervention in Czechoslovakia had occurred and Yugoslavia itself was in danger, not from NATO, as he had heretofore assumed, but from the Soviet Union; no longer did he view the Soviet military presence in the Mediterranean with benign approval. He candidly admitted that the events in Czechoslovakia and the Middle East "demonstrated that we were not altogether in the right."[36] Though maintaining that the new Soviet strategic course still seeks to thwart American policy, he acknowledged that he had been in error in assuming that the "essence" of that course inhered in a desire to help other countries maintain their independence "without anyone's, or any kind of, external interference." It is now clear that the new Soviet strategic course has a global character "which exceeds the bounds of the camp in which it is allegedly permissible and even obligatory, in terms of internationalism, to intervene militarily in the name of 'loftier goals.' "[37] Gabelić claimed that the Soviet Union is interested not in demilitarizing the Mediterranean and eliminating Great Power confrontation from it, but rather in "the affirmation of its own military power . . . for the purpose of bringing political influence to bear on *internal trends,* on the *internal affairs* of various countries" (emphasis added). In a word, Moscow has imperial ambitions in the Mediterranean, which Belgrade had previously discounted. In June 1967 Belgrade thought Moscow had come to help the Arabs; now it believes Moscow has come to help

[36] Andro Gabelić, "The Strategic Tolerance and Irreconcilability of the Superpowers," *Review of International Affairs,* Vol. xix, No. 446 (November 5, 1968) , p. 23. See also his article in *Borba,* November 28-30, 1968, p. 9.
[37] *Ibid.*

itself, with the Arabs the pawns in the Great Power struggle.[38]

That Belgrade perceives the influx of Soviet influence in the Middle East in increasingly pessimistic fashion may also be gleaned from the changed tone of the commentaries found in *Borba*. Belgrade is uneasy over Algeria's apparent encouragement of an influx of Soviet military advisers and technicians to maintain the naval base at Mers-el-Kebir, which France relinquished in late 1968.[39] Even more disturbing to Yugoslav leaders, and assuredly to Tito himself, are signs that Cairo, in formulating its position on the situation in Czechoslovakia and on the desirability of a new nonaligned conference, has been swayed by Moscow, and that it is, moreover, even beginning to sanction hints in its press that Yugoslavia is pursuing a line detrimental to the cause of socialism and anti-imperialism.[40] Could it be, asks Milutin Milenković, one of *Borba*'s leading editorialists, that Egyptian leftists are veering toward the Soviet position on Czechoslovakia, without taking "into consideration all of the consequences which might result from the use of the theory of 'limited sovereignty' [i.e., the Brezhnev Doctrine] in the Near East as well?" When Modibo Keita was deposed in Mali by a military coup on November 19, 1968, there was no outcry from Belgrade, no rash of diplomatic activity comparable to that which it generated when Nkrumah was deposed; this suggests that Yugoslav leaders were not too unhappy over Keita's deposal because he had expressed support for the Soviet intervention in Czechoslovakia and opposed Tito's initiative for a nonaligned conference, presumably at Moscow's request.[41]

If this analysis of changing Yugoslav views on Soviet objectives in the Middle East is correct, it would suggest the introduction of certain strains into the hitherto close rela-

[38] V. Vladisavljević, "Mediterranean Confrontation," *Review of International Affairs*, Vol. xix, No. 449 (December 20, 1968), p. 3.
[39] *Borba*, December 4, 1968.   [40] *Borba*, November 16, 1968.
[41] *Borba*, November 21, 1968.

tionship between Tito and Nasser, strains arising out of differing priorities assigned to nonalignment, differing perceptions of the long-term danger of an expanding Soviet presence in the Middle East, and differing national responses to the situation each finds itself in today.

Economic Cooperation

Though political priorities have overshadowed economic ones since June 5, 1967, the latter remain important for the future of both countries. In the 1950's the Yugoslavs had great hopes for expanded economic ties, seeing in them a substitute for the markets they had lost in the Soviet bloc in 1948. They viewed the Third World as a potential major consumer of the manufactures of Yugoslav infant industries.

The first agreement on Trade and Economic Cooperation with the Nasser Government was signed on July 30, 1953. At first trade in both directions amounted to less than five million dollars. During the 1954-1956 period Yugoslavia imported (mainly raw cotton) almost twice as much from Egypt as it exported. Since then Yugoslav exports have generally exceeded imports, with an attendant perennial balance of payments problem. The long-term agreement on trade, economic cooperation, and payments concluded on June 26, 1957, has served as the basis for subsequent bilateral accords. The trade turnover has expanded steadily, reaching approximately 36 million dollars in 1964, 42 million in 1965, and 48 million in 1966. Indicative of the economic importance of the U.A.R. for Yugoslavia is the fact that it is Yugoslavia's most important trading partner in Africa, consistently accounting for almost 40 percent of Yugoslavia's total trade with the area. Notwithstanding the record of gradual growth, Yugoslav officials maintain that economic relations with the U.A.R. have been neither fully explored nor fully exploited.

An important step in the direction of increasing economic cooperation was taken during President Nasser's visit of June 1960 with the establishment of a Mixed Commission for Economic Cooperation. Meeting annually and alternately in each capital, the Commission reviews the record and problems of trade between the two countries and makes recommendations for expanding exchanges. It deals also with cooperation in industry, investment, agriculture, and tourism.

The knottiest problem centers on the need to bring exports and imports into balance, while increasing the level of trade. This trade gap resulted in a slackening of interest in the U.A.R. market by Yugoslav exporters and a curtailment of U.A.R. imports from Yugoslavia. An interim solution adopted in December 1963 turned the U.A.R. debt of 8 million dollars into a three-year credit. In addition, Yugoslavia has granted investment credits of more than 50 million dollars to help finance the import of Yugoslav goods and complete various technical projects. One reason for this chronic imbalance has been the nonfulfillment by the U.A.R. of cotton exports, which represent 70 to 80 percent of Yugoslav purchases. Cairo has had to accord priority to cotton commitments to the Soviet bloc to repay for extensive loans and, when possible, has preferred to dispose of the remainder in hard currency areas. As a result, in some years it delivered as little as 60 percent of the promised amount to Yugoslav firms.

Two steps have been taken since 1964 to overcome this difficulty. First, Yugoslavia agreed to include a number of U.A.R. manufactures in its list of imports, e.g., auto tires, textile fabrics, and various electrical products, in addition to the usual imports of cotton, fruits, and vegetables. Second, the agreement reached by the Mixed Commission in October 1965 provided for the joint production of certain industrial and semimanufactured goods. The development of a phosphate mine in the U.A.R. is part of the plan to expand the number of cooperative projects, the finished products of which will be used to repay Yugoslav credits. There are plans to extend this cooperation to the electrical equipment industry and to the production of processed foods. Apart from the obvious economic possibilities of this type of arrangement, officials in both countries envision it as the prototype for expanded economic cooperation and trade among the nonaligned countries. They anticipate the joint appearance on the world market of Yugoslav-U.A.R. goods, which would be produced and marketed in accordance with an agreed upon division of labor and profits, and would reap the benefits of economies of size, thereby making possible a more competitive position for the two countries in the markets of Africa and Asia.

Yugoslavia contributes valuable technical assistance to the economic development of the U.A.R. Though dwarfed by the enormous Soviet effort, this aid is not unimportant. There were approximately 500 Yugoslav technicians in the country in 1966, in comparison with the fewer than 100 a decade earlier. Among them are doctors, agronomists, engineers, and road construction specialists. Of particular importance to the U.A.R. is the land reclamation project undertaken by the "Ingra" enterprise of Zagreb. Work has commenced on this 20-million-dollar project, which aims at the reclamation of 12,000 acres of desert by 1970, the building of 180 miles of interconnecting roads, and the preparation of an irrigation system and a water supply capable of providing for 20,000 people. More than 200 Yugoslav technicians will work with 1,200 Egyptians on the road-building phase alone.

Yugoslav officials believe it was at the Belgrade Conference that Nasser came to the full realization of the urgency for developing closer cooperation in international economic relations. Ever since the Conference, the two countries have explored their mutual economic concerns, an activity in which they were joined by India in October 1966. The emphasis on economic problems gained momentum during Tito's visit to Cairo in February 1962. A joint communiqué identified the difficulties faced by the developing countries and paved the way for the Cairo Economic Conference of July 1962. With the U.A.R. and India, Yugoslavia emerged as one of the leaders of the Conference. Vladimir Popović, the chief Yugoslav delegate, presented a comprehensive assessment of the key international economic problems and offered a series of concrete recommendations. These included increased trade between the developing countries, financial compensation to the primary producing countries for losses of foreign exchange earnings due to fluctuations in commodity prices, the abolition of discriminatory import restrictions imposed by industrial countries upon the products of the new industries of developing countries, and closer cooperation among the developing countries in transport, monetary affairs, industrial production, short-term investments, and technical assistance. These proposals received extensive examination at the first UNCTAD Conference, which was the lineal creation of the Cairo Conference.

Yugoslavs believe that the U.A.R. will eventually become their most important trading partner in the Third World. Though India now absorbs more Yugoslav exports, the U.A.R. is considered a better long-term prospect. For one thing, it is closer geographically—a factor keeping transportation costs to a minimum; second, there is no serious competition from resident, well-established European firms, most of which have been nationalized or forced into bankruptcy; third, the U.A.R. can readily absorb many of Yugoslavia's exports. Still, the constricting problem of payments remains. However much the U.A.R. would like to lessen its growing dependence on trade with the Soviet bloc, it realizes the inherent limits of Yugoslavia's capacity as a supplier and consumer. But both Yugoslavia and the U.A.R. are determined to explore all the possibilities for new forms of cooperation and economic interdependence which they hope will enhance their economic, as well as political, viability in international relations.

The Yugoslav Impact on the U.A.R.: Foreign Policy

Tito has had an impact on Nasser greater than that of any other leader. Because of their friendship, Yugoslav views have received respectful hearings and can be perceived in Cairo's approach to world affairs. As always in a relationship between equals, the process of interaction is complex, and clearcut identification of what each contributed to the position of the other is difficult. Despite the need for caution in ascribing in too simplistic a fashion the outlook and behavior of one country to the ideas and influence of another, there are nonetheless legitimate grounds for speculation.

It is possible to argue that the U.A.R. would have evolved its present international disposition even if it had not developed close ties with Yugoslavia: that Nasser would independently have moved toward the internationalism implicit in Tito's conception of nonalignment; that he would by trial and error have learned to take from the West and the East; that he would have become vitally interested in international economic problems. But from the earliest days of Nasser's rule the similarity in the diplomatic problems and pressures of each country, and the extraordinarily intimate friendship that grew between the two men who in the final accounting determined the basic policies of their nations, all suggest that Yugoslavia brought various elements to the present orientation of the United Arab Republic toward international issues, especially those not touching on developments in the Arab world. And in its impact on the U.A.R. one can detect some principal components of Yugoslavia's attraction for other nonaligned countries.

First, Yugoslavia demonstrated the ability of a small country to withstand Great Power pressures. Tito's defiance of Stalin and refusal to deny his ideological heritage, as some in the West expected and some in the East wanted, seemed proof that a small country could pursue an independent foreign policy, while resisting the ubiquitous pressures of the Great Powers. Yugoslavia's success in asserting and preserving its national identity and forging a sense of national unity impressed Egyptian leaders, who sought these same goals in the years after 1952.

Second, Tito helped bring Nasser into the forefront of nonalignment. As the ruler of Egypt, Nasser was already a personage in his own right, especially after the Suez crisis, which made him a household figure in the Arab world. The head of a strategically important country, he would probably have been included in inner councils of the nonaligned as a matter of course. However, Tito's invitation to meet with him and Nehru at Brioni in July 1956 did mark the beginning of Nasser's association with the ambitious conception of active nonalignment, which Tito was then beginning to formulate. Their friendship, and Nasser's undisguised respect for the Yugoslav leader, led Cairo to assume a more active role in nonalignment than had theretofore been contemplated. His inclusion at that time was testament to Tito's prescience, political luck, or both.

Third, Tito helped broaden Nasser's horizons toward the potentialities of nonalignment. Nasser's hostility toward "imperialism" and embrace of "neutralism" for what assistance it might afford in the struggle against Britain were set in a broader cast: from Arabcentrism to internationalism. Tito alerted Nasser to the relevance of disarmament, neocolonialism, and international economic problems to the securing of U.A.R. national interests. More than any other international figure, Tito influenced the maturation of Nasser's views on international politics; the theoretician of nonalignment, Tito conceptualized nonalignment and offered an integrated explanation of international developments. His evaluations of the Cold War and the changing international environment have found general agreement in Cairo.

Fourth, while Cairo long sought to avoid entanglement with any Great Power bloc, Belgrade went a stage beyond: it mastered the art of accepting material assistance from both the West and the East without surrendering its political independence. Nasser has acknowledged his admiration for Tito above any other leader "because he showed me how to get help from both sides without joining."[42] While genuine in its desire to minimize Cold War tensions, Yugoslavia was a pioneer in exploiting the Cold War to its

[42] *The New York Times*, January 12, 1968.

advantage. For this, many nonaligned countries owe it a political debt. Tito showed that if a nonaligned country held a strategic position, and if its internal system were strong enough to resist the inevitable cascade of external pressures, it could, because of its nonalignment, obtain generous assistance from both Cold War protagonists, each of which was anxious to forestall any departure from nonalignment if this meant a shift to the opponent's camp. Both the United States and the Soviet Union seem willing to accept a country's adherence to nonalignment as the preferable alternative to membership in a competitor's bloc; moreover, they are ready to pay for the continuation of such a status to a degree that can redound significantly to the strengthening and development of the particular nonaligned country that is being courted. Nasser learned this principle early and well, and on occasion Nehru was frank to admit that "India benefits greatly from the Cold War."[43]

Fifth, Yugoslavia tried to convince the U.A.R. of the importance of the United Nations. After the dramatic events of October-November 1956, Cairo did not need to be told of the salutary part that the U.N. played in safeguarding Yugoslav security during Belgrade's maximum period of insecurity in 1949-1952 to appreciate the world organization; by then Nasser owed his own political survival to the U.N., which made possible Soviet-American cooperation in countering the attack against Egypt. But to this cognizance (well developed even before 1956) of the political and security functions of the U.N., Belgrade perhaps added a heightened awareness of the extent to which international organizations could promote the position of the economically less-developed countries. Economic development of developing areas had brought forth Egyptian initiatives from the earliest postwar days, but the Yugoslavs added persistence and a capacity for mobilizing widespread sup-

---

[43] Alvin Z. Rubinstein, *The Soviets in International Organizations: Changing Policy Toward Developing Countries, 1953-1963* (Princeton: Princeton University Press, 1964), p. 51.

port for new proposals. Together with Yugoslavia and India, a U.A.R. "presence" is evident in most U.N. organs. Through his emphasis on the economic preconditions for socialist development and the political consequences of economic weakness, Tito may have alerted Nasser to a dimension of international relations for which his background had not fully prepared him.

Sixth, Yugoslavia has persuaded the U.A.R. to support its initiatives for convening international conferences and Nonaligned Summits, though Cairo does not attribute the importance to them that Belgrade does. Not part of any regional grouping, Yugoslavia consciously seeks to keep the nonaligned countries active and functioning as a group, if only to confirm its membership in a political constellation. The U.A.R., on the other hand, is regionally-oriented: it is less reluctant to ask, "What's in this meeting for the U.A.R.?" Nasser has even become disenchanted with Arab Summits.[44] He originated the idea in 1963, only to abandon it in 1966 because he failed to dominate the conferences. This represented a shift from a strategy of "unity of goals" (meaning readiness to cooperate *ad hoc* with all Arab regimes, irrespective of their "conservative" or "reactionary" character) to one of "unity of ranks" (denoting an emphasis on appeals to the masses for the revolutionary overthrow of anti-Nasser leaderships). He agreed to an Arab Summit at Khartoum in August 1967 only because of the defeat at the hands of the Israelis and the desire to muster support behind an anti-Israeli stand, the only issue capable of generating a semblance of Arab unity. The Khartoum Conference was also intended to formulate the Arab diplomatic and political stand in the international arena, especially at the United Nations.

Cairo favors the establishment of more exacting criteria to determine whether a country is truly nonaligned or not. It has come to this position since the unproductive Second Nonaligned Conference in Cairo in October 1964, because of the growing manifestations of what it regards as

[44] *Mideast Mirror*, Vol. 18, No. 25 (June 18, 1966) , p. 2.

Western interference in the Middle East on behalf of "reactionary" Islamic regimes, and as a result of the ineffectiveness of the nonaligned nations, as a group, in rallying behind Cairo after the June 1967 defeat. The Yugoslavs are opposed to tightening the criteria for two reasons: first, they argue that nonalignment cannot aspire to an influential international role unless it includes India, though it is Cairo's uneasiness over India's fence-sitting propensities that leads it to question the usefulness of having "so-called" nonaligned states attend conferences of the non-aligned; second, Belgrade fears that to define the conditions for nonalignment too rigorously might mean to limit membership, which in turn might discourage the current erosion of bloc cohesiveness. Whereas Cairo's thinking is largely conditioned by its policy and aims in the Arab world, Belgrade's remains broader in conception, and hence more flexible. Belgrade also prefers to avoid subjecting the criteria for nonalignment to too rigorous an examination because the open and growing Soviet military presence in the U.A.R. since the June war makes it uneasy over the extent to which the U.A.R. really fits the description of a nonaligned country today.

The Yugoslav Model and the Development of Socialism in the U.A.R.

Every new nation experiments in search of a viable political system; and every political system is unique, the concatenation of chance historical occurrences and evolved political-cultural traditions. Whereas social scientists talk of models and patterns of development, national elites are eclectic, borrowing piecemeal what seems relevant and adaptable to their particular environment. The U.A.R. variant of socialism is a conglomerate of Egyptian, Islamic, and Marxist influences. Notwithstanding the extensive economic and military reliance on the Soviet Union, the U.A.R. has been influenced more by the Yugoslav system than by the Soviet. Its involvement in nonalignment at the international level "brought Egypt closer to such countries as Yugoslavia whose policy and economic organization (with its original emphasis on central planning and the use of cooperatives) became increasingly appealing."[45] One career civil servant in Cairo stressed the importance of Tito's ideas in the evolution of Nasser's views on socialism: "If anyone has influenced President Nasser inside or outside of the U.A.R. it has been Tito." To overlook this is to miss a seminal insight.[46]

Talks between Tito and Nasser are not restricted to foreign policy but cover matters of internal policy. In a speech dealing with the critical events in Hungary, Poland, and Egypt, delivered at Pula (Istria) on November 11, 1956, Tito gave these details of his first meeting with Nasser:

> When I met Nasser for the first time, on my return voyage from India, he gave me an exact account of all their difficulties in Egypt, which is an underdeveloped country without industry, with a very low standard of living, and without any strong internal organization— a political party on which one could rely. When he was setting forth these difficulties, they really seemed to us almost insurmountable. . . .
>
> It was our view and I expressed it in conversation with Nasser, that they should first strengthen within, that they should create an internal political organism and a strong and firm army, that they should raise themselves economically, endeavoring to get credits wherever they can, and that they should let the people see something of the new state authority so they might straight away feel a certain improvement. These were our suggestions and proposals which they readily accepted.

[45] Salah El Serafy, "Economic Development by Revolution: The Case of the UAR," *The Middle East Journal*, Vol. 17, No. 3 (Summer 1963) , p. 224.

[46] For example, in discussing the 1961 reforms and the evolution of "Arab Socialism" in Egypt, Malcolm H. Kerr makes no mention of the Yugoslav influence on Nasser's thinking. "The Emergence of a Socialist Ideology in Egypt," *The Middle East Journal*, Vol. 16, No. 2 (Spring 1962) , pp. 127-144.

Lacking background and experience in the political-organizational-economic essentials for carrying out the modernization of a tradition-bound, undeveloped society, Nasser and his military colleagues turned to trusted sources for assistance. They exchanged delegations with the Yugoslavs, who freely shared their developmental experience, careful not to impose their approach or model.

By the late 1950's Nasser started a brand of socialist development that was, ironically, falling out of favor in Yugoslavia: nationalization of basic industries; central economic planning; centrally generated investment and subsidies in the public sector; weakening of the private sector; and a commitment to the equalization of wages. This extension of state control over the economy was hailed by Yugoslav writers as "progressive" and pertinent for the U.A.R. at its level of development:

> The only way in which the process of building up such an [underdeveloped] economy can be completed within the shortest possible time, the only way of making good the neglect of decades and getting into step with the rest of the developed world is to keep it within the firm grasp of the state as both the administrator and a direct economic factor.[47]

Thus, at a time of renewed ideological disputation with Moscow, at a time when Belgrade had adopted a new Party Program (1958) calling for further decentralization and de-etatization, it expressed enthusiasm for Cairo's turn to centralization and statism, to a Soviet-type solution to development.

Nasser is no ideologue. His muddled socialism is pragmatic and Egyptian, motivated more by Mohammed than Marx.[48] He accepts the quest for social justice inherent in traditional Islam and the economic equality inherent in

[47] Josip Djerdja, "Notes on an Anniversary: Development and Problems of the United Arab Republic," *Review of International Affairs*, Vol. x, No. 226 (September 1, 1959), p. 7.
[48] *Arab Observer* (June 6, 1966), pp. 38-40.

Marx, some of the postulates of Marxism, but none of the pervasive hostility to religion. Indeed, the government is committed to preserving religion, ruling out a completely secular state. Opposition from the deeply conservative Moslem Brotherhood remains an ever-present danger to the government.

The U.A.R.'s search for an effective, integrating political institution within the framework of a one-Party system has not yet been successful. The National Union Party (1958-1961) established at the time of the abortive union with Syria was impotent, dominated as it was by factionalist rivalries. It was succeeded by the Arab Socialist Union (ASU), which proved as ineffective. In the spring of 1968, as a consequence of the June war, the Arab Socialist Union underwent a major overhaul intended to make it more responsible to centralized control by President Nasser. Student unrest and widespread bitterness against the vested military bureaucracy impelled Nasser to try to invigorate the feeble ASU, through a purge of key officials and a reconstitution of local ASU councils.[49] He has shown renewed interest in the operation of the Socialist Alliance, the all-inclusive mass organization enabling Yugoslav leaders to dominate political, social, and economic life. However, the driving force behind the Socialist Alliance is the League of Yugoslav Communists, and since there is no equivalent to the LYC in the ASU, Egyptian leaders still need to create a disciplined, responsible elite to provide the necessary leadership for the mass organizations. Earlier, with the adoption of the new Yugoslav Constitution in 1963 and the election of the first National Assembly in the U.A.R. in 1964, Cairo promoted an exchange of parliamentary delegations to investigate the functioning of Yugoslav governmental institutions.

The U.A.R. has also tried to emulate Belgrade's efforts to curb bureaucratism and decentralize most governmental functions. Its own bureaucracy, the legacy of Ottoman and British rule, is incredibly sluggish, inept, and, until

[49] *Los Angeles Times*, June 23, 1968.

273

recently, corrupt. The ennui (or was it duplicity?) of the bureaucracy was legendary: A few years after the July Revolution it was discovered that the National Bank was still paying several million dollars a year in tribute to the defunct Ottoman Empire! For four decades no one had questioned an annual outlay that supposedly ended with World War I. Though corruption is being eradicated, the creation of a competent bureaucracy is proving more difficult.

Cairo has long been fascinated by Yugoslavia's system of Workers' Councils and self-management and has discussed them frequently with Yugoslav leaders, including Edvard Kardelj, Tito's most prominent socio-political architect.[50] The U.A.R.'s Corporations Law, adopted in early 1966, clearly reflected Yugoslavia's experience with autonomy for plant managers.[51] The reorganization of public-sector enterprises has incorporated industrial management principles found in Yugoslav firms.[52] Interested though they are, Egyptian officials are aware that self-management requires a fairly high standard of literacy, interest, and initiative at the grass-roots level, and a stable, supportive institutional framework—conditions presently absent in the U.A.R.

In other areas, too, Yugoslavia's experience has appeared relevant. Trade union delegations have been exchanged, with discussions focusing on labor-management relations, social insurance programs, the training of unskilled workers, and methods of stimulating productivity. Agricultural specialists have studied the system of cooperatives in Yugoslavia, which is more akin than the Soviet kolkhoz to the land-owning pattern of small farmers still prevalent in the U.A.R.[53] Vitally concerned with encouraging modern-

50 *The New York Times*, November 17, 1960.

51 Phillip Dorn, "Egypt's Paralyzed Revolution," *The New Leader* (January 30, 1967), p. 12.

52 Le Commerce du Levant (December 12, 1966), cited in *International Financial News Survey*, Vol. xix, No. 3 (January 27, 1967).

53 In the U.A.R., as in Yugoslavia, the question of the degree of control to be exercised over agriculture is continually debated: the radicals press for collectivization and expansion of the public sector;

ist attitudes among the youth, Egyptian leaders have embraced the Yugoslav experience by organizing and marshalling the energy and idealism of youth to build roads and other public works projects. A group of organizers from the Yugoslav Youth Organization visited the U.A.R. in 1966 and helped to establish "Youth Brigades" throughout the country. Given the mutual attachment to "socialism," the existence of familiar sets of development problems, and the friendship of Nasser and Tito, the U.A.R. seems likely to be receptive to suggestions from the Yugoslav experience, borrowing when promising and adapting where feasible.

The Impact of the U.A.R. on Yugoslavia

Yugoslavia has not been untouched by its friendship with the U.A.R. More than is generally appreciated abroad, Yugoslavia's policy toward Western and Eastern Europe has been conditioned by its interaction with the Third World and especially by its relationship with Cairo.

The Belgrade-Cairo entente is important to Tito. He considers friendship with the U.A.R. as Yugoslavia's best insurance for continued membership in the inner circle of the nonaligned nations. Irrespective of any remaining quixotic expectations he may hold for the Soviet Union, Tito knows that nonalignment has brought Yugoslavia a position of leadership on the international scene that affiliation with the Soviet camp would have denied; that it affords Yugoslavia an opportunity to advance the spread of socialism; that it has enabled Yugoslavia to transcend the limitations of geography and limited resources. Thus, there is no likelihood of his returning to the Soviet fold, a possibility some foreign commentators raised anew during the third Arab-Israeli war, when it was reported that Yugoslavia was considering the grant of special fueling conces-

---

the moderates defend the mixture of permissiveness and persuasion. Nasser finds the Yugoslav method far more appropriate than the Soviet or Chinese because he understands the *fellahin*'s passion for their own piece of land and the implications this has for the future of his rule.

sions to Soviet naval vessels. Mindful of the capriciousness of inter-nation fealties, one must, however, allow for the possibility that Tito's successors may not, for a variety of domestic and diplomatic reasons, place a comparable premium on friendship with the U.A.R., or, indeed, the Third World.

In the Middle East, Yugoslav diplomacy follows in Cairo's wake. Though wont to range far and wide in search of friends and tangible economic ties, Belgrade refrains from initiatives in the Arab world which would not meet with the complete approval of Nasser, whose preeminent interests in this domain it respects. The glaring exception, of course, has been Israel and that mainly for historical reasons: Yugoslavia recognized Israel before becoming an intimate of the U.A.R. Being pragmatists, the Egyptians overlooked the trade connections, especially since diplomatic relations were kept in low key. They were satisfied with the frequent expressions of Yugoslav support for the Arab position on Palestine.[54] But since June 1967, Cairo's attitude has hardened, as Kardelj discovered during a visit in March 1968. Having broken off diplomatic relations with Israel to demonstrate solidarity with the U.A.R., Belgrade finds it difficult to justify continued commercial ties, much less any restoration of *status quo ante bellum*, at least until Israel pulls back from Egyptian territory.

Yugoslavia took the U.A.R. position when Mauritania and Kuwait applied for admission to the United Nations. Mauritania's application, in November 1960, was challenged by Morocco, which claimed that Mauritania had historically been part of Morocco, to which it should again be joined. Most of the Arab states, including the U.A.R., supported Morocco. Yugoslavia sided with the U.A.R. A similar situation arose in late 1961 when Kuwait applied

[54] During a visit to Cairo in February 1966, Edvard Kardelj, then Vice-President, noted "the consistent support of our country for a just solution to the question of the Arab people in Palestine in the spirit of the UN resolutions and of the recommendations of the Cairo Conference." *Politika*, February 4, 1966.

for membership. Iraq maintained that Kuwait was part of Iraq and should be so recognized. However, Nasser was then at odds with Iraq, and hence opposed assimilation by Iraq of oil-rich Kuwait. Contravening his position during the Mauritanian affair, Nasser this time did not call for a final obliteration of the territorial demarcations from the colonial period. He preferred independence for Kuwait rather than its merger with Iraq, which would have benefited enormously economically and would have become an even more potent rival for leadership in the Arab world. Once again Yugoslavia took the U.A.R. position.

However, nowhere was the contrast between declaration and deed in Yugoslav diplomacy more unflatteringly exposed than in Belgrade's singularly uncritical support of Cairo's military intervention in Yemen. A poor, mountainous country with a highly traditional and tribal society, Yemen was ruled from 1948 by a tyrant, Imam (King) Ahmed Ibn Yahya, who died on September 19, 1962. A week later his son Mohammed El-Badr, a moderate and a relatively enlightened man, who refused to follow Nasser's lead in foreign affairs, was overthrown by Colonel Abdullah al-Sallal, the head of the palace guard, who immediately proclaimed Yemen a republic. Unable to effect a complete military victory over the royalist guerrillas, Sallal requested assistance from Cairo. Nasser intervened on the side of the republican forces to gain a foothold on the Arabian peninsula. He hoped to undermine the position of his arch Arab rival, Saudi Arabia, to bring his brand of revolutionary ideology to the area, and to influence the outcome of the struggle for leadership in Aden and the Trucial States as they approached independence. Nasser therefore committed between 60,000-80,000 troops to the fighting in Yemen, a move he was later to admit had been a "miscalculation."[55] Friendship bound Tito to acclaim Nasser's expansionist adventure "a new phase of a more decisive struggle for national and social emancipation" and to strain the definition of "noninterference" in the internal affairs

[55] Attwood, op.cit., p. 67.

of another country—one of the key principles of nonalignment and peaceful coexistence. No doubts over the wisdom or propriety of Nasser's course appeared in the Yugoslav press, itself a commentary on the effectiveness of self-censorship in matters pertaining to foreign policy. Not even well-documented reports by the International Red Cross of the use of poison gas by U.A.R. fliers in Yemen[56] could crack the phalanx of selective reporting. Tito's partisanship extended even to undermining the effectiveness of a U.N. peace-promoting effort: a light reconnaissance squadron, contributed by Yugoslavia to the U.N. Peace Observation team that operated in Yemen in late spring and summer of 1963, came with "preconceived ideas and very definite orders" whose net effect was to serve the Sallal-Nasser policy.[57] The Egyptian intervention ended—one consequence of the defeat in the June war—by mutual agreement of the major Arab protagonists at Khartoum in August 1967. The civil war in Yemen continues, with neither the republican nor royalist forces capable of gaining the upper hand, and with complications of tribal and personal rivalries.

The internal "image" disseminated in Yugoslavia of Nasser and the U.A.R. is extraordinarily favorable and assiduously reinforced. Though quick to deplore the repression of Communist Parties or other "progressive" forces in the Third World, Yugoslavia has maintained silence on the harassment of Communists in the U.A.R. There are no critical commentaries about either the U.A.R. or Nasser in Yugoslav newspapers or scholarly journals. Although the Yugoslav press carries more information about the U.A.R. than the U.A.R. press carries about Yugoslavia, the reason is obviously that Cairo is the more important political center, being the hub of the Arab world. Yet Yugoslav leaders have reason to feel satisfied with the oft-reported observations of foreign visitors that every villager in the

[56] *The New York Times*, June 3, 1967.
[57] Carl von Horn, *Soldiering For Peace* (New York: David McKay Company, 1966), pp. 366-376.

U.A.R. knows "Nasser-Tito." Belgrade also attributes importance to details such as Belgrade's having been the first capital to which Nasser (in 1960) sent a permanent newspaper correspondent. (Cairo has had permanent newspaper correspondents in London since the 1930's and in New York since the mid-1940's.)

A desire to help its friend, coupled with concern over the pronounced militarization of the Mediterranean area since June 1967, resulted in nongovernmental initiatives by Yugoslav officials. At the invitation of Josip Djerdja, a member of the Presidium of the Federal Conference of the Socialist Alliance, representatives of sixteen parties from eleven countries convened in Rome in April 1968 after preliminary meetings had been held in Bologna and Rome in September 1967 and January 1968, respectively. The Conference was ostensibly aimed at mobilizing support for the victims of "Israeli aggression" and coping with the intensified threat from "imperialist forces" seeking to open a new "front" in the Mediterranean. However, the Yugoslavs were also interested in a "thinning out" of Great Power fleets from the area, in the creation of a peaceful, denuclearized Mediterranean littoral that would be increasingly nonaligned in character. For Djerdja, who was proceeding without any avowed support or expectations on the part of LYC leaders, the Conference was a bitter disappointment. It refused the demand of the Yugoslavs for the inclusion of "all progressive, peaceful, popular and national forces and parties in the Mediterranean," preferring instead to limit the participants in accordance with Moscow-formulated dictates. Djerdja subsequently noted:

> This failure is all the more deplorable since this move was hampered not by objective difficulties or objections of an objective nature, but most frequently by subjective approaches and narrow-mindedness of some of the participants who were not yet able to subordinate the momentary and narrow considerations or reserves to the advantages that a broad and active participation of

strong national and democratic forces would give this significant effort of the progressive policy in the Mediterranean.[58]

Furthermore, the Yugoslav delegation did not even sign the final statement because it failed to demand the removal of all foreign influences, i.e., American and Soviet, from the area, though this was implicit in the communiqué issued in January. Contrary to the intentions of the Yugoslavs, the Conference did not assume a sufficiently nonaligned coloration.[59]

Tito and Nasser: An Unfinished Portrait

The Belgrade-Cairo entente is the handiwork of a relationship rare in international politics. One may acknowledge the propitiousness of the times for close ties, but without an understanding of the catalytic effect of personality on politics an adequate understanding of this relationship is not possible. Rarely have two leaders enjoyed such active and intimate good relations, attended by mutual respect and a sense of reliability.

From the beginning each saw his country's national interests as consonant with the general outlook and behavior of the other. In February 1955 Nasser was in a quandary: to turn to the West or to the East? Both demanded a price of sorts. Nasser perceived in the Yugoslav experience guidelines for Egypt. Tito, too, was casting about for a resolution to political dilemmas. And, to his credit, he alone among the Third World leaders of the time sensed that through Nasser something new and important was happening in Egypt. More than any non-Arab leader, Tito gave Nasser support and loyalty, even though in 1967 it created greater dissonance in the Party than any other foreign policy issue had in more than a decade.

[58] Josip Djerdja, "The First Phase of the Mediterranean Action," *Review of International Affairs*, Vol. XIX, No. 432 (April 5, 1968), p. 7.
[59] RFE Research Report, "Whose 'Mare Nostrum' is it?", April 23, 1968.

Their friendship, remarkable for the differences in out-look and aspiration that it encompasses, may wane as a consequence of the emergence since 1967-1968 of national priorities that are in certain ways not only divergent but antithetical. Tito is the genuine "internationalist" and the one who has the most to lose from the erosion of nonalignment's influence in world affairs. A strategist, he sees nonalignment in its global context, against the setting of the Cold War and the objective forces impelling change and tension in the world. He believes in the need to broaden the base of nonalignment, to accept a country as nonaligned if it claims to be so, on the assumption that it may one day become a truly nonaligned nation. By keeping the criteria flexible, he hopes to attract new adherents and enhance the group's international solidarity. He knows it is nonalignment that, in the final analysis, makes possible Belgrade's ambitious international role. And for him, one goal of nonalignment is the reduction of Cold War tensions and Great Power rivalries.

By contrast, Nasser is a regionalist, preoccupied with Pan-Arabism, who sees nonalignment primarily in terms of its ability to advance his aims in the Arab world. A tactician, pragmatic, fatalistic, and generally reactive in foreign affairs, Nasser is much less concerned than Tito with sweeping theoretical explanations for changing international trends. To discredit his opponents in the Arab world, he favors criteria for nonalignment that would exclude his rivals. For him, the Great Power rivalry in the Middle East is a source of threat but also of largesse, whose diminution because of any Soviet-American détente would seriously compromise his domestic position and regional prestige. Unlike Tito, Nasser regards Soviet-American rivalry, especially since 1967, as beneficial, and is seemingly not disturbed by the rapid naval buildup of the Soviet Union in the Mediterranean.[60] His military aid is now

---

[60] In an interview with the Political Editor of the French magazine *Paris Match*, on October 28, 1968, Tito said of the growing Soviet naval

exclusively Soviet, and welcomed. A great power détente could only slow the flow of Soviet munificence. A fatalist ever since his early days in power, when he moved hesitantly from weakness only to find that his opposition faded away, Nasser believes that he has "a pact with the stars."

There is no gainsaying the observation that each has influenced, and derived benefit from, the other. Because Tito was a world figure when Nasser was still relatively unknown and insecure, presumably his was the stronger influence in the formative years of their friendship. Tito helped broaden Nasser's horizons and served as a model for him to emulate in dealing with the Great Powers; he enhanced Nasser's appreciation of the problems of bringing an undeveloped society to socialism and of the importance of international economic issues. Tito involved Nasser in international concerns transcending the Arab world. The benefits to Belgrade have been considerable. Nasser's trust helped establish Yugoslavia's credentials among the many revolutionary Arab-African groups that operated out of Cairo in the mid-1950's, the most important for Yugoslavia being the Algerian FLN. Possessing no geographic or ethnic ties to these groups, and somewhat set apart by its adherence to Marxism-Leninism and its unique relationship with the Soviet bloc, Yugoslavia found relations with these groups facilitated by virtue of its closeness to Cairo. Nasser has generally given his support freely to the initiatives and activism that established Tito as a leading figure among the nonaligned countries. Though dubious about the usefulness of nonaligned conferences, he went along with the 1964 Cairo Conference. However, since June 1967, Nasser has been less enamored of such gatherings, despite his continuing regard for Tito.

Nasser acquired fame, but his achievements are limited to the Arab world. He has suffered defeats and repeated re-

presence in the Mediterranean: "When the Soviet fleet entered the Mediterranean after so many years of the presence of the American fleet, we regarded that positively. We regarded that as some kind of assistance to the Arab countries that would help reach some solution there. Now quantity is turning into quality." *Borba*, November 14, 1968.

buffs in his efforts to unify the Arab world (e.g., in Syria in 1961 and in Yemen) and in his attempts to dominate Jordan and Iraq; and since 1967 his home base has become less secure than at any other time since 1954-1955. Tito remains wedded to Nasser's policy in the Middle East, and he tends to accept Nasser's evaluations of developments in non-Arab Africa, often to the apparent detriment of Yugoslav interests. For the moment Tito has placed his African eggs in Nasser's basket, but there are signs that he may not allow his policy to be shaped indefinitely by a commitment to a politically capricious partner. To paraphrase an Arab proverb, "The friend of my enemy is my enemy."

Continued close relations with Nasser is a principal objective of Tito's diplomacy. The U.A.R. has been a loyal associate, and Tito would prefer not to trim his sails to ride out the stormy days ahead in a cove of circumspect detachment. His friendship with Nasser militates against such a course. But friendships wane, while national interests remain. Beyond the Tito era lies a period of uncertainty for Yugoslav-U.A.R. relations in which internal developments in Yugoslavia and the U.A.R. will figure prominently.

CHAPTER VIII

Tito's Acentric Communism[1] and Sino-Soviet Rivalry in the Third World

Yugoslavia has preserved its independence since 1948 despite periodic pressures from the Soviet Union. The course it staked for itself in the Third World at first brought contumely from Moscow (particularly prior to 1962) but more recently, emulation. Yet among many in the West the view persists, though it is diminishing, that Yugoslavia has, sometimes consciously and sometimes inadvertently, served Moscow's purpose by undermining Western influence in developing countries and promoting communism and Soviet interests.[2]

In foreign policy, Yugoslavia is a nonaligned country with a security interest in keeping Balkan tensions minimal; internally, it is a Communist country, ruled by leaders shaped by a Marxist-Leninist mode of viewing and analyzing reality, and with a propensity for friendship with "socialist" countries. Unlike the other nonaligned states, Yugoslavia is linked to the socialist camp by geography, ideology, and political ambition. Its internal liberalization and its foreign policy of nonalignment create barriers which Yugoslav leaders try to minimize by seeking agreement with their Soviet counterparts on other international

[1] The term "acentric communism" was suggested by Ross Campbell, former Canadian Ambassador to Yugoslavia.

[2] Examples of the collusion concept abound in Western writings. The more sophisticated versions, however, generally contain qualifications. Thus, one eminent specialist wrote that "Soviet and Yugoslav policies in Africa (as elsewhere) are likely to be increasingly coordinated. For the Soviet Union, the Yugoslavs can be most useful in Africa as intermediaries in such countries as Guinea, where Moscow . . . met with humiliation." He prudently qualified this, noting that "Soviet-Yugoslav alignment toward Africa is unlikely to be either total or permanent"; and that "the Yugoslavs are likely to insist on retaining some capacity for independent action." William E. Griffith, "Yugoslavia," in *Africa and the Communist World*, edited by Zbigniew Brzezinski (Stanford: Stanford University Press, 1963), p. 141.

issues. These efforts have, at least temporarily, been sharply diminished since post-August 21, 1968 developments in Czechoslovakia. Indeed, no event since their expulsion from the Cominform so stunned the Yugoslavs as the Soviet occupation of Czechoslovakia. It signified the ascendancy of the neo-Stalinists in the Kremlin and a setback to liberalization in Eastern Europe. It also called into question the sanguine assumptions underlying Yugoslav analyses of the future of East-West relations, the erosion of military-political blocs, and the transformation of the Cold War in Europe.

Prior to Czechoslovakia, evidence of intimacy and, inferentially, of conniving was neither lacking nor unimposing. Yugoslav leaders condemned NATO but were sparing in admonishment of the Warsaw Pact. They leaned heavily toward the Soviet position on such issues as German unification, Berlin, Cuba, Vietnam, nuclear testing, and disarmament. In stressing their commitment to oppose colonialism and imperialism, they betrayed an unmistakable presumption that culpability was solely Western: thus, they considered heinous the embargo on Cuba by the Organization of American States, but lauded the one adopted by the Organization of African Unity against the Congo as exemplary regional cooperation; they were annoyed at Sukarno, especially after Singapore seceded, for pressing the confrontation with Malaysia, but would not criticize Indonesia because Britain was involved on the other side; though insisting that they judge issues dispassionately and support the party that is for peace, they did not criticize Soviet policy during the Berlin crises of 1958 and 1961, though both were precipitated by Soviet actions which could have upset a precarious status quo. Tito refused to condemn Moscow's unilateral resumption of nuclear testing on the eve of the Belgrade Conference, and he backed the Afro-Asian resolution calling for the removal of the U.S. naval quarantine against Cuba before any indication was forthcoming of a withdrawal of Soviet missiles.

These biases are tangible and upsetting to Westerners,

reflecting as they do deep-rooted Yugoslav suspicion of Western policies and motives. However, they also exist in the policies and attitudes of many non-Communist non-aligned countries, which suggests that the evidence and the criteria for determining the allegedly surrogate role of Yugoslavia in Soviet diplomacy in the Third World need to be examined in greater depth.

The only act that can unequivocally be ascribed to the Communist character of the Yugoslav leadership was recognition of East Germany in October 1957. It was the price Tito paid to keep his status as a Communist in good standing in Moscow; it had nothing to do with nonalignment. Very possibly Moscow thought Yugoslav recognition would make it easier for East Germany to obtain diplomatic recognition from the nonaligned. But there is no evidence— even from extensive interviewing of diplomats from non-aligned countries—to indicate that the Yugoslavs ever attempted to persuade any of the nonaligned to extend such recognition. To have pressed this issue would have ingratiated Belgrade to Moscow and Pankow, but it would only have raised doubts among the nonaligned nations about the extent of Yugoslavia's independence. Belgrade would have had much to lose and little to gain. Yugoslavia fully understands that its unique position among the new nations rests on the belief that it is pursuing *national* interests that are consonant with the *national* interests of the developing nations. Though Belgrade may have been tantalized in the mid-1950's by the prospect of acting as a bridge between the socialist camp and the nonaligned countries, there is no evidence that, with the possible exception of recognition of East Germany, it tailored its policies to fill such a function or pursued policies for reasons other than the furtherance of national interests. Sinister though it may be to Westerners, and much as it may titillate some Yugoslavs, the notion that Yugoslavia advises Moscow on developments in the Third World has to be treated with utmost skepticism: Moscow has its own views of what is occurring and does not take kindly to Yugoslav interpretations, though it may on occasion be persuaded on some minor matter.

On a number of issues vital to Belgrade, the Yugoslav and Soviet positions diverge. In the United Nations they differ on peacekeeping, finances, the role of the Secretary-General, assistance to developing countries, and the fundamentals of international economic policy as formulated at the UNCTAD conferences. They disagree on the purposes of international Communist conferences and international trade unions. Belgrade and Moscow differ significantly in their conceptions of nonalignment and its role in international affairs. And Yugoslav leaders go their own way in policies toward Western Europe, tourism, foreign private capital, and the building of socialism. In de Gaulle's words, "Ideology is transcended by facts."

Yugoslav leaders are driven by their ideology to international activism, and their commitment to Communist ideology makes them interesting for developing countries. In response to the question, how does being a Communist country influence Yugoslav policy, one French diplomat in Belgrade replied:

> If Yugoslavia were not a Communist country, it would have a less ambitious foreign policy. The foreign policy of Yugoslavia is important not because of the fact of its policy, but because other countries are interested in it —and this subjective and conspicuous interest stems from the fact that it is a Communist country.

Being Communist no more predicates performing a proxy function for Moscow in the Third World than it does being subservient to the Soviet Union. The assertion of collusion or cooperation between Belgrade and Moscow in this area cannot be substantiated by the known facts. Indeed, the opposite may be more readily demonstrated by an examination of the Sino-Soviet dispute as it involved Yugoslavia and the nonaligned nations.

Estrangement: *1956-1961*

Soviet policy toward Yugoslavia during this time was shaped by developments in the Soviet Union and in Eastern Europe, and by the Kremlin's Sisyphean effort to find a basis for accommodation with China. Yugoslav-Soviet relations did not result in a second schism, but they were discordant and acrimonious.

A reconciliation having been effected at Moscow's initiative in May 1955, Belgrade again drew close, but warily. Then the Soviet intervention in Hungary in October-November 1956 opened old sores and created new difficulties. In his Pula speech on November 11, 1956, Tito criticized the Hungarian leaders for calling in the Red Army to quell the demonstration in Hungary and counselled the Soviet leaders against reverting to Stalinism in preference to continuing the relaxation within intrabloc relationships. The Chinese, after experiencing some upsetting domestic disturbances, had second thoughts about destalinization and attacked revisionism. In November 1957 at the Moscow Conference of Communist Parties they induced Moscow to take a stiffer stand than it had initially intended against revisionism and Yugoslavia, who became the symbol for heresy in the bloc. Tito's refusal to sign the Declaration of Unity strengthened China's hand and coincided generally with Peking's advocacy of renewed militancy in foreign policy.[3] Soviet criticism of Yugoslavia intensified,

---

[3] Zagoria writes: "It is not accidental that Yugoslavia became the major target of Peking's venom. In periods of international calm, when the strategy of the Right allows cooperation with socialists, neutralists, and moderates, Bloc relations with Yugoslavia tend to improve. At such times there is no great need for iron discipline within the ranks. Conversely, in periods of international tension, when Left foreign policy is in the ascendant and cooperation with socialists, neutralists and moderates yields to revolutionary and direct-action tactics, the errant Yugoslavs are the first to feel the burden of the change. At such times, it is necessary for the Bloc to close ranks and unify policy-making. Hence, in the spring of 1958, the beginning of the Sino-Soviet conflict manifested itself in divergent attitudes toward Yugoslavia. The Russians wanted to increase pressure on Tito, but not to the point where the strategy of the Right would be jeopardized. The Chinese, on the other hand, were calling for an abandonment of the strategy of the

especially after the adoption of a new Program by the League of Yugoslav Communists in March 1958. The Program formalized a decade of heretical rebukes of Soviet policy and society. Yugoslavia reiterated its adherence to nonalignment and openly proclaimed that socialism could come about in developing countries by parties other than Communist Parties. Belgrade thus served notice on Moscow and Peking that it would go its way in defining a different formula for realizing peace and socialism in the Third World.

Moscow reacted promptly. At the Congress of the Bulgarian Communist Party in June 1958 Khrushchev derided Yugoslavia for "the alms" it sought from "imperialist countries" and implied it was a Trojan horse in the socialist camp. At the Twenty-first Congress of the CPSU in February 1959, the "Yugoslav revisionists" were accused of betraying "proletarian internationalism" and, "in their narrow national and chauvinistic interests," of assisting "the imperialists in their subversive activity in the countries of Asia and Africa":

> The revisionists, hoping to disorient individual political leaders in the young republics of the East, seek to instill in them a mistrust of Soviet policy and the policy of other socialist countries. The actions of the revisionists are harming the real interests of the peoples of Asia and Africa.[4]

Khrushchev desired to tarnish Yugoslavia's prestige in the Third World, but his abuse rarely reached the level of Chinese vituperation. In the period between Congresses these attacks persisted, though more on a Party than state level.

Right and, consistent with this, for an all-out assault on Yugoslav revisionism. The connections between intra-bloc relations, external revolutionary strategy, and foreign policy are direct." Donald S. Zagoria, *The Sino-Soviet Conflict, 1956-1961* (Princeton: Princeton University Press, 1962) , p. 151.

[4] Quoted in *Current Soviet Policies: III*, edited by Leo Gruliow (New York: Columbia University Press, 1960) , p. 107.

Yugoslav analysts countered Soviet efforts to discredit Belgrade in the nonaligned world. One commentator denounced the attempts "to persuade the Arab countries that Yugoslavia is in 'imperialist service' and that it consequently represents a threat to the anti-colonialist and anti-imperialist aspirations of the Arab peoples,"[5] citing Yugoslavia's past support of the Arab states, though skirting mention of the Palestine problem. In answer to epithets hurled at Tito during his Afro-Asian trip (December 1958-February 1959) to the effect that he was a "stooge of imperialism," the Secretary of the Federal Assembly's Political Committee for Foreign Affairs castigated Soviet leaders for myopically continuing to implement "the dictum that who is not with them is against them."[6] That they defame Yugoslavia for supposedly serving Western interests and undermining Soviet influence in the Near and Far East is, he argued, a measure of "the magnitude of their blindness and lack of understanding of this world."[7] Unlike the USSR, Yugoslavia does not, he said, recognize the division of the world into two military-political camps, nor does it seek to bring countries into the Soviet camp. Another writer comments on the attempts made by the "Eastern countries" to compromise Yugoslavia's cooperation with the new nations: he sees these attempts as evidence of a spurious commitment to the policy of active coexistence, the product of momentary interests only, and as an expression of the fundamental hostility to Yugoslav support for a policy of nonalignment instead of loyalty to the socialist bloc.[8] A leading Party theoretician asserted that divergent points of view are inevitable even among socialist countries and cannot be papered over by invoking the principle of "pro-

[5] Dragan Stojiljković, "A Foredoomed Venture: The Attempt to Discredit the Yugoslav Attitude Towards the Arab Peoples," *Review of International Affairs*, Vol. IX, No. 205 (October 16, 1958), p. 5.

[6] Maks Baće, "Tito's Trip and Its Critics," *Review of International Affairs*, Vol. X, No. 214 (March 1, 1959), p. 2.

[7] *Ibid.*

[8] R. Kozarac, "The Fiction About a 'Third Bloc,'" *Review of International Affairs*, Vol. X, No. 216 (April 1, 1959), p. 4.

letarian internationalism," and that "the conception of the camp is nothing but a political formula for ignoring the national contradictions inherent in socialism."[9] He noted that Yugoslavia had national interests "in the outside world" which it pursued independently of any consensus manufactured in Moscow. He also linked Yugoslavia's championing of equal rights and independence for countries abroad to the promotion of free and equal decisionmaking among all the nationalities in Yugoslavia, and implied that one reinforced the other. One publicist, generally sympathetic to the socialist camp, upbraided Moscow for disparaging Tito's meetings with nonaligned leaders and for failing to realize "the importance and role of the nonaligned countries and the progressive forces outside the socialist camp." He pointed out that it is just these countries that, "with Yugoslavia support the numerous initiatives of the Soviet Government for the liquidation of the Cold War."[10] In a major speech at Titovo Užice in July 1961, Tito said that Soviet vilification of Yugoslavia harmed the cause of socialism in developing countries:

> People in countries who know the truth about us ask why such an attitude is taken toward us, what intentions are concealed behind it. This then creates doubt and mistrust, not only toward individual socialist countries but toward socialist States and social relations in general.[11]

Especially galling to the Yugoslavs were Soviet charges that Belgrade was a handmaiden of the Western powers. But by 1961 Belgrade could tolerate even these with mingled impunity and sadness; it had established itself as a prominent member of the nonaligned grouping and hosted the first Conference of Nonaligned States.

Yugoslav policy toward the nonaligned nations during

[9] Kiro Hadži Vasilev, "Internationalism and the Unity of Socialist Forces," *Socijalizam*, Vol. III, No. 5 (1960), p. 56.

[10] Mladen Iveković, "Inconsistency in Policy of Co-existence," *Review of International Affairs*, Vol. XI, No. 246-247 (July 1, 1960), p. 4.

[11] *Yugoslav Facts and Views*, No. 128 (July 10, 1961), p. 7.

this period shows no signs of Yugoslavia's being a proxy and no evidence of a strategy planned in cooperation with Moscow. The Soviet accusations and insinuations, and their failure to find a receptive audience in the nonaligned countries; the Yugoslav refutations that inevitably cast doubt on the disinterestedness of the Soviet policy of aiding developing countries; and the absence of statements critical of the Yugoslavs by officials in those countries—all suggest that Belgrade's policy was carried on without advice, assistance, or encouragement from Moscow. Indeed, in time, Moscow faced the same dilemmas as Belgrade, and approached them in remarkably similar fashion.

The origins of the Sino-Soviet dispute have been documented with Talmudic scrupulousness and need no recounting here. For our purposes a few observations may add perspective to the autonomous nature of Yugoslav and Soviet policies toward nonaligned countries. After Khrushchev's effort to heal the deepening rift with the Chinese failed at the November 1960 Conference of Communist Parties, he devoted more attention to the extension of Soviet influence among the developing countries, which had become a key area of competition with the Chinese. As Tito's prestige rose, Khrushchev hoped to use a Soviet-Yugoslav rapprochement to demonstrate that his "socialist commonwealth" was being placed on a new basis. The open split with the Chinese by the time of the Twenty-second Congress in October 1961 was to dispose him more kindly to the Yugoslavs and lead him to observe that "on the question of the struggle for peace, our position and that of Yugoslavia coincide in many ways." The serious differences over internal policies were overlooked as foreign policy positions coalesced.

Tito was attracted by the prospect of increased Soviet trade and assistance to offset the losses suffered as a result of Yugoslav domestic difficulties and the threat posed by the exclusivity of the Common Market. Other advantages have been succinctly described by one noted authority:

It [rapprochement] would provide the more orthodox Yugoslav Communist *apparatchiki* with a renewed sense of ideological assurance and "fraternal solidarity," and Ranković and the Serb Communists with a perhaps necessary source of support to counter the probable increase in Croat and Slovene hostility toward Serb Communist hegemony after Tito's death. Furthermore, Tito and his associates viewed the Sino-Soviet dispute as a great opportunity for Yugoslavia to renew and expand its influence within the Communist world while at the same time maintaining its activity in nonaligned areas.[12]

Though Yugoslav-Soviet relations generally improved during the 1962-1968 period, fluctuations between coolness and cordiality were frequent. These were determined by internal developments in Yugoslavia and the Soviet Union and by events in Eastern Europe rather than by changes in the Sino-Soviet dispute, on which positions had hardened to intransigence. As China intensified its diplomatic activity in the Third World, it challenged the policies of Belgrade and Moscow. Both Yugoslavia and the Soviet Union were confronted by dilemmas in their relations with nonaligned countries because the policies they offered were not as militant as those advocated by China. Moscow's problem may have been greater in proportion to its power, material commitments, and hypersensitivity to Peking's ideological challenge in the international Communist movement. Yugoslavia followed its own course, wanting to maintain its ties to the socialist camp, but mainly struggling to keep nonalignment from being fragmented by the Sino-Soviet dispute and manipulated for bloc purposes. At times, as will be evident, Belgrade and Moscow took similar paths, though their reasons for doing so differed. The complex relationship between them, and between each of them and the nonaligned world, can be best illustrated by reference to specific developments on the international scene.

[12] William E. Griffith, *The Sino-Soviet Rift* (Cambridge: The M.I.T. Press, 1964), pp. 45-46.

The Sino-Indian Border War: 1962

Serious fighting, precipitated by the Chinese, broke out on October 20, 1962, between China and India, along India's northeastern border areas and in the province of Ladakh. For the first time Yugoslav (and Soviet) leaders had to make a choice in a major political crisis between a socialist and a nonaligned country. For more than two weeks *Borba* straddled the issue. On October 24, in a speech delivered on the occasion of U.N. Day, Tito expressed concern over unresolved international disputes which lead to armed conflict and cited the Sino-Indian border problem as an example.[13] The following day, obviously immersed in the Soviet-American crisis over Cuba, he called for a meeting of the General Assembly to bring about a peaceful solution of the Cuban crisis, but was silent on the fighting in the Himalayas. The first reaction that appeared in the Soviet press on the Sino-Indian fighting, on October 25, was mildly pro-Chinese. *Borba* published reports from Moscow indicating that the Soviet Government supported China's proposal for a solution of the dispute; it gave accounts of the fighting; and it reported the accusation of aggression leveled against China by the Communist Party of India.[14]

---

[13] *Borba*, October 24, 1962.

[14] *Borba*, November 2, 1962. *Borba*, November 3, 1962, quoted the resolution passed by the CPI, to wit, "the incorrect attitude of the Chinese Government strengthens the Rightwing reactionary parties in India and all the opponents of the policy of nonalignment."

Yugoslav Party officials were optimistic over Titoist possibilities for the CPI, which had split as a consequence of the Chinese attack. One analyst at the Institute for the Study of the Workers' Movement, which is subsidized by the Central Committee, wrote: "An evolution in the attitude of the CPI from a blind copying of the 'Russian' and 'Chinese' road to socialism and a sectarian trend to overthrow the government, to the adoption of a position of peaceful transition to socialism and to a fixing and adjusting of its policy to Indian conditions (constructive opposition to the Congress government and cooperation with the progressive elements outside the CPI to effect social changes and to build an independent and economically strong India), and to the urgent task of working out a new CPI programme" may develop as a result of recent developments. Ksenija Dragišić, "The Evolution in the Attitudes

But not until November 6 did the first criticisms of the Chinese as the instigators appear in the Yugoslav press (a Soviet editorial in *Pravda* the previous day had adhered to a position of neutrality). V. Teslić editorialized that the evidence "clearly points to the side which crossed the demarcation line," noting that "the Chinese themselves recognized that they crossed the MacMahon Line because they never acknowledged that they did not."[15] He then placed the Chinese action in the framework of Sino-Yugoslav relations:

> And still something else—as a comment. We must look at the action of China and beyond to that aspect of Chinese policy toward our country. Opposed to all the principles of peaceful coexistence, Chinese policy toward Yugoslavia throws doubt on the motives of Chinese actions as a whole. Exactly on the example of Yugoslavia the leaders of China clearly showed not only their lack of understanding but also a quite specific policy of intolerance toward the idea and practice of nonalignment. . . .

On the following day, the Sino-Indian fighting was featured on the front page of *Borba,* though not until early December did the influential *Review of International Affairs* carry an article on the subject. Belgrade had resolved its dilemma; Moscow hesitated a while longer, no doubt because of a lingering hope for a settlement with Peking.

Yugoslav indecision, relatively short-lived though it had been, was not greeted kindly in New Delhi. The Indian Government was disappointed by the failure of the leading nonaligned nations (and the Soviet Union) to condemn the Chinese attack, and pressure for a reevaluation of its commitment to nonalignment mounted from its rightwing

---

of the Communist Party of India on International Problems as an Aspect of its Independent Course," published in *Društvene Snage i Savremena Politička Kretanja u Nerazvijenim Zemljama* (Beograd: Institut Za Izučavanje Radničkog Pokret, 1963) , pp. 430-431.

[15] *Borba,* November 6, 1962.

parties.[16] The United Arab Republic, for example, had informed New Delhi of its intention to remain benevolently neutral in the hope that by keeping open channels of communication to China (with which it enjoyed good relations) it might help end the conflict and in this manner aid India more effectively than by taking a partisan stand. On October 28 Nasser sent a note to Chou En-lai offering the services of the Afro-Asian countries in settling the issue. Six nonaligned countries met in Colombo in February 1963 but failed in their attempt to arrange direct talks between India and China. (Irate though India was with the nonaligned countries in 1962, it welcomed the reluctance of the nonaligned Moslem countries to take sides in its war with Pakistan three years later: these countries would not oppose Pakistan on religious grounds, but were sympathetic toward India as a fellow nonaligned country.)

There are differences of opinion as to whether division existed in Yugoslav Party and governmental circles over the issue of open denunciation of another socialist country. In off-the-record discussions most officials deny that there was any dilemma. One member of Tito's "Kitchen Cabinet," for example, noted that Yugoslavia had been critical of China, even when India had cordial relations with China, and that it did not have any illusions about Peking's foreign policy: "As we know from our experience with the Soviet Union in 1948, a socialist country is not automatically free from all chauvinistic elements. We did not receive the impression from official Indian sources that there was disappointment that Yugoslavia had not come out more openly in support of India in October 1962, though such views did and do exist." A Bureau chief in the

---

[16] For a careful examination of the effect of October 1962 on Indian thinking see Cecil V. Crabb, Jr., "The Testing of Nonalignment," *The Western Political Quarterly*, Vol. XVII, No. 3 (September 1964), pp. 517-542. Another writer has observed that India's voting pattern on Cold War issues in the U.N. General Assembly underwent an almost complete reversal during the three years after the Chinese attack—from alignment with the Soviet Union to alignment with the West. Theodore L. Shay, "Nonalignment Si, Neutralism No," *The Review of Politics*, Vol. 30, No. 2 (April 1968), p. 236.

Secretariat for Foreign Affairs also emphasized the absence of illusions about the Chinese and contended that the Yugoslav Government had not seen itself as having to choose between a nonaligned and a socialist country. In fact, Yugoslavia had not been uncritical of India at a time when the Nehru Government had been friendly to China and had shown "not too great" attention, considering its interests, to nonalignment. During the 1956-1962 period, the Bureau chief remarked, India had been playing "games with the Great Powers" instead of promoting nonalignment, and this had redounded to its detriment when the military showdown with China came. He said that, contrary to the Indian view of Yugoslav equivocation, Yugoslavia had been far more explicit in supporting India than had many of the other nonaligned countries. Different officials, including one who had been stationed in New Delhi at the time, speculated that Belgrade's seeming hesitancy had stemmed from a bureaucratic oversight in New Delhi, resulting in Belgrade's not being informed promptly of the gravity of the situation and thus thinking initially that the fighting was another in a long series of minor skirmishes. This view was, however, denied by colleagues who had then been in Belgrade.

Nevertheless, some officials acknowledge the dilemma and the leadership's ideological doubts about the wisdom of condemning China. An official in the Office of the President said there had been a prevailing reluctance to criticize a socialist country. Furthermore, he admitted, the Yugoslavs had been unwilling to provoke a polemic with the Chinese, in part because it would be useless, and in part because it would not be politic to engage in acrimony with China at the same time some of their nonaligned friends remained well disposed toward China. Fearing that condemnation might complicate their relations with the nonaligned nations, the Yugoslavs proceeded cautiously, although President Tito did express his firm support for Nehru in private messages. When asked why Tito aligned himself immediately with the U.A.R. in June 1967 whereas he had delayed for two weeks in the case of India in 1962, a high-ranking member of the LYC said, "There were some conflicts of interest; between Yugoslavia's position in Europe and its policy in Asia there is a difference, since the closer a development is to one's home base, the more one must think in day-to-day terms."

In late December 1962 Edvard Kardelj went to India for discussions (at approximately the same time that Tito went to Moscow "to confirm and publicize the already extensive Soviet-Yugoslav rapprochement and to discuss with Khrushchev its future intensification").[17] Belgrade was concerned over the rising pressure from Nehru's right-wing parliamentary critics to ally India with the West and the Indian Government's apparent reappraisal of the utility of nonalignment. Though it is unlikely that Kardelj had to convince Nehru of the long-term advantages of non-alignment, he did, from all reports, help to allay Nehru's anxiety over the intentions of the Soviet Union, which had not yet come out forthrightly against the Chinese. Kardelj satisfied Nehru that the conflict of interests between the Soviet Union and China was inevitable and irreconcilable, that India need not fear that the Soviet Union would join China against India, and that China could not carry out a major war against India while isolated from the Soviet camp and from the rest of Asia. If these surmises are correct, Kardelj's visit may have brought Nehru the extra ammunition he needed to withstand his critics and adhere to nonalignment, despite his momentary need for military assistance from the West.[18]

[17] Griffith, *op.cit.*, p. 85.

[18] A Yugoslav diplomat, long resident in India, said that both the Soviet Union and the United States were guilty of trying to interfere unduly in the political affairs of India: the Soviets, by relying too heavily on the advice and assessments of the pro-Moscow wing of the Communist Party of India; the Americans, by lecturing the Indians too often on what they should and should not do. He said that after the Chinese attack, John Kenneth Galbraith, who was American Ambassador, went around stating that nonalignment was now clearly impossible and that India should discard it and align more closely with the West. "In this," he mused, "Galbraith was more a professor than a diplomat."

In short, during the Sino-Indian crisis of 1962, Yugoslav leaders formulated a policy that suited their interests. Though based on certain expectations concerning Sino-Soviet relations, it did not emerge from any prior consultations with Moscow. Soon afterward the Soviets emulated the Yugoslav position. They decided after Cuba that their interests, at least for the moment, lay in détente with the United States, and after the border war that their stake in China was lost and that they had to cultivate India as a potential ally against China for the future. Friendship with India took precedence over reconciliation with China, which demanded too much for what it offered in return.

The Cairo Conference of Nonaligned States: 1964

The Second Conference of Nonaligned States was held in Cairo from October 5 to 10, 1964, in an international environment of relative calm. The United States and the Soviet Union had surmounted the Cuban missile crisis and negotiated a Limited Nuclear Test-Ban Treaty in August 1963, lessening the immediate danger of nuclear war and creating a favorable political climate for further agreements. Not only were East-West relations changing, but within NATO and the Soviet bloc there were indications that formal adherence to a military-political alliance system need no longer determine a nation's foreign policy: France and China were calling into question old assumptions about bloc cohesion. Decolonization proceeded in Africa. UNCTAD had been held, and though the results disappointed the developing countries, hopes were still strong for economic concessions. Vietnam was a cloud that had not yet become ominous. The Yugoslav-Soviet rapprochement continued apace, the Yugoslavs hoping that it would strengthen Khrushchev and his policies and help the "more up-to-date tendencies" to prevail in the socialist world.[19] At a Plenum of the Central Committee of the

19 Dj. Jerković, "Widening of the Zone of Peace," *Review of International Affairs*, Vol. xiv, No. 306 (January 5, 1963) , p. 4.

LYC on May 18, 1963, Tito exuded optimism: he spoke with obvious elation of fraternal ties with the Soviet Union, and stressed that these were not inconsonant with Yugoslavia's desire to maintain good relations with the Western countries; he also castigated Peking, asserting that because Yugoslavia "enjoys great prestige in the Asian and African countries, especially in the nonaligned and developing countries, and because of its peaceful policy," the Chinese cast unwarranted aspersions on the socialist nature of Yugoslav society and the anti-imperialism underlying its foreign policy.[20]

The initiative for the Cairo Conference had come from Tito and Nasser, especially the former. The increased number of new nations, the uncertainty expressed in various quarters over the functions of nonalignment in a period of incipient détente, and the challenge raised by militant Chinese propositions were motivating factors. During the preparatory phases the Indonesians questioned the opportuneness of a new nonaligned conference, preferring instead a second Bandung, i.e., Afro-Asian gathering.[21] According to a leading Yugoslav diplomat, "there were frequent attempts to impose upon the constructive and principled policy of the nonaligned countries artificially contrived dilemmas."[22] Yugoslav-Indonesian relations, once friendly, deteriorated noticeably prior to the Conference, accelerating a trend that had set in since Sukarno's shift to

[20] *Peti Plenum Tsentralnog Komiteta Savezna Komunista Jugoslavije* (Belgrade: Komunist, 1963) , pp. 20-27. Of Khrushchev, Tito said: "Thanks to Comrade Khrushchev and the rest of his collaborators, we have slowly and steadily succeeded in improving our relations with the Soviet Union and the other socialist countries. That improvement in relations to the USSR and the other socialist countries has enormous positive significance not only for Yugoslavia and for these socialist countries but also for the revolutionary workers' and progressive movement in general. It strengthens the unity not only of the socialist countries but also of all the progressive forces in the struggle for peace and for constructive, active, and peaceful coexistence."

[21] Josip Djerdja, "New Stage in the Evolution of Nonalignment Policies," *Medjunarodni Problemi*, Vol. XVI, No. 3 (1964) , pp. 9-24.

[22] Mišo Pavićević, "The Second Conference of Nonaligned Countries," *Socijalizam*, Vol. VII, No. 5 (May 1964) , p. 672.

a pro-Peking position in late 1961.[23] Yugoslav-Cuban relations also took a turn for the worse because Tito sponsored an invitation for Venezuela, Castro's bitterest enemy in Latin America. Castro, meanwhile, dependent on the Soviet Union for economic and military assistance, but resentful over Khrushchev's settlement with Kennedy, vented his ire by adopting a Maoist line on the feasibility of exporting revolution by violent means. This set him in direct opposition to Tito (and Khrushchev), who advocated a policy of peaceful coexistence.

The widening of the Sino-Soviet rift that resulted from the Cuban crisis and the Sino-Indian border war brought Moscow closer to Belgrade's position on nonalignment. Moscow's opening to the West and to the nonaligned countries further infuriated the Chinese. Sino-Soviet hostility spilled over into the Third World. Peking tried to prevent Soviet participation in the militant and marginalist Afro-Asian forums, where the Chinese were influential—e.g., the Afro-Asian Peoples' Solidarity Conference at Moshi (Tanzania) in February 1963—on the ground that the Soviet Union was a European not an Asian country. Moscow, in contrast to its reserved attitude toward the Belgrade Conference three years earlier, fully backed Yugoslav efforts to promote a Conference of Nonaligned States, which it believed would better serve its own interests in the Third World than another Bandung Conference dominated by Peking's views. In February 1964 it enthusiastically endorsed the convening of a Nonaligned Conference. Animosity toward Peking moved Moscow toward Belgrade's corner.

The main antagonists at Cairo were Tito and Sukarno:

[23] By late 1961 Sukarno had moved sharply to the left in his domestic policies. He established informal but intimate ties with the pro-Peking Indonesian Communist Party (P.K.I.), in part out of frustration with the resistance to his domestic policies from the mélange of conservative, often corrupt, political parties which ostensibly supported him, and in part out of admiration for the organizational talent and drive of Aidit's P.K.I., which he hoped to manipulate for his own purposes. Also, the greater became Sukarno's appetite for foreign expansionism at the expense of his neighbors, the more he looked to Peking.

the first championed nonalignment, active and peaceful coexistence, and cooperation through the United Nations as the main political organization of the international community; the other, exclusivity predicated on racial and ethnic ties among Afro-Asian states, unremitting struggle against "reactionaries" and the West, and the creation of a new militant organization of Afro-Asians outside the framework of the U.N.

Tito held that adherence to the principles of peaceful coexistence as the "norms governing the life of the international community" implied no lessening of the struggle against imperialism or colonialism. The policy of nonalignment had never been, nor could it ever be, construed as "a policy of passive resistance to the division of the world, or a policy of equidistance"; it was always "principled and universal in its approach, committed when the preservation of peace and the protection of the fundamental rights of peoples and States were involved."[24] Tito impatiently condemned those who "accept peace and coexistence in one area" [between the superpowers], while invoking ideological or racial motifs and Cold War methods in another [the Third World], for playing into the hands of the imperialists and others who favor aggravating tensions and adventurist policies, "not even precluding the possibility of a general conflagration."

Sukarno, on the other hand, denied the universality or desirability of "peaceful coexistence": the principle could be applicable only "between powers of equal strength," not in cases where one country or group of countries was strong and the other weak. Only through solidarity and by struggle and confrontation with the West could the Afro-Asian countries overcome their position of weakness in the world. As if to emphasize the irreconcilability of his premises with those of peaceful coexistence, Sukarno made his area of conflict so broad as to encompass virtually all of international politics:

[24] NAC-II/Heads/PV.2 (Provisional Verbatim Record of the Second Meeting of the Conference of the Heads of State of Nonaligned Countries), p. 44.

. . . since all kinds of colonialism, imperialism, neo-colonialism, racial discrimination and apartheid are forms of domination, peaceful coexistence cannot be fully practiced the whole world over until these evils have been finally eradicated.[25]

Belgrade interpreted Sukarno's extremism as being linked to Peking's aims of isolating Yugoslavia and the Soviet Union from the nonaligned Afro-Asian countries and polarizing relations between the developing and developed countries, to the detriment of efforts such as UNCTAD and the Limited Nuclear Test Ban Treaty, and other steps designed to loosen bloc ties and ease Cold War tensions. Yugoslav officials denounced Sukarno's formulation in "pseudo-revolutionary phraseology" of a conflict between decolonization and coexistence, arguing that these objectives were not incompatible and focusing on the positive achievements of nonalignment.[26]

To assert, as Western commentators did, that Tito was "essentially taking a Soviet view of the Cold War situation"[27] was inaccurate. Tito was upholding a position he had been associated with for almost a decade; it was the Soviet leaders, newcomers to lauding nonalignment, who were now advocating views that accorded with Tito's.

The Cairo Conference ended on October 10, 1964. Four days later Nikita S. Khrushchev was deposed, and the following day Peking detonated its first atomic bomb, ushering in a new phase in the Sino-Soviet dispute and rivalry in the Third World.

The Failure of the Militants: Algiers and Havana

Prior to the Cairo Conference, Sukarno had induced a group of Afro-Asian nations to discuss the convening of a Second Bandung. At the preparatory meeting in April 1964 in Jakarta, the Indonesians maneuvered not only

[25] NAC-II/MIN/R.3/Add. 2, p. 2.
[26] Mišo Pavićević, "The Policy of Nonalignment in the World at the Cairo Conference," *Socijalizam*, Vol. VIII, No. 11-12. (November-December 1964) , pp. 1527-1531.
[27] *The New York Times*, October 7, 1964.

to prevent the Second Conference of Nonaligned States but also to discredit Yugoslavia for proposing it. They attacked India, too, for suggesting that, should a Second Afro-Asian Conference be held, the Soviet Union be invited as an Asian country and a supporter of national liberation movements, contentions which Peking disputed through its Indonesian proxy. After considerable wrangling, the preparatory meeting agreed to convene a Second Bandung in June 1965, but in Algiers, which was a keen disappointment to Sukarno who wanted the prestige of acting as host. Yugoslavia was excluded because it did not have any geographical basis for claiming, as did the USSR, that it was an Asian country. However, this did not stop Yugoslav commentators from flailing China for its "cheap, demagogic, and quasi-revolutionary" proposals, which clearly revealed ambitions for primacy and hegemony over Afro-Asian countries.[28]

Peking's efforts to ensnare Algeria's Ben Bella had not succeeded, but Tito was sufficiently concerned in April 1964 to visit Algeria to reinforce Yugoslav-Algerian ties and thus keep Ben Bella's growing militancy concentrated within a nonaligned rather than an Afro-Asian framework. Tito was successful, at least to the extent of encouraging Ben Bella to remain neutral in the Sino-Soviet rivalry during the sessions of the Afro-Asian Preparatory Committee for the Algiers Conference. The ouster of Ben Bella on the eve of the Conference, forcing its postponement to November 5, 1965, was a sharp setback for the Chinese. During the intervening months, many invitees began to harbor grave doubts about a Second Bandung and Chinese intentions. The abortive coup by the Indonesian Communist Party on September 30, 1965, tacitly encouraged by Sukarno himself, gave them pause to reconsider the implications of Chinese radicalism. As a result of developments in Indonesia and the air of uncertainty surrounding the Boumedienne government in Algeria, the Second Bandung

---

[28] M. Mirić, "Consolidation of the Anti-Colonial Movement," *Review of International Affairs*, Vol. xv, No. 338 (May 5, 1964) , p. 8.

Conference, scheduled for Algiers, was postponed indefinitely.

In Indonesia the non-Communist military leaders suppressed the coup and dealt harshly with Communists throughout the country. They skillfully isolated Sukarno from his bases of political power and within a year ended his two decades of rule. Sukarno faded swiftly from the international scene, his vainglorious design for leadership of the Afro-Asian nations shattered by the turnabout in Indonesia's domestic politics. The father of his country and a genuine national hero, he unleashed forces he could not control and became another historical memento of showy grandeur. Since 1965-1966, Indonesia's leaders have rejoined the moderates of nonalignment, inclining toward cordiality with the Western countries more than with the socialist camp.

Yugoslav leaders were not unhappy with the humbling of Sukarno, but were upset by what they judged to be the pronouncedly pro-Western, albeit officially nonaligned, bent of the new Indonesian Government. A pointed example of ambivalence in Yugoslav officialdom appeared in the spring of 1966. On April 18, 1966, *Borba* published the substance of an interview which its correspondent D. Simić had just obtained in Jakarta with Adam Malik, the new Foreign Minister, to the effect that the Indonesian Government reaffirmed its commitment to nonalignment and its desire to improve relations "with other nonaligned countries, especially Yugoslavia."[29] However, the following day an editorial written by V. Teslić, a Party spokesman, appeared in *Borba* and suggested that in attempting to extirpate the Communists "Indonesia has resorted to a by no means less harmful extreme position than the one taken in recent years."[30] Teslić acknowledged that energetic measures were necessary against "the errors or treason committed by *individual people* from progressive parties" but expressed dismay at their widening scope

[29] *Borba*, April 18, 1966.   [30] *Borba*, April 19, 1966.

which seemed geared to liquidating "all progressive forces in Indonesia" (emphasis added). Disturbed by the overthrow of Nkrumah in February and Ghana's shift toward the West, Belgrade feared that Indonesia would exchange Sukarno's pro-Peking loyalties for equally pro-Western ones, thereby further weakening nonalignment. In the subsequent period Indonesia has maintained its nonaligned status, but its leaders have concentrated on domestic difficulties and established friendly relations with the Western Powers, choosing in the process to remain relatively inactive in nonaligned councils.

To salve their disappointment over Algiers, the Chinese backed Cuba's convening in Havana in January 1966 of a Conference of the Afro-Asian-Latin American Peoples' Solidarity Organization, a potpourri of representatives from about sixty parties and movements who did not officially represent their respective governments. This Tri-Continental Conference refused to admit observers from Yugoslavia. Both Havana and Peking denounced Yugoslavia for kowtowing to the United States, abjuring armed revolutionary struggle, and advocating a mealy brand of coexistence. Havana parroted Peking's anti-Yugoslav invective.

Belgrade blamed Peking for the failure of the conference to invite observers from the Yugoslav League for Peace, Independence, and Equality of Peoples, which had been represented at previous Afro-Asian nongovernmental conferences, attributing this hostility to the attempts by "dogmatic and pseudo-ultra-radical forces" to discriminate against the policy of nonalignment and peaceful coexistence.[31] Officially, the Yugoslavs feigned surprise and disappointment at being barred. Actually, their being blackballed had advantages. According to Western diplomats resident in Belgrade at the time, the Yugoslavs privately expressed relief that they had been excluded. It would have been difficult for them to be there under the domination of Cuba with its pro-Peking line, and with the baiting

[31] *Borba*, January 3, 1966.

and denunciation of Belgrade; further, it would have compromised them in the eyes of the Latin American governments (of Venezuela, Colombia, and Brazil, for example) with which they were trying to improve economic and political relations. As it turned out, Soviet participation in the Conference and acquiescence in the resolution calling for armed support of revolutionary forces seeking to overthrow existing governments in Latin America set back Moscow's efforts to expand its ties with countries in the region.

Incongruent Conceptions of Nonalignment

The convergence since 1962 of Yugoslav and Soviet positions on issues involving the nonaligned countries has partially obscured the persisting and profound differences of outlook which shape their approaches to nonalignment. Despite the agreement in many of their current policies toward the nonaligned countries, the differences in their general conceptions of nonalignment reflect the assumptions and aspirations that must inevitably bring the two into frequent contention. These differences have generally been overlooked by Western writers because of their understandable but unfortunate propensity for looking at nonalignment through the prism of Soviet-American relations and not in the light of views from the Third World.

Prior to 1961-1962, Yugoslavia went its own way during the years of separation from the Soviet bloc. It pioneered nonalignment and established sound and intimate relationships with the leading Afro-Asian nations. Its view of nonalignment was consistent with its policy among the nonaligned. On the other hand, the Soviet Union is an Ivan-come-lately to nonalignment. Despite Khrushchev's official scrapping in February 1956 of the Zhdanov "two-camp" thesis and his enunciation of the "zone of peace" concept, with its implicit acceptance of a transitional role for developing countries trying to build "socialism," and despite the occasional patronizing congratulatory remarks about the role played by nonaligned countries in opposing "imperialism" and fighting for peace, Soviet leaders *in practice* treat nonaligned countries in a manner that may best be described as friendship with enemies of their enemies rather than friendship with friends. The widening rift with Communist China, the felt need to compete with Peking in the Third World, and the growing stake there of Soviet diplomacy, led them to bestow an element of respectability upon nonalignment. The Yugoslavs, pleased by the rift and continually mesmerized by the vision of linking the socialist countries to the nonaligned countries in a grand constellation of "progressive" forces, labor to bring the Soviet Union in line with nonalignment. But political reality is not the clay of the sculptor; it has an implasticity that defies grand designs.

Despite the partial congruence of current Yugoslav and Soviet policies toward nonaligned countries, there is no evidence of systematic coordination. Yugoslavia is still suspect in Moscow (this was true even before August 1968); it is tolerated, not accepted for what it is and seeks to be. And the unregulated differentiation, part of which Moscow attributes to "revisionism" (i.e., Yugoslav ideas and practices), spreading within the Soviet camp is definitely not to Moscow's liking. Indeed, the incompatibilities between Yugoslav and Soviet concepts of nonalignment, which many Yugoslav officials in private grudgingly acknowledge, may lead Yugoslavia in the future to give its formulations of nonalignment a less institutionalized anti-Western bias than has heretofore been the case; for, ironically, the ultimate purposes of Yugoslavia and the Soviet Union in the Third World may prove to be less congenial than those of Yugoslavia and some nations of the West, e.g., France and Great Britain.

First, unlike the Soviet Union, Yugoslavia, which is not a member of the Warsaw Pact, is committed to the abolition of blocs and camps. As the Yugoslavs see it, the acme of nonalignment is a no-camp world. To Moscow this is anathema. At a time of Yugoslav-Soviet tension, Vladimir Bakarić, the Croatian Party leader and one of the most influential figures in Yugoslavia, retorted to Soviet charges that Yugoslavia by its revisionist policies was intent on undermining the unity of the socialist camp. Dismissing as peevish Moscow's complaint that Yugoslavia was violating the principles of proletarian internationalism by refusing to join the "socialist camp," he noted that "there exist also firmer links than those of formal agreements."[32] Yugoslavia had discovered to its disillusionment that in dealing with the Soviet Union "agreements are concluded, declarations are signed, and then something entirely different goes on than what the documents contained." He said the Soviet endeavor to convert the socialist world into a "camp" is older than the "camp" itself:

> Stalin was its protagonist. He was the protagonist of "negotiations" at the expense of others and, by this token, he was one of the creators of a policy from positions of force. That is not the same as the strengths of the socialist movement and socialist states. . . .[33]

Bakarić asserted that Moscow thinks only in terms of blocs: "They say we are sitting on two chairs. It only looks that way to them, for they see nothing beyond blocs. They are the ones who believe in blocs. . . ."[34] On another occasion, shortly after the 1957 Moscow Conference of Communist Parties, Aleš Bebler answered Soviet critics of Yugoslav nonparticipation in blocs:

> Politics is not geometry. Politics is an effort to achieve certain objectives, close at hand or more remote. The principal aim of non-bloc policy is international non-bloc cooperation. Efforts in this direction may lead to an attitude which sometimes draws closer to, or even coincides with that of one or another country included or not included in any of the blocs, i.e., dependent on the essence of the question involved.[35]

[32] Vladimir Bakarić, "Speech at the Fourth Congress of the LYC of Croatia," *Review of International Affairs*, Vol. x, No. 217 (April 16, 1959), p. 3.

[33] *Ibid.*   [34] *Ibid.*

[35] Aleš Bebler, "Role of the Non-Bloc Countries," *Review of International Affairs*, Vol. ix, No. 186 (January 1, 1958), p. 2.

At a press conference on January 30, 1959, a spokesman for the Secretariat of State for Foreign Affairs replied to Khrushchev's statement that the essence of the Soviet-Yugoslav dispute was the LYC's effort to convince everyone that there are in the world two blocs, two military camps:

> It is true that we speak of the existence of two blocs and of the negative effect of any bloc policy. We, however, also say that socialism cannot accommodate itself to "camps." On the contrary, those who do so, actually make camps—theoretically and practically—military ones.[36]

For the Yugoslavs the advancement of socialism on a global scale is a goal transcending the confines of any particular camp. The concept of a "camp" implies discipline and subordination to a central authority, a readiness to sacrifice national interests for those of the leader of the "camp." None of this suits Belgrade, which dares not forget 1948; nor is it apt to find favor among the new nations, whose political quest in this century is to overcome the vestiges of a colonial past. A relative calm in relations between Belgrade and Moscow in no way means that a resolution of this issue has been reached.

Second, the Yugoslavs regard the developing countries as national entities seeking, like themselves, an independent existence and a voice in decisions affecting war and peace in the world of which they are an integral part. However, to the Soviet Union the developing countries are "a potential strategical reserve which may be helpful in achieving ascendancy over a rival or attaining world dominance" and not partners with whom cooperation on a plane of equality is possible.[37] Moscow approaches the nonaligned countries primarily as "a no-man's land or free-hunting ground" where it can extend its control to improve its overall political-strategic position relative to the West; it seems po-

---

[36] *Yugoslav Facts and Views*, No. 88 (February 6, 1959).

[37] Dj. Jerković, "Comments on the Change," *Review of International Affairs*, Vol. XII, No. 260 (February 5, 1961), p. 9.

litically incapable of dealing for long with weaker countries on a basis of equality, as if driven to dominate all within its grasp. A Yugoslav journalist who spent many years at the U.N. said that from the very beginning of the postwar period the Soviet Union placed heavy emphasis on the colonial question in the world organization only as a lever in the Cold War. It saw the colonial peoples as "the reserves of the socialist revolution," to be set against the West, but at no time did Stalin regard them as important in their own right.

More recently Yugoslavia opposed Moscow's convocation of an international Communist conference in June 1969 to tighten bloc discipline, isolate the Chinese, and, in particular, reassert within the socialist camp Moscow's hegemonic role, which has been flaunted since 1964 by Romania and was for a brief time jeopardized in Czechoslovakia, which had experienced a startling and unforeseen liberalization under Dubcek. Moscow's reimposition of discipline on the socialist camp contravened Belgrade's position of relaxing bloc ties. Moscow also undermined the Yugoslav-sponsored Mediterranean Conference on the Middle East by ensuring that the resolutions conformed to its immediate political needs instead of trying, as Belgrade urged, to accommodate as many progressive and non-Communist movements as possible from among the nonaligned countries. The Yugoslavs saw in Moscow's obdurate stand a dismaying reminder that Soviet leaders had learned little from their experience with the Third World. Belgrade reiterated its familiar argument of more than a decade: that under present conditions the Marxist socialist parties "no longer have a monopoly over the ideology of peace."[38] In a pointed allusion to Moscow's inability to discard outmoded Stalinist formulations, one noted publicist states:

> It is obvious that obsolete ideas about the "vanguard" and "reserve," and the old concepts and methods of

---

[38] N. Opačić, "International Cooperation of the League of Communists of Yugoslavia," *Review of International Affairs*, Vol. xix, No. 404 (February 5, 1968), p. 26.

cooperation and common activity, are untenable under the complex conditions of contemporary development.[39]

A corollary of Moscow's tendency to use developing areas as political arenas for weakening the West is the proposition that socialism can be built only by Communist Parties—an ideological tenet discarded by the Yugoslavs in 1958.

Third, though Yugoslavia considers itself a socialist country and a part of the socialist world (which is never interpreted as synonymous with the socialist camp), it maintains also that it is a nonaligned country. It insists there is no incompatibility between the two. Moscow has yet to accept this proposition, which remains a bone of contention between them. To the question, how would you distinguish the main differences between Yugoslav and Soviet views of nonalignment, one brilliant Yugoslav analyst said simply: "Yugoslavia is a nonaligned country and the Soviet Union is not. The USSR is a superpower; it has a position in the world, with interests and aims designed to strengthen its camp." Ruminating for a moment, he added: "Perhaps after all there are two types of nonalignment: the nonalignment of the superpowers who are trying to align others to it, and the nonalignment of the nonaligned countries who are not trying to align anyone because they neither can nor wish to do so."

Finally, the Yugoslavs have worked hard at formulating the theoretical bases of nonalignment and the relationship of nonalignment to international trends.[40] They are also deeply concerned with the relationship between the policy of nonalignment and the evolution of socialism as a social system and process of development. A longtime member of Tito's inner circle pointed out that the Soviet Union, by contrast, has no well thought out stand on nonalignment. The Soviets object to Yugoslavia's membership in

[39] *Ibid.*
[40] For example, two carefully presented monographs are: Gavro Altman, *Politika Nesvrstavanja Posle Kaira* (Belgrade: Komunist, 1964) and Leo Mates, *Neangažovanost: Začeći, Razvoj, Perspektiv* (Belgrade: Sedma Sila, 1964).

the nonaligned group, claiming Yugoslavia is not a fully socialist country because it aligns itself with nonsocialist countries. Moreover, "though on occasion Soviet policy takes a positive view of nonalignment, basically Moscow is skeptical and reluctant to discuss nonalignment, especially with the Yugoslavs." Indeed, according to Yugoslav informants, Soviet leaders believe that in the future the nonaligned group will become a more disparate conglomerate and thus more easily managed, a factor underlying Soviet foreign aid policy. The Soviets anticipate and welcome fragmentation in the Third World; the Yugoslavs seek to promote cooperation and integration, both economic and diplomatic.

The Yugoslavs argue that it is theoretically and politically unjustified to draw any artificial demarcations between socialist and nonaligned countries. They see both types contributing to a world process that is transforming international life. To perpetuate their differences in the interest of narrow political goals would be tragic. A thoughtful Yugoslav correspondent has written:

> Still more harm would be done by holding nonalignment to be a kind of lower foreign policy in relation to the "socialist foreign policy," even if the policy of nonalignment was viewed with sympathy. The socialist countries should not merely "sympathize" or "support" the policy of nonalignment but should identify themselves with it, irrespective of the fact that, owing to the relation of forces in the world or to some other reasons, some of them are not in a position to act as "nonaligned" in every respect at this moment.[41]

Whether Moscow is listening is a debatable—or perhaps not a debatable—point.

Peaceful Coexistence: Active and Adaptive

Integrally related to, but distinct from, the Yugoslav and Soviet views of nonalignment are their differing interpre-

[41] Gavro Altman, "Responsibility of the Policy of Nonalignment," *Socialist Thought and Practice*, No. 15 (July-September 1964) , p. 94.

tations of peaceful coexistence. At the present time it is difficult to be sure of the differences because Soviet views have varied over the years and according to the context in which they were proffered. To the Yugoslavs peaceful coexistence means the parallel coexistence of states regardless of their social and political systems; to the Soviets the term, which had its origin in Lenin's writings, implies a recognition of the existence of two hostile blocs. As one Yugoslav epitomized the Soviet interpretation, it reduced itself to the notion—we are here, they are there, and let's keep it that way. Underlying the Yugoslav disagreement with Soviet ideologues is the Yugoslav assumption that peaceful coexistence between blocs is temporary and unstable, and would lead other countries to a choice between blocs and to an eventual war. For this reason Yugoslavia's view of coexistence is anti-bloc. The idea of permanent coexistence of blocs is antithetical to its belief that every nation has the right to deal with problems within its own country in a manner that suits it best. Genuine coexistence does not perpetuate existing bloc divisions, but tends to break down blocs formed along ideological, military, and political lines. As Tito noted in his speech on December 25, 1958, at Bandung, "coexistence is in essence a dynamic progressive process in the course of which there should be achieved an easing of tensions, a gradual elimination of blocs." He also observed that it was erroneous—an allusion to the Soviet view at the time—to consider coexistence "a question of tactics—of respite and truce, and not a lasting need, a need for peace and fruitful international cooperation":[42]

> It is, in actual fact, an erroneous conception regarding the possibility of coexistence between blocs, proceeding from the already attained bloc positions. It is clear that such a concept of coexistence is in contradiction with the very essence of coexistence.

[42] Quoted in "Yugoslavia's Views on the Policy of Active Peaceful Coexistence," *Yugoslav Survey*, Vol. III, No. 8 (January-March 1962), p. 1202.

In his 1958 New Year's Day message Tito put the issue even more forcefully:

A lasting, constructive coexistence between the blocs is impossible, whatever some people may think, for it would be no coexistence. It would be just a kind of truce full of dangers of new conflicts. Coexistence should replace the blocs, for the division of the world into blocs is contrary to the idea of coexistence, since the blocs really represent an ideological division of the world which naturally makes them so bitter. The ideological division of the world means the division into a capitalist and a socialist system.[43]

Yugoslav writers go to great lengths to stress that peaceful coexistence is not a rationalization for the maintenance of either colonial or Great Power domination over large parts of the world; nor is it a policy for preventing internal liberalization. According to Kardelj:

The policy of coexistence neither is nor should it be a policy of defence of the *status quo* in international relations and even less in internal social relations. It simply means renouncing war as an instrument for the settlement of international contradictions and taking the line of relying upon the results of the internal social development which will ultimately change international relations as well.[44]

Implicit in this statement are three aspects of Yugoslav sensitivity: to Soviet interference in its internal affairs; to Soviet intervention in the countries of Eastern Europe; and to any belief that it tacitly sanctions a continuation of colonialism, under any guise, out of fear of precipitating a war. The Yugoslavs say that in the policy of the Soviet Union—peaceful coexistence between blocs—the interests of small countries in the bloc do not receive proper weight.

[43] Quoted in Jože Smole, *Yugoslav Views of Coexistence* (Belgrade: Jugoslavija, 1961) , pp. 30-31.
[44] *Ibid.*, p. 41.

Some maintain that a change has occurred in recent years, even though the same term continues to be used. Others argue that nothing basic has altered, giving as illustration the proposal of the Soviet Union for a treaty of non-aggression between the Warsaw and NATO Pacts, i.e., between blocs. To Yugoslavs, peaceful coexistence should be the active promotion of exchanges between individual governments, and between nongovernmental, scientific, and cultural groups and individuals, in order to have beneficial impacts on political systems. In a major address in Dar-es-Salaam on February 26, 1968, Edvard Kardelj emphasized that what is involved in active coexistence "is not a sort of *modus vivendi* in mutual relations among peoples with different social systems, but active mutual cooperation in all fields where this is possible, regardless of differences of systems."[45]

Unlike the Soviet Union, Yugoslavia predicates its conception of peaceful coexistence on the assumptions that the small nations can exert an influence on world developments and must actively seek to do so, and that for lasting political agreements to emerge the two blocs must consider the interests of the developing countries. From its "objective" condition of being a small country, it sees the Third World in a different light, as an ally to be galvanized to action in the common interest rather than as a quarry to be stampeded through fear and blandishments. Realizing that the potential of the small nations for influence is limited and can be wielded primarily in a period of relatively low tension between the Great Powers, it espouses the coexistence of states and an enhanced role for the nonaligned countries in the effectuation of a noncamp world.

Observations

The Sino-Soviet rift has had the effect of moving the Soviet Union closer to Yugoslavia's position on nonalignment, and not of bringing Yugoslavia back to the Soviet fold. Moscow, not Belgrade, accommodated in order to en-

[45] *Yugoslav Facts and Views*, No. 38 (March 20, 1968), p. 1.

hance its respectability and persuasiveness among the non-aligned. Thus, it was Moscow that embraced (and indeed went beyond) the Yugoslav view of Chinese "adventurism" and "pseudo-radicalism" in meetings of the nonaligned nations; and it was Moscow that, at least in its dealings with the nonaligned countries, shifted to a position of lauding active and peaceful coexistence (i.e., the Yugoslav variant), the international importance of nonalignment, and the "progressive" character of non-Communist nationalist leaders in the Third World. By contrast, on no major issue involving nonalignment has Belgrade abandoned or altered a previously held position out of deference to Soviet wishes. (The nearest thing to such a reversal occurred at the Belgrade Conference when Tito avoided criticizing Moscow for its unilateral resumption of nuclear testing.)

If we realize that prior to 1961 the Soviet Government showed little understanding of nonalignment, and even less approval of Yugoslav policy in the Third World, the extent to which Moscow's attitude has altered becomes amply evident. However, Moscow has not permitted apprehension over the challenge from Peking to blind it to pitfalls inherent in some of the views advanced by the Yugoslavs. Thus, it resists equating the nonaligned and the socialist countries ideologically in terms of their "progressiveness"; it avoids discussions with nonaligned countries of the disutility of blocs, since it does not favor the abolition in the foreseeable future of the Warsaw Treaty Organization, one of the last institutional levers it retains for exercising control over Eastern Europe; and it does not agree with the Yugoslav proposition that socialism can be built in the nonaligned world by non-Communist parties.

Most Afro-Asian countries view the Sino-Soviet dispute with mingled annoyance and bewilderment, as a limitation on their ability to maneuver freely between East and West. When Yugoslavia alone bore the brunt of Chinese denunciations, they did not sympathize very much because they did not fully understand the broader issues involved. Indeed, for a short period (1962-1965), the "verbal radicalism" of the Chinese made Yugoslav proposals seem tame and unattractive by comparison. After China's smashing defeat of India, which was enthusiastically acclaimed in Indonesia, where anti-Indian feeling was then strong, Peking made some inroads among the militants of non-alignment through Sukarno. But by 1965-1966 a reaction set in and Chinese influence waned. Just as in India there had not been much understanding of, or attention paid to, the rift before 1962, so now among the African militants there is only minimal awareness of its issues and stakes. The African militants desire that Sino-Soviet unity be reestablished so they can rely on support from the East in their disputes with the West, which they continue to regard as their principal threat.

Reviewing the confusion wrought in the ranks of the nonaligned by the dispute, the difficulties experienced by Yugoslavia in trying to explain the issues and its reasons for upholding the Soviet position, and the persistence of illusions about Chinese policy in a number of nonaligned countries, one Yugoslav, who had served for years at the United Nations and in one of the nonaligned countries, ruefully commented on the character of international relations:

> Perhaps after all in international relations, as in personal development, one must actually experience the difficulties. Before one can mature, one must go through the experience of dealing with these issues, of dealing with the Soviet Union and China. The vote of India in 1951 in support of the Yugoslav resolution regarding the Soviet danger to Yugoslavia was quite a victory for Yugoslavia because the Indians did not really understand why and about what the Yugoslavs were concerned; they did not understand the Cominform dispute at all. Today many nations may have to go through a similarly direct confrontation with China to understand the concrete issues involved in the Sino-Soviet dispute and what they signify for them. Certainly the Indians understood little before adversity forced them to face facts.

Yugoslavia has benefited from the Sino-Soviet rift.[46] Moscow's diminished authority within the Communist world resulted in decreased Soviet pressure on Belgrade and the development generally in Eastern Europe of an environment more conducive to liberalization and national, not Muscovite, communism. At the same time it is reasonable to assume that Yugoslavia does not want the Soviet Union or the idea of communism discredited in the Third World, since this would minimize the uniqueness of Yugoslavia as a Communist state and its importance among the nonaligned.

There is no reason to believe that Yugoslavia has been compromised in the eyes of the leading nonaligned countries by its identification with the Soviet position in the dispute between Moscow and Peking.[47] Since the Yugoslav attitude toward nonalignment has not changed, the nonaligned countries have no cause to question it. Also, after working closely with the Yugoslavs for more than a decade, they have made a differentiation which is felicitous to the Yugoslavs: they view them as a breed of Communist quite different from the Soviet or Chinese; and they respect them for their pragmatism, their abstinence from attempts to disseminate their brand of Marxism-Leninism, and their avoidance of interference in the domestic affairs of nonaligned countries. Yugoslavia will not sacrifice its vested interest in its achievements by becoming Moscow's proxy. It has earned a role and a status in the nonaligned world out of all proportion to its size and power, and it is not apt to jeopardize them to service Soviet diplomacy.

[46] Some Yugoslavs say that the benefits were not unqualified. Until August 1968 the Sino-Soviet rift served to blur Yugoslavia's basic disagreements with Moscow, and thereby probably helped the conservative elements in the League of Yugoslav Communists to retain influence on the basis of their close ties to Soviet leaders.

[47] This does not mean that Yugoslavia supports the Soviet Union on every issue; for example, both Yugoslavia and Communist China have condemned the Soviet intervention in Czechoslovakia and held that socialism cannot be built by bayonets.

CHAPTER IX

Beyond Nonalignment

YUGOSLAV LEADERS find nonalignment at the crossroads. They are searchingly examining the problems and the alternatives in order to suggest new forms and new directions for the nonaligned countries. The shortcomings of nonalignment are not mainly their own, and the correctives are not self-evident.

Nonalignment originally emerged as a reaction to the alliances and antagonisms of the Cold War and the attempts of the Great Powers to enmesh the newly independent nations in their ideological, political, and military struggles. The new nations resisted, pioneered timely forms of small power cooperation, and became an autonomous and courted force in international politics. Through nonalignment they kept out of blocs and may even have contributed to the weakening of alliance systems. But with blocs eroding and international relationships less fixed than in the bipolar world of the 1940's and 1950's, nonalignment has lost much of its early utility as a contrast and alternative to membership in one of the major blocs.

Beyond their desire to avoid entangling alliances with Great Powers and to follow an independent policy, the nonaligned nations are in basic disagreement over purposes, priorities, and procedures. Their dissonances drown out their demands and their influence has been sharply reduced—the consequences of changes in the leadership of the nonaligned, in the attitude of the Great Powers, and in the international environment. No one is more dismayed than the Yugoslavs by this diminished status, no one more determined to alter this course which if continued must surely undermine nonalignment, and no one more ready to act on the assumption that "if the courses be departed from, the ends will change."

The confidence Yugoslav analysts convey in their writings about the future of nonalignment is often belied in private discussions where they frankly cast about for hopeful signs that may signify the emergence of new trends. For a time many expected more countries to become nonaligned, acquire incremental influence, and develop within a general framework of socialism. But the Cold War of the early postwar decades has changed, and its alliances and aims are now, in Dickens' words, "but shadows of things that have been." In adapting to this unanticipated development, the Yugoslavs maintain that what is important is the actual policy followed by a country and not its formal allegiance. It is no longer essential that a country not belong to a military bloc—though they prefer that it does not— as long as it pursues a constructive policy: France under de Gaulle was a member of NATO but practiced an independent, anti-bloc policy; and Pakistan, though part of SEATO, does not support the Vietnam war. On the other hand, some countries are nominally nonaligned, but are on the periphery of a bloc. In a period of transition, argue the Yugoslavs, it is the trend not the formal tie that is important. Moreover, they believe that many of the small nations will be forced back to nonalignment because of China's rise to prominence and its interference in their affairs.

The parameters of nonalignment are ambiguous. The criteria formulated at the Cairo Preparatory Conference in June 1961 have not been formally violated but have been broadly interpreted. At that time the participants agreed on the following:

(1) A country should follow an independent policy based on peaceful coexistence and nonalignment, or should be showing a trend in that direction;

(2) It should consistently have supported movements for national independence;

(3) It should not be a member of multilateral military alliances concluded in the context of Great Power conflicts;

(4) If it had conceded military bases these concessions should not have been made in the context of Great Power conflicts;

(5) If it were a member of a bilateral or regional defense arrangement, this should not be in the context of Great Power conflicts.

Yet even these criteria are subject to discussion and review, for as one Yugoslav noted, "political history is not physics—where one repeats experiments and searches for constants."

Designed as a protection against Great Power pressure, nonalignment does not preclude the temporary acceptance of assistance from one or another Great Power. India and the U.A.R. receive considerable aid and Kenya and Tanzania called in British troops to quell domestic disorders, yet presumably all are still nonaligned. The Yugoslavs accept the Indian and Egyptian view that a country may seek help from a Great Power in moments of national peril, provided it retains its independent foreign policy even while cooperating with the Great Power for some specific purpose and for some limited time. After the Chinese attack of October 1962, the United States and Great Britain held joint military air exercises on Indian territory at the invitation of the Indian Government. While the Chinese publicly charged the Indians with discarding nonalignment, the Soviet Government expressed its concern privately; the Yugoslavs were upset but kept silent. Should, as has occasionally been hinted since the 1967 Middle East war, the Egyptians or Algerians grant the Soviet Union a naval base at Alexandria or Mers-el-Kebir, respectively, Belgrade would be forced to water down further its criteria for nonalignment to meet this departure from the formulations adopted in 1961.

The Yugoslavs see the international system as experiencing three revolutions simultaneously: technology and science knitting the world tightly together so that interdependence is no longer a rhetorical flourish for ritualistic occasions but an undeniable reality; the quest for independence and equality of nations becoming more nearly universal than at any other time in history; and decolonization occurring in a remarkably short time. They grant the difficulty of cooperation among the nonaligned, yet insist that the widening gap between the poor nations and the rich nations will strengthen the bonds of the developing countries, which share a desire to resist foreign meddling in their internal affairs and accelerate the process of nation-building. The cementing "unity of interests" the Yugoslavs ascribe to the nonaligned is, however, often hard to discern. Indeed, as the charismatic personalities who gave a sense of solidarity pass from the scene, and as national concerns absorb ruling elites, disunity becomes epidemic.

What is especially disconcerting to the Yugoslavs is the inability of their Afro-Asian colleagues to agree among themselves on the meaning of nonalignment. To some it signifies aloofness from the alliances and imbroglios of the Cold War; to others, a selective partiality which posits participation in some international decisions, the basis for involvement being determined by their partisan interests and not by any principled concern for the critical issues facing the international community; still others assume the nonaligned can perform a magisterial function and settle Great Power disputes because of an alleged objectivity; and so on. It does seem excessive to argue, as one noted Western analyst does, that by attempting to manipulate the Great Powers and advance their own interests in the process, the nonaligned countries have a "demoralizing" effect on the stability of the international system and "adverse effects on both the Great Powers and the uncommitted themselves":[1] the weak can scarcely be blamed for luring the powerful to expansionism and war. However, he is on firm ground in pointing out the manner in which many of the nonaligned countries have been remiss in practicing *vis-à-vis* their own neighbors "the kind of power politics which they urge the great powers to abjure."[2] There are as many different interpretations of nonalignment as there are countries, and

[1] Henry A. Kissinger, "Reflections on Power and Diplomacy" in *The Dimensions of Diplomacy*, edited by E. A. J. Johnson (Baltimore, Md.: The Johns Hopkins Press, 1964) , p. 34.
[2] *Ibid.*, p. 35.

the Yugoslavs may well be trying to organize something that cannot be organized.

Only on economic issues do the nonaligned countries seem capable of agreeing on constructive courses of action. Undeterred, Belgrade insists they will be listened to by the developed countries if they remain united and give proper attention to nonstrategic issues. Increasingly, it sees the economic route as the one to follow to forge a greater unity.

Shortly after the Middle East war of 1967, three major interviews with Nijaz Dizdarević, a member of the eleven-man Executive Committee of the Central Committee of the League of Yugoslav Communists, appeared over a four-month period in the Yugoslav press.[3] Dizdarević dwelt on the state of nonalignment, socialism, and the Middle East. He said nonalignment had to adjust to the new conditions that had matured since 1964, which he identified as follows: (1) The struggle of the former colonies for political independence is "more or less over—though not one hundred per cent"; (2) The absence of stable economies, socio-political structures, and state institutions continually jeopardizes this independence; (3) The new nations find themselves in a relationship of persistent economic dependence on the former colonial powers; and (4) There is a shortage of trained cadres to run many of the new nations. He expressed at some length his disappointment at UNCTAD's paucity of progress in redressing the disparity between the developed and the developing countries. Though laying the blame primarily on the Western countries that dominate international trade relations, he was also critical of the Soviet bloc countries for their unwilling-

[3] *Nin*, August 27, 1967; *Nin*, September 3, 1967; *Narodna Armija*, January 26, 1968, as translated by the Joint Translation Service, No. 4803 (September 1, 1967), No. 4804 (September 2, 1967), and No. 4928 (January 30, 1968), respectively.

In a major reorganization of the executive bodies of the LYC undertaken at the Ninth Congress in March 1969, Nijaz Dizdarević retained key positions: he is a member of both the 15-member Executive Bureau and the 52-member Party Presidium, the supreme body of the LYC (the Central Committee has been abolished on the federal level).

ness to forego their concern with narrow commercial considerations in relations with developing countries, and their reluctance to work jointly with them to realize a fundamental alteration in international economic relations, which would establish strong bonds between the socialist and the developing countries. Noting the failure of new economic relations to keep pace with new political relations, Dizdarević held that a struggle between the haves and have-nots, between what the Chinese call the "world urban areas" and the "world rural areas," would be avoided only if the developed countries responded promptly to the needs and aspirations of the Third World, wherein reside the seeds of war, whether in the Middle East, Latin America, or Southeast Asia. In their emphasis on UNCTAD as a suitable instrument for advancing such a program, one sees that the Yugoslavs continue to place great store in functional economic cooperation for the future of nonalignment and democratization of international relations; but the reeds with which to build are few.

Expectations

In the absence of reliable data it is difficult to gauge the extent of the gap between expectation and actuality. One leading political figure rejected the view that the Yugoslav leadership, having had great expectations for nonalignment, felt keenly disappointed by recent developments: "Others ascribe illusions to Yugoslavia which Yugoslavia does not have." President Tito, he said, had always maintained that nonalignment could not be expected to develop in linear fashion, that setbacks were inevitable, that progress must wait upon public opinion and changed governmental attitudes in what was destined to be a lengthy process. There is no guarantee of success, he noted, and no easy road, but since nonalignment is the best alternative available to the new nations it warrants continued support: "It exerts an enormous influence on the general approach and thinking of the new nations, though the difficulties in finding suitable means of cooperation are serious." Another official—a thoughtful, fair-minded person with long experience in diplomacy—rejected the term "illusions." He believed Yugoslavia had been correct in its expectation that the Third World would have a special role to play in world affairs, and that it would inevitably have an influence on international law and relationships. Where Yugoslav leaders may have erred, he suggested, was in their "wrong appraisals" of the tempo of change at particular moments and in particular situations. Another distinguished specialist on foreign affairs thought expectations may have been exaggerated during the Kennedy-Khrushchev period. In addition, he said that some of the analyses on which policymakers relied may have been made by people of limited or no experience in the Third World who wrote overly optimistic reports of developments in Africa, Asia, and Latin America in terms of what they thought the leadership wanted to hear.

Overall the Yugoslav Government was never too far out of line with reality. It hoped for cohesion, was dismayed by setbacks, but was not surprised by instability. Notwithstanding the frustrations of the "progressives" in the nonaligned world, it remains convinced of the historical necessity of nonalignment and the urgent need for accelerating economic development. And it believes in the inevitability of a flexible and pluralist socialism.

Impact

If Yugoslav leaders have played a major role in the evolution of nonalignment, they have in turn been transformed as a consequence of their involvement. Nonalignment helped break once and for all the psychological isolation of the Yugoslav Communists from the outside world. It led to the discarding of the legacy, dating from the Bolshevik Revolution and ritualized during the Stalin period, of the beleaguerment of Marxist-Leninist parties in a capitalist battleground. Out of necessity the Yugoslavs shed much of the unregenerate hostility toward all non-Communists that typified their Soviet counterparts, and adopted an approach based on cooperation with non-Marxist groups.

Nonalignment widened the horizons of Yugoslav leaders, most of whom had only secondhand information about the world beyond Europe. It enhanced their confidence and helped them to mature. By contributing toward a more realistic awareness of the outside world, it brought Yugoslavia into a felicitous relationship with Afro-Asian leaders and made possible a deeper understanding of the West. Before 1948, during what Yugoslavs call their "dogmatic period," they perceived international developments only in terms of conflicts between capitalism and communism, between West and East. Gradually they came to see them in terms of a North-South conflict, of developed societies versus developing ones. No longer was the question whether capitalism or communism would triumph in the Third World, but rather how best to advance the spread of socialism through diverse, flexible, national byways. Nonalignment reshaped the Yugoslavs' conception of the world and restructured their national attitudes.

Contact with the West acted as a catalyst for internal liberalization. With ever growing frequency, Western solutions—those of the socialist camp were known and in disfavor, and the Third World had little to offer—were studied. When the postwar Constitution was revised in the early 1950's, Western embassies in Belgrade were asked for copies of their countries' constitutions. Greater contact with the non-Communist world brought Yugoslav leaders to more liberal attitudes on exchanges and travel; they realized that these did not threaten Yugoslavia or its commitment to socialism. Personal and continual experience with the West was essential to breaking the cast of narrow-minded, self-satisfied, prescribed ideas that had been theirs in the socialist camp. A critical and questing spirit emerged, which strengthened the anti-dogmatic and anti-sectarian forces internally and in foreign policy. The differentiated policy toward developing countries influenced the approach of Yugoslav leaders to their own backward regions, leading them to grant larger measures of autonomy, usher in a period of accommodation and coexistence with religion, and regard foreign private capital in a new light.

Tito and the comrades of his generation, Communists through conversion and not inheritance and reared in Moscow's Comintern hothouse, may still feel the emotional tug of Moscow but their heads are elsewhere—in the Third World and the markets and technology of the West. They fully understand the integral relationship between their political independence and leading role in nonalignment, and their need to develop a prosperous, productive economic system which of necessity must be linked to the convertible currency areas of the West. The internal liberalization to which they have firmly committed themselves by the economic reforms of 1965 is intended to impel Yugoslavia toward economic viability, which is prerequisite for continued leadership among the nonaligned: for without a strong economy Yugoslavia cannot hope to conduct an ambitious foreign policy.

There are also compelling domestic reasons for adherence to nonalignment: it is the only foreign policy that has proven acceptable to all factions of the LYC, to the different republics within the Yugoslav federation, and to the main strata of the population—serving as a compromise policy both for those who at various periods favored closer ties with the Soviet camp and for those who generally prefer a more West European orientation. As a leader among the nonaligned countries, Yugoslavia has acquired prestige abroad, which has been a source of pride to most Yugoslavs. In nonalignment Yugoslavia found a truly "national" foreign policy for the first time in its history, thereby contributing to the development of a sense of unity. Looking to the future, Yugoslavia's ability to withstand the probable strains of the post-Tito succession crisis depends on the continued containing of nationality tensions, and this can best be managed within an expanding and decentralized economic and social system, and by a foreign policy capable of unifying the diverse elements in the country. In few countries are the relationships between domestic difficulties and foreign policy alternatives so plainly evident.

Of unknown and crucial importance are the attitudes and ambitions of the generation now coming of political age. It does not have the umbilical ties to Moscow of Tito's Partisans, nor does it share their early dreams of comradeship with the Soviet Union and the socialist camp. 1948 may be beyond their ken, but 1968 is not: the crassness of Soviet bullying tactics in squashing Czechoslovakia's liberalization will not soon be lost on anyone but the most dyed-in-the-red pro-Russian Yugoslav. The Soviet invasion of Czechoslovakia has wrecked another incipient Yugoslav-Soviet rapprochement. Internationally, the disarray in the world Communist movement, the polarization within it that Tito contributed to by his domestic revisionism and relations with the nonaligned world, and Chinese and Cuban hostility, all limit Tito's options. Domestically, the commitment to liberalization, the evolution of political pluralism along nationality lines, the importance of economic, cultural, and scientific ties to Western Europe combine to make nonalignment the most feasible policy for Yugoslavia. Caution spiked with ambition will keep the leadership feinting like a boxer, alternately to the East and then to the West, but with its feet set firmly on nonalignment.

What Role for Yugoslavia?

If one looks beyond the Tito era to a more developed Yugoslavia linked even more closely to Europe for its economic well-being, and no longer automatically accorded a seat in the inner councils of the nonaligned by virtue of past contributions and respect for one of the founders, the question of Yugoslavia's role looms large. For Yugoslavia, as well as for the Afro-Asian countries, nonalignment needs a new framework. Unless it is imbued with a fresh spirit and promotes development and nation-building, it may well become the barren refuge of the poor and the weak. Thus far the nonaligned countries have not demonstrated any notable capacity for solving their own critical problems: India, Indonesia, the United Arab Republic, Syria, Algeria, Burma, Mali—the list is as long as the problems are complex. The birth pangs of nationhood do not elicit sustained sentiment or readiness to share from the international community, seldom known for its humaneness or vision.

Yugoslav leaders are conscious of the imperative need for inventive proposals. They are active, but neither new forms nor new modes of behavior are readily fashioned in international politics; the tradition of self-interest, selfishly defined, is strong. The shortcomings inhere in nonalignment itself and not in Yugoslav diplomacy. The Vietnam crisis, for one, has shown how powerless the nonaligned are to restrain a Great Power. Since January 1968, Tito has lobbied for "a conference of Heads of State of Nonaligned and other peaceful countries." He did this during his visits to India, Pakistan, Cambodia, Ethiopia, and the U.A.R. in January-February 1968, and to Japan and Iran two months later. His attempts to enlist support for new initiatives to settle the Vietnam war and Middle East crisis, to organize resistance to the spreading danger from "neocolonialism," and to give impetus to U.N. programs for helping developing countries have not attracted the attention they once did in the West.[4] In a speech delivered in Leskovac on October 20, 1968, Tito noted that Yugoslavia's initiative for convening "a summit meeting of the nonaligned countries with a wish to make it more extensive than the ones held in Belgrade and Cairo" had "met with a very poor reception among the leaders of some socialist countries:"[5]

> Previously the Western capitalists were against it. The Western imperialist states did not like the idea and now it is the others who do not like it. Meanwhile, everywhere, particularly in Africa and Asia, invented stories are being circulated that this is a lost cause, that Yugoslavia

[4] For example, there were no accounts of Tito's 1968 trip to the Far East in *The New York Times*.

[5] *Yugoslav Facts and Views*, No. 47 (October 25, 1968), p. 7.

has failed with this idea, that it has damaged Yugoslavia itself, that there is no longer any sense in proposing a meeting.

While the Soviet Union has opposed a summit of non-aligned states, fearing criticism of its intervention in Czechoslovakia, the Afro-Asian countries, too, have been slow to respond affirmatively. For them the prospect of still another conference has a taste of staleness.[6]

Tito may continue to think that "the idea of nonalignment and the principles adopted at the Belgrade and Cairo Conferences are equally valid today," that "they have not lost their value or role for a single moment,"[7] but he is too much a realist to see them as safeguarding the peace or Yugoslav national security. An astute student of history, he understands the limited role of personality in influencing international affairs; he realizes that for Yugoslavia to retain its present privileged status among the nonaligned countries, it will have to rely on the force of its ideas and not on the prestige of any leader. This implies that Yugoslavia will have to induce nonalignment to undergo a revitalization that is nowhere in sight.

Though the endless round of U.N. meetings is producing few tangible benefits for developing countries, they will remain the principal focus of Yugoslav endeavors if only because the machinery is available for extensive economic reforms; what is absent is the cooperation of the developed countries. Yugoslav diplomats acknowledge that even in

[6] But Tito's diligence was not without any reward: a Consultative Meeting of 51 nonaligned countries was held in Belgrade between July 8 and July 12, 1969, and agreed "on the desirability of holding, with adequate preparation, a conference of Heads of State and Government of nonaligned countries." The participants, however, did not set a date for the Third Conference of Nonaligned Countries.

While attending the twenty-fourth session of the U. N. General Assembly, representatives of 53 nonaligned states met on September 27, 1969, and called for the convening of a Preparatory Meeting to be held in Tanzania in the spring of 1970 in order to reach agreement on the time, place, and agenda of the proposed Nonaligned Summit Conference itself.

[7] Interview with C. L. Sulzberger, *The New York Times* (May 24, 1968).

the U.N. the organized activity of the nonaligned countries is less evident today than in the past. Many new nations are beholden to one or the other Great Power and are reluctant to organize *qua* nonaligned for fear of offending it. For their part, the Great Powers, though generally tolerant of the nonaligned countries, do not want them to organize as a cohesive voting group; they accept the coalescence of the developing countries into larger groupings on specific issues, for example, in UNCTAD and on anticolonialism, but are unhappy at any emergent grouping clustered around the concept of nonalignment. This situation is, needless to say, discouraging to the Yugoslavs. They will make do during this period of political ebb because the U.N., notwithstanding its limitations, still offers the best framework for promoting economic cooperation.

Yugoslavia faces an uncertain relationship with an increasingly pluralistic nonalignment. Regionalism not internationalism is the probable pattern, and cooperation that is constructive not rhetorical will center on specific issues, largely economic in character. Politically, nonalignment lacks strength; moral power may influence a particular policy or shape a temporary mood, but it is not yet the basis on which international problems are settled. A combination of developments has brought nonalignment to this state of affairs: the erosion of bloc cohesiveness which has altered the once bipolar complexion of the Cold War and lessened the distinctions between formal and informal nonalignment; the unwieldy membership which suffers from the lack of a unifying concept or ideal to which nations can attach their foreign policies, now that anti-colonialism is passing as a political priority and catalyst; the growing attention to national problems which reflects the pragmatic bent of the postliberation generation to concentrate on building a nation; and the feeling of helplessness which has become more pronounced toward changing the basic attitudes of the Great Powers, who have become less interested in catering to the nonaligned and more concerned with staking out some crucial areas for limited détente between themselves; the effect of the Sino-Soviet split in the nonaligned world; the weaknesses of nonaligned countries unable to cope with their special political, economic, social, and demographic problems; and the indifference of the developed countries to the plight of the developing countries.

The national interests that originally spurred Yugoslav involvement in nonalignment are essentially the same now. If the next generation takes to heart the passionate insistence of one of the elders of the present leadership that "Yugoslavia must not lose its soul and become another anonymous developed country, but retain a leading role in world affairs," Belgrade may successfully continue to serve in the vanguard of nonalignment. The greater uncertainty is whether nonalignment has the potential for influencing international affairs that Yugoslavia believes it has.

Selected Bibliography

A. Books

Bartoš, M., *Osnovi Pojmovi O Ujedinjenim Nacijama*, Belgrade, 1953.

———, *Pravni Aspekti Mirne Aktivne Koegzistencije*, Belgrade, 1956.

Brecher, M., *India and World Politics: Krishna Menon's View of the World*, New York, 1968.

Bulajić, M., *Pravo Naroda Na Samoopredeljenje u Društvu Naroda i Ujedinjenim Nacijama (1917-1962)*, Belgrade, 1963.

Burton, J. W., *International Relations: A General Theory*, London, 1965.

———, ed., *Nonalignment*, London, 1966.

Campbell, J. C., *Tito's Separate Road*, New York, 1967.

Crabb, C. V., Jr., *The Elephant and the Grass: A Study of Nonalignment*, New York, 1965.

Čvorović, M., and M. Ristić, *Yugoslavia in the System of Multilateral International Economic Cooperation*, Belgrade, 1967.

D'Arcy, F., A. Krieger, and A. Marill, *Essais sur L'économie de L'Algérie nouvelle*, Paris, 1965.

Duroselle, J. B., and J. Meyriat, eds., *Les nouveaux états dans les relations internationales*, Paris, 1962.

Farajallah, S. B., *Le groupe Afro-Asiatique dans le cadre des nations unies*, Geneva, 1963.

Gosović, B., "UNCTAD: North-South Encounter," *International Conciliation*, No. 568 (May 1968).

Hoffman, G. W., and F. W. Neal, *Yugoslavia and the New Communism*, New York, 1962.

Jansen, G. H., *Afro-Asia and Nonalignment*, London, 1966.

Jeremić, Z. S., *Pomoć Zemljama u Razvoju Preko Ujedinjenih Nacija*, Belgrade, 1964.

Johnstone, W. C., *Burma's Foreign Policy: A Study in Neutralism*, Cambridge, 1963.

Jugoslavija u Ujedinjene Nacije, Belgrade, 1955.

Jugoslavija i Privredni Razvoj Zemalja u Razvoj: Materijali Simposijuma (unpublished), Ljubljana, 1966.

Kardelj, E., *Socialism and War: A Survey of Chinese Criticism of the Policy of Coexistence*, New York, 1960.

Karunakan, K. P., ed., *Outside the Contest: A Study of Nonalignment and the Foreign Policy of Some Nonaligned Countries*, New Delhi, 1963.

Katić, D., *Društveno-ekonomske Osnove Arabskog Nacionalizma*, Belgrade, 1959.

Lall, A., *The UN and the Middle East Crisis 1967*, New York, 1968.

London, K., ed., *New Nations in a Divided World*, New York, 1963.

Lyon, P., *Neutralism*, London, 1963.

Mallik, D. N., *The Development of Non-alignment in India's Foreign Policy*, Allahabad, 1967.

Martin, L. W., ed., *Neutralism and Nonalignment: The New States in World Affairs*, New York, 1962.

McWhinney, E., *International Law and World Revolution*, Leyden, 1967.

Mitrović, T., *Codification of the Principles of Peaceful and Active Coexistence*, Belgrade, 1964.

Ninčić, D., *Načela Koegzistencije i Njihova Kodifikacija*, Belgrade, 1964.

"Nonalignment in Foreign Affairs," *The Annals*, Vol. 362 (November 1965). Special Issue.

Oreščanin, B., *Vojni Aspekti Borbe za Svetski Mir Nacionalnu Nezavisnost i Socijalizam*, Belgrade, 1962.

Pečar, Z., and V. Zagorac, *Egipat: Zemlja, Narod, Revolucija*, Belgrade, 1958.

Pečar, Z., *Alžir Do Nezavisnosti*, Belgrade, 1967.

———, *Alžir*, Belgrade, 1959.

Peti Plenum Tsentralnog Komiteta Savezna Komunista Jugoslavije, Belgrade, 1963.

Petković, R., *Dvadeset Godina Ujedinjenih Nacija*, Belgrade, 1965.

———, *Nesvrstani u Akcija*, Belgrade, 1968.

Račić, O., *Odnos Izmedju Ujedinjenih Nacija i Specijalizovanih Ustanova*, Belgrade, 1966.

Radojković, M., *Kodifikacija Načela Aktivne Miroljubive Koegzistencije* (unpublished), Belgrade, 1961.

Radovanović, Lj., *Politika Neangažovanih Zemalja: Vanblokovske Zemlje na Beogradskoj Konferenciji*, Belgrade, 1961.

———, *Neangažovanost i Aktivna Koegzistencija: Načela, Praksa, Dokumenti*, Belgrade, 1964.

Šahović, M., *Shvatanja Savremene Teorije Medjunarodnog Prava o Koegzistenciji*, Belgrade, 1961.

Sayegh, F. A. ed., *The Dynamics of Neutralism in the Arab World*, San Francisco, 1964.

Sen, C., *Against the Cold War: A Study of Asian-African Policies Since World War II*, Bombay, 1962.

Smole, J., *Yugoslav Views on Coexistence*, Belgrade, 1961.

Stanovnik, J., *World Economic Blocs: The Nonaligned Countries and Economic Integration*, Belgrade, 1962.

Stepanovsky, J., et al., *Foreign Policy of Nonalignment*, Prague, 1964.

Šuhović, O., *Položaj i Uloga Generalnog Sekretara Ujedinjenih Nacija*, Belgrade, 1967.

Tito, J. B., *Borba za Socijalističku Demokratiju*, Belgrade, 1953.

———, *Tito: Selected Speeches and Articles, 1941-1961*, Zagreb, 1963.

The Conference of Heads of State or Government of Unaligned Countries, Belgrade, 1961.

Vuković, B., *Socijalistička Orientacija u Nerazvijenim Zemljama*, Belgrade, 1967.

Wilcox, F. O., *UN and the Nonaligned Nations*, New York, 1962.

Worsley, P., *The Third World*, Chicago, 1964.

B. ARTICLES

Aćimović, Lj., "The Peaceful Settlement of Disputes Within the UN," *Medjunarodni problemi*, Vol. VII, No. 3-4 (1955), 51-84.

———, "The Relationship Between the Security Council and the General Assembly in the Peaceful Solution of Disputes," *Jugoslovenska revija za medjunarodno pravo,* Vol. III, No. 2 (1956), 286-296.

Altman, G., "Responsibility of the Policy of Non-alignment," *Socialist Thought and Practice,* No. 15 (July-September 1964), 79-95.

Anabtawi, S. N., "Neutralists and Neutralism," *The Journal of Politics,* Vol. 27, No. 2 (May 1965), 351-362.

Andrassy, J., "Review of the Charter and Collective Measures," *Jugoslovenska revija za medjunarodno pravo,* Vol. II, No. 2 (1955), 197-204.

Bartoš, M., "Legal Aspects of Peaceful Active Coexistence of States," *Jugoslovenska revija za medjunarodno pravo,* Vol. II, No. 3 (1955), 321-339.

———, "Progressive Tendencies in the Principles of the New Positive International Public Law and the Inadequacy of the Defense of its Essential Principles," *Jugoslovenska revija za medjunarodno pravo,* Vol. IV, No. 3 (1957), 321-332.

———, "Some Observations on Peaceful and Active Coexistence," *Jugoslovenska revija za medjunarodno pravo,* Vol. VII, No. 2 (1960), 216-227.

———, "The Contribution of New Yugoslavia to the Development of International Law," *Jugoslovenska revija za medjunarodno pravo,* Vol. VIII, No. 2 (1961), 180-186.

Bebler, A., "Foreign Policy Relations," in *Enciklopedija Jugoslavije,* Vol. 5, Zagreb, 1962, 140-154.

———, "On the Congo," *Socijalizam,* Vol. VIII, No. 1 (January 1965), 89-98.

Bell, C., "Nonalignment and the Power Balance," *Australian Outlook,* Vol. 17, No. 2 (August 1965), 117-120.

Božović, A., "United Nations and the Decolonization Process," *Medjunarodni problemi,* Vol. XV, No. 2 (1963), 53-66.

Bulajić, M., "Sovereignty Over Natural Wealth and Resources," *Jugoslovenska revija za medjunarodno pravo,* Vol. IX, No. 3 (1962), 379-400.

Campbell, J. C., "Yugoslavia: Crisis and Choice," *Foreign Affairs*, Vol. 41, No. 2 (January 1963), 384-397.

Chametzky, J., "Yugoslavia," *Atlantic Monthly*, Vol. 222, No. 1 (July 1968) 19-21.

"Cooperation Between the Socialist Alliance of the Working People of Yugoslavia and Progressive Parties and Movements in Africa, Asia, and Latin America," *Yugoslav Survey*, Vol. VI, No. 22 (July-September 1965), 3207-3215.

Crabb, C. V., Jr., "The Testing of Nonalignment," *The Western Political Quarterly*, Vol. XVII, No. 3 (September 1964), 517-542.

Djerdja, J., "Yugoslavia and the New Asian States," *Politique étrangère*, Vol. 20, No. 1 (January-February 1955), 17-26.

———, "The Policy of Nonalignment in a Divided World," *Medjunarodni problemi*, Vol. XIII, No. 3 (1961), 7-22.

———, "The Policy of Nonalignment in a Divided World," *Naše teme*, Vol. V, No. 12 (1961), 1761-1772.

———, "New Stage in the Evolution of Nonalignment Policies," *Medjunarodni problemi*, Vol. XVI, No. 3 (1964), 9-24.

Djordjević, A., "The Principle of the Sovereign Equality of States," *Jugoslovenska revija za medjunarodno pravo*, Vol. XI, No. 1 (1964), 42-54.

———, "The Situation of Underdeveloped Countries in Agreements Concerning the Granting of Aid," *Jugoslovenska revija za medjunarodno pravo*, Vol. XI, No. 3 (1964), 432-446.

Dragomanović, T., "A Review of Yugoslavia's Economic Relations with Developing Countries," *Medjunarodni problemi*, Vol. XVI, No. 2 (1964), 157-162.

Frenzke, D., "Coexistence and Socialist Internationalism in the Yugoslav Constitution and International Law Doctrine," *Modern World*, Vol. 5 (1965/1966), 99-119.

Gott, R., "The Decline of Neutralism: The Belgrade Conference and After," in *Survey of International Affairs 1961*, London, 1965, 365-387.

Grahek, Z., "On Neocolonialism," *Socijalizam*, Vol. VII, No. 9 (September 1964) , 1190-1215.

Griffith, W. E., "Yugoslavia," in *Africa and the Communist World*, edited by Z. Brzezinski, Stanford, 1963, 116-141.

Hazard, J., "Codifying Peaceful Coexistence," *The American Journal of International Law*, Vol. 55, No. 1 (1961), 109-120.

Hehn, P. N., "Yugoslavia and the Afro-Asian Bloc," *Review*, No. 7 (1968), 618-642.

Hudson, G. F., "The Neutrals and the Afro-Asians," *World Today*, Vol. 20 (December 1964), 542-548.

Ibler, V., "Revision of the Charter and the International Court," *Zbornik pravnog fakulteta u Zagrebu*, Vol. 5, No. 3-4 (1955), 157-162.

Jha, C. S., "Le non-alignement dans un monde en évolution," *Politique étrangère*, Vol. 32 (1967), 349-367.

Južnić, S., "The Process of Social, Economic, and Political Changes in Latin America," *Medjunarodni problemi*, Vol. XIII, No. 3 (1961), 23-54.

Kardelj, E., "Evolution in Yugoslavia," *Foreign Affairs*, Vol. 34, No. 4 (July 1956), 580-602.

————, "Yugoslav Foreign Policy—Some Topical Problems of International Relations," *India Quarterly*, Vol. 14, No. 4 (October-December 1958), 337-350.

Keep, J. L. H., "Belgrade and Moscow: A Calculating Courtship," *Orbis*, Vol. X, No. 3 (Fall 1966), 754-781.

Kiefer, D., "La Yougoslavie et l'Amérique Latine," *Est et Ouest*, Vol. 16, No. 328 (October 1964), 6-9.

Krajger, S., "Economic Integration and the Development of Economic Relations with Foreign Countries," *Socijalizam*, Vol. VII, No. 2 (February 1964) , 163-188.

Lang, R., "The Problems of Economic Development of Underdeveloped Countries," *Ekonomski pregled*, Vol. II, No. 5 (1951), 294-308.

La Rue, P. A., "Yugoslavia's Neutralism," *Politique étrangère*, Vol. 26, No. 4 (1961), 327-342.

Mates, L., "Facing the Beograd Conference," *Socialist Thought and Practice*, No. 2 (1961), 2-29.

————, "Nonaligned Countries in International Relations," *Medjunarodni problemi*, Vol. xiv, No. 2-3 (1962), 7-24.

————, "Increased Role of the Developing Countries in International Relations," *Medjunarodni problemi*, Vol. xvi, No. 2 (1964), 9-22.

————, "Social Factors Conditioning the Policy of Nonalignment," *Medjunarodni problemi*, No. 3 (1966), 17-35.

————, "The Policy of Nonalignment Today," *Socijalizam*, Vol. x, No. 5 (May 1967), 581-592.

Milbank, D. L., "Yugoslav Policy Toward Algeria in Perspective," *SAIS Review*, Vol. 12, No. 1 (Autumn 1967), 4-14.

Nayar, N. P., "Nonalignment in World Affairs," *India Quarterly*, Vol. 18, No. 1 (January-March 1962), 28-57.

Nikezić, M., "Why Uncommitted Countries Hold They Are Neutral," *The Annals*, Vol. 366 (July 1961), 75-82.

Ninčić, Dj., "The Problem of Collective Measures," *Jugoslovenska revija za medjunarodno pravo*, Vol. iii, No. 1 (1956), 33-40.

————, "The Question of a United Nations Force," *Jugoslovenska revija za medjunarodno pravo*, Vol. vii, No. 2 (1960), 227-233.

————, "Yugoslavia and the United Nations," *Arhiv za pravne i društvene nauke*, No. 1-2 (January-June 1961), 114-123.

Opačić, N. N., "Nonalignment," *Coexistence*, Vol. 3, No. 2 (July 1966), 123-135.

Palmer, N. D., "Changing Balance of Power: The 'Neutral' Nations in the United Nations," in *Studies in Political Science*, edited by J. S. Bains, London, 1961, 38-76.

Petković, R., "The Middle East and the Creation of the Yemen Arab Republic," *Medjunarodni problemi*, Vol. xv, No. 1 (1963), 99-116.

Račić, O., "Problems of Financing UN Operations," *Medjunarodni problemi*, Vol. xv, No. 1 (1963), 117-128.

Radojković, M., "The Codification of the Principles of Peaceful Coexistence," *Jugoslovenska revija za medjunarodno pravo*, Vol. ix, No. 2 (1962), 161-184.

Rana, A. P., "The Intellectual Dimensions of India's Non-alignment," *The Journal of Asian Studies*, Vol. xxviii, No. 2 (February 1969), 299-312.

Rubinstein, A. Z., "Reforms, Nonalignment, and Pluralism," *Problems of Communism*, Vol. xvii, No. 2 (March-April 1968), 31-40.

Rus, V., "The Peoples of Asia and Africa as Exponents of Coexistence," *Medjunarodni problemi*, Vol. viii, No. 1 (1956), 3-48.

Rusinow, D. I., "Yugoslavia Reaps the Harvest of Coexistence," *Southeast Europe Series*, Vol. xi, No. 1 (Yugoslavia). American Universities Field Staff Reports.

Shay, T. L., "Nonalignment Si, Neutralism No," *The Review of Politics*, Vol. 30, No. 2 (April 1968), 228-245.

Stanovnik, J., "The Problems of Development of Underdeveloped Countries in the World Economy," *Ekonomska revija*, Vol. iii, No. 3-4 (1952), 143-193.

———, "International Assistance to Underdeveloped Countries in the Light of World Economic Development," *Medjunarodni problemi*, Vol. ix, No. 4 (1957), 3-31.

———, "The Problems of Economic Development of Underdeveloped Countries," *Socijalizam*, Vol. iii, No. 2 (1960), 80-109.

———, "Some Problems of Theory and Policy of Economic Development in the Light of the Cairo Conference Declaration," *Medjunarodni problemi*, Vol. xiv, No. 2-3 (1962), 25-46.

Sukijasović, "The Nature of the UN Intervention in the Congo," *Medjunarodni problemi*, Vol. xiv, No. 2-3 (1962), 65-86.

———, "Characteristics of Economic Agreements Concluded Between the SFR Yugoslavia and Underdeveloped Countries," *Medjunarodni problemi*, Vol. xvi, No. 2 (1964), 35-58.

Šuković, O., "The Question of Financing UN Operations in the Congo and Near East," *Jugoslovenska revija za medjunarodno pravo*, Vol. xi, No. 3 (1964), 484-494.

Triska, J. F., and H. E. Koch, Jr., "Asian-African Coalition and International Organization: Third Force or Collective Impotence?", *The Review of Politics*, Vol. 21, No. 2 (1959), 417-455.

Vujović, V., "New Tendencies in the Socialist Development of the UAR," *Socijalizam*, Vol. v, No. 1 (1962), 103-115.

————, "Some Actual Problems of the Development of Algeria in the Light of the Work of the Congress of the National Liberation Front," *Socijalizam*, Vol. vii, No. 5 (May 1964), 680-688.

"Yugoslavia's Views and Actions in Connection with Israel's Aggression Against the Arab Countries," *Yugoslav Survey*, Vol. viii, No. 4 (November 1967), 131-162.

Index